D1739075

Epistolary
Responses

Epistolary Responses

The Letter
in 20th-Century
American Fiction
and Criticism

Anne Bower

The University of Alabama Press
Tuscaloosa and London

Library of Congress Cataloging-in-Publication Data

Bower, Anne L.
Epistolary responses : the letter in 20th-century American
fiction and criticism / Anne L. Bower.
p.   cm.
Includes bibliographical references and index.
ISBN 0–8173–0836–9 (alk. paper)
1. American fiction—20th century—History and criticism.
2. Epistolary fiction. American—History and criticism.
3. Criticism—United States—History—20th century.   4. Letters in
literature.   I. Title.
PS374.E65B69   1996
813′.509—dc20   96–3595
CIP

British Library Cataloguing-in-Publication Data available

For Rachel, Aviva, and Isaac—always present
no matter how long the absence or how far the distance

Contents

Preface: Dear Reader

June 26, 1995

Dear Reader,

Ever since I was a child I have loved letters. An envelope received from the dark of the mailbox crackles with promise, waiting for my fingers to expose its enshrouded gift. This letter was once held by its writer and is now held by me, so that the page forms a physical bridge between sender and receiver. E-mail's convenience has its advantages but lacks the contact point of a *shared* page; its speed and effortlessness also reduce the "gift" quality. E-mail has become part of my communications system, but I still prefer the old-fashioned letter, an attachment some of my friends see as "romantic." Carefully drawn or impatiently ripped from the envelope, a letter brings not only a message, a presence, a relationship, a memory, a secret, a possibility, a joke, an invitation, or a thank you, but traces of its sender (from handwriting to a mere smudge at the fold line).

What particularly marked letters as special in my early years was discovering that what I wrote down and enclosed in an envelope made a difference to others. The essays for Mrs. Brown's fifth grade got A's, but those grades were negated by their overwhelming negative consequences: the girls in class teased me for being a teacher's pet, and the boys disdained me, preferring the girls who received lower grades. Poems I wrote embarrassed my parents, who preferred limericks to my efforts at lyric or philosophic expression, and my early efforts at journalism brought forth only head pats, fleeting smiles, and other gestures of condescension. But letters . . .

When I wrote to my grandmother, I gave her *my* version of our family trip to Washington, D.C., and my written version lived. She believed it, she believed me, she used my writing to affirm or deny what others told her. When I wrote letters home from camp, my scribbled begging brought forth cookies, money, the wished-for phone call. When I wrote my pen pal a description of my appearance, my words created the body she saw. In letters, where for a while I controlled both the content and form of what was said, my words had power.

As I grew older and corresponded with friends, lovers, and faraway family members, I continued to enjoy the particular powers of letters, without ever articulating those powers to myself. But over the past few years, finding myself drawn to epistolary novels, I began to wonder more and more about this discourse form. I investigated histories and theories about letter communication, focusing on fiction, realizing all the while that fictitious letters derive much of their power from the same impulses and qualities embodied in "authentic" letters (and beginning to realize too that those "authentic" letters embodied many fictional elements). I also wondered to what effect the letter form might be used within critical discourse. As I was soon to find out, instead of residing in back-(or front)-of-the-journal ghettos in *PMLA* or *College English,* letters had already moved to the upscale neighborhood of actual articles.

This book grows out of a personal interest and pleasure in the letter—a form of writing with the power to encourage intimacy and enhanced one-to-one understanding of difficult issues. Naturally, letters can be used for distancing and dissimulation as well; that possibility makes attempts at connection and truthfulness more intriguing. In a time of alienation (one can question when that time began) letters still proffer some sense of physical connection, enduring material substance, individualized or private (confidential) language. Each letter in its envelope is also a package of aesthetic, conceptual, and emotive qualities, derived from the writer's circumstances, but existing within the context still of his or her society and its values.

This book you are holding is not a letter, yet I want to maintain the fiction that it can function as one. You receive it as a complete entity, anticipating that the reading experience ahead of you, unlike "real life" experience, will have a perceivable beginning, middle, and end. Now, a letter is written by a particular person to a particular person, and it is written to elicit a response. Letter writers, whether they know an addressee well or slightly, create that person in their letters: projecting and imagining the reader. As I do you. (Sometimes you're a graduate student, sometimes a librarian, at other times a professor, sometimes a security guard reading under fluorescent lights at a gray metal desk; sometimes you're female with long earrings or none, in jeans or maybe a suit; sometimes a male in tweeds, at other times wearing shorts and a tee-shirt.) While they write, letter writers are active; their encoding of a message, no matter what that message, is a form of action; they know themselves alive, they know themselves as makers of meaning, and they maintain a sense of their addressees as present. Then they send their letters off and hope for replies. Whether or not they receive return mail, they maintain the sense that response is possible—they are not, therefore, seeing themselves as completely isolated or without at least the possibility of a community of some sort.

Any book, fiction or criticism, can elicit a response from the reader. Presumably one of our motives for writing or reading is that we want that kind of give and take. To posit a book as a letter is to emphasize the dialogic nature of the critical undertaking. Most research writing comes to some kind of closure, but in spite of its traditional "Yours Truly" or other formalized ending, a letter often does not. A letter is a fragment of discourse, a communication sent off before the whole story is known. I would hope to maintain some of that open quality in this study. My text includes "authentic" letters, but it is mostly about fictional letters. And it concludes with an exploration of letter criticism. To stress critical work as letter is to seek for readers and writers alike the possibility that we engage in more personal interchange (although not necessarily autobiographical), with renewed interest in each other's styles and methods, with more interest in correspondence and less in competition.

Prefatorily,

Anne Bower

Acknowledgments

Without the readerly attention, discussions, and comments of my Ohio State University colleagues this book could not have come into being. Over the past years—too many—Marcia Dickson and Debra Moddelmog provided especially insightful, thorough, good-humored, and tough-minded input, but comments from Lynda Behan, Stuart Lishan, Murray Beja, and Jim Phelan also helped greatly. I credit, too, the inspiration of instructors at the School of Criticism and Theory (summer 1988), especially Nancy K. Miller and Mary Ann Caws. And my enduring thanks go to Tim Adams, Cheryl Torsney, and Dennis Allen, all of West Virginia University's English Department; they saw parts of this study in an earlier manifestation and cheered me on.

My thanks as well to The Ohio State University-Marion for a quarter free of teaching—invaluable to this text's creation—and for a grant that supported research using Vassar College's collection of Jean Webster's papers. A small grant from the OSU College of Humanities (funds from the Virginia Hull Award program) also supported research for this project.

Without the cooperation of authors and critics and authors' estates who contributed letters for this book, the enlivening enactment of correspondence within *Epistolary Responses* could not have taken place. To each of them, my heartfelt thanks:

Letter from John Barth used by his permission.

Letter from Ana Castillo used by her permission, copyright © 1995 by Ana Castillo.

Letter from Dorothy Combs Hill used by her permission.

Letter from Linda S. Kauffman used by her permission.

Letter from James A. Schiff used by his permission.

Letter from Upton Sinclair (October 25, 1949) quoted by permission of Jean Sinclair, literary property rights holder, and Lilly Library, Indiana University, Bloomington, Indiana.

Robert Stepto's unpublished lecture, "Let Me Tell Your Story: Fraternal Authorship in Narratives of Slavery, Revolt, and Incarceration—Douglass, Montejo, and Wideman," delivered July 1988 at the School of Criticism and Theory, Dartmouth College, used by his permission.

Letter from John Updike used by his permission.

Letter from Jean Webster (24 July 1913) quoted by permission of Ralph Connor, literary property rights holder, and the Special Collections at Vassar College Library.

Epistolary
Responses

1

Introduction

I was teaching at a federal prison, and we were discussing a short story, when one of the more forthright students interjected a real conversation stopper: "What's this for?" he asked. Ben wanted one clear-cut answer to his question; a precise man, a stickler for detail (counterfeiting had brought him to prison), he expected me to authoritatively and comprehensively tell him some end product he would receive from reading and studying fiction, nonfiction, drama, and poetry. In subsequent classes he, I, and the other students articulated ideas about interpreting, analyzing, "mastering," and enjoying literature, and celebrated possibilities for making connections between ourselves and literature and between texts, frustrating Ben's desire for one true answer. Everyone else seemed happy with multiple possibilities, but Ben never found that kind of approach acceptable.

In no way do I seek one answer, but in putting together this book, I have found myself returning to Ben's question, asking myself: what's this for? What is it about letters—in fictions and critical essays—that seems deserving of special attention; why in thinking about what *literature* is for do I find myself returning again and again to the *letter*?

I come to literature—whether it is "high" art or popular and regardless of genre—not for a specific intellectual or emotional end product, but for a series of interactive *responses*. Sometimes in reading we seek an author's response to a problem—how a narrative enacts the writer's reaction to an event such as the Civil War or twentieth-century ghetto life. Sometimes the search is for an author's response to more formal issues—experimentation with a particular genre or the use of time or intertextual recuperation of another text. At other times we are more interested in the depiction of a character's responses to people or to a changing self. And sometimes we seek our own responses to various textual elements . . . that positive sense that a narrative, through its handling of characters and point of view, setting, structure, story, and language, has allowed expansion of old definitions of time, history, space, gender, race, language, certain emotions, even self.[1]

Of course we can also respond negatively to aspects of a text. Nevertheless, even when resisting some change a text offers, we have the opportunity to explore the meanings of that rejecting response. For instance, a reader may find a character in a novel revolting. In Judith Fetterley's terms, we, as readers, may refuse "to identify with a selfhood that defines itself in opposition to" our own selfhood (*Resisting Reader* xii). Still, that very resistance begins a response that can yield changed attitudes, beliefs, or even actions.

Epistolary works frame and feature these response processes. The reading of any text can provide the opportunity for exploring one's attitudes and beliefs, in concert with an author and the characters, places, and events within that text. However, the lettered text, with its repeated rectangles capturing one writer's reactions, then moving to another writer's expression or the same writer's subsequent recordings, privileges literature's power to provide a special protected space and time for these responses. I use the word *responses* to embrace the variety of possible intersections and reactions of readers, literary characters, and authors (with plenty of room for the question of intertextuality, too). More than other narrative forms, letters, with their grounding in the ups and downs, ins and outs of people's daily lives, emphasize how written responses are enacted in pieces, with revisions, discontinuously. The kind of responsiveness we find in (and through) letters is rather like the responsive attitude Mary Catherine Bateson generalizes about in *Composing A Life:* a "mode of action [that] is responsive rather than purposive: it is based on looking and listening and touching rather than the pursuit of abstractions" (234). In addition, even though the word *responses* also carries the meaning of answers or replies to questions and statements that certainly could be abstractions, in that usage the word still includes such things as a congregation's spoken or sung reaction to a minister's words, so the emphasis again moves to give-and-take. This word appeals to me also because of its verbal link to reader-response theories, with their probing into processes of reading.

Although literature in general can prompt our own intellectual and emotional insights and reappraisals, for each of us some *forms* of literature stimulate response more readily than others. For me the epistolary is such a form. Traditionally associated with women and with the "private" as opposed to the "public" sphere, the letter form engages many feminist issues. At the same time, with its emphasis on the act of writing and writing as act, the letter permits exploration of postmodernist questions. The back and forth of letters, their desire for reply, their incomplete ownership of information, their concomitant play on ideas of absence and presence, and their apparently personal and private nature, model an interactive openness (although one always knows, paradoxically, that this seeming openness can be used for manipulation and deception). If we see letters as a written attempt at conversation (slow and gap-riddled as it may be), then John Barth's statement that "we converse to convert, each the other, from an Other into an extension of oneself; and we converse conversely" (*Friday Book,* 2–3) helps to begin my own conversation about epistolary fiction and critical prose as particularly productive sites of literary response. Letters call forth responses from the writing character and the addressee (or internal reader), from the external reader, and from authors, whose responses to their own or others' letter texts may then yield readers new perceptions about the ways texts "mean."

Janet Altman uses the term "mediation" to cover the letter's way of allowing characters to move back and forth in time and space, among levels of confidence and even among levels of communication success itself (*Epistolarity* 14–43). Linda Kauffman applies this idea of mediation to the formal aspects of epistolary work, finding intertextual turnings in which texts "look backward and forward, as remembrance and prophecy" of epistolary traditions (*Special Delivery* xiv). I take this to mean that letter novels have special formal abilities to place the traditional and the experimental face to face, to create conversations between past and present texts, and to make us party to those conversations in highly self-conscious ways. Kauffman concentrates on what she calls the "epistolary mode" as opposed to the epistolary genre, with mode implying that one can borrow bits and pieces of letters' qualities in an experimental, adaptive way and genre demanding the "complete external form" of letters from Dear so-and-so through signature (*Special Delivery* xiii).

With full respect for Kauffman's provocative and valuable work, I must admit that, in fiction and other forms of writing, I love the epistolary genre itself, for narratives and essays that persist in repeating the actual shape of correspondence attest to our need for personal contact, material production, for something to hold in the hand, to store and return to, for bodied writing, if you will. In addition, the letter form asserts belief in the power of writing to make a "critical" difference. Writing is the supreme action of the epistolary character or epistolary critic; all is lodged in the individual's ability to write to another individual.

Independent scholar Susan Koppelman, a prolific letter writer, emphasizes certain qualities she finds in letter exchanges: writing them she has a strong feel for her audience; receiving them she enjoys "the special feeling of being addressed"—whether directly or as a second, "eavesdropping" reader (76); and, contrasted with essay writing, she finds letters more personal, dialogic, and emotional (77). E-mail, fax, and satellite phone systems may seem to disengage us from the old-fashioned need for the physical form of the letter, but we return to our need for something that seems permanent when we print out e-mail or transcribe a phone call; fax, of course, always results in hard copy. Even then, it seems a loss to me that the "hard copy" has never been touched by the sender.

The sense of touch (we say that someone's work "touches" us, eliding the differences among physical, emotional, and intellectual responses) is probably more central to our reading and writing than we have admitted. So when another scholar, Shari Benstock, asserts that the "constituent textual elements that play presumably tangential roles in representing subjectivity" are in fact the "bricks and mortar" of fiction (xv), I find myself nodding vigorously in agreement. Letters' "bricks and mortar" elements include replicated salutations and closings, the white spaces that stand in for the time and space between each segment of the correspondence, the idiosyncrasies captured through an individual's less formal writing style, the oddness of long sections of dialogue and description when made part of a letter. These representations consistently bring us up against the writing act. We would lose ourselves in fiction? Allow a critic's argument to sweep us along? The letter's form, placing repeated frames around segments of discourse, interrupts such naturalizations. The symbolic rectangle of the letter heightens awareness of self and text in responsive process.

Perhaps I also choose to look at critical and fictional works presented in full epistolarity because I am fascinated in part by the very thing that drew John Barth to this form when he undertook *LETTERS*. In that novel, a character named John Barth, who just happens to be writing an epistolary novel, explains what attracts him to eighteenth-century novelists' use of letters: "I was impressed with their characteristic awareness that they're *writing*—that their fictions exist in the form, not of sounds in the ear, but of signs on the page, imitative not of life 'directly' but of its documents" (52–53). The epistolary *re*presents what is already a *re*presentation.

Nevertheless, the most distinctive thing about the letter form as a literary device may be that no matter what else it does, it always attempts to elicit or offer a response. Designating the reactive nature of letter writing, we use the term *correspondence*. Yet each writer necessarily writes alone. (Most often each reader also reads alone.) While letter writing, each individual (whether fictitious character or literary critic, the two kinds of letter writers at the center of this study) becomes responsible for his or her subjective reactions and reportings; as the solo occupier of the epistolary space, the letter writer can elaborate for both the internal and external reader one set of replies to particular issues or to others' actions.

Letter writers, "real" or fictitious, attempt to create and revise both self and addressee; they must believe they have this power or they would not write. (Whether they succeed is another question.) Although not necessarily mightier than the sword, the pen can arm any writing self or character with special offensive and defensive possibilities for moving unsatisfactory relationships into more satisfactory states. In the private space of letters, women, so often silenced in public life, have personal freedom in which to rewrite the self and even, sometimes, to rewrite others.

At times letters can be so private as to appear almost indistinguishable from diaries. One thinks, for instance, of Celie's "Dear God" letters in Alice Walker's *The Color Purple* or Ivy Rowe's letters to her sister Silvaney in Lee Smith's *Fair and Tender Ladies*. One

strong difference between diaries and letters is that the latter form
seeks a response, even if only the illusion that a response is possible.
Letter writers may expect a return letter, a gift, money, or some physical item; they may hope for a change of attitude or action on the
part of the letter recipient. Frequently, letter writers wish, like diarists, to rewrite themselves. Reaching out to the absent addressee a
letter writer may also change the notion of herself or himself held by
the letter's intended recipient. In this sense, letter writers are more
daring than diarists, for, to a limited extent, they "go public" with
their subjective perceptions, questions, and desires.

The author choosing epistolary form necessarily foregrounds
issues of power and agency, even if, as in Ring Lardner's recently
reissued *You Know Me Al,* or John Updike's *S.* (which I discuss
later), the protagonist's power to know self and surrounding world
is heavily satirized. No matter what constraints the letter writer suffers, for the moment, he or she has pen in hand, and so has the
potential to control the discourse. This power of agency enables protagonists from the Portuguese Nun to Celie in Alice Walker's *The
Color Purple* to hold onto their desire and subjectivity and to overcome, in one way or another, the absence of the addressee.

"In the first place, let us draw what all letter-writers instinctively
draw, a sketch of the person to whom the letter is addressed," writes
Virginia Woolf as she begins the first letter of *Three Guineas* (5). The
letter writer's power always exists within this condition of the absent
other. Indeed, letter fictions and letter criticism face absence as a
central issue. Letters highlight the gap (physical space, time, emotional difference, slippage between sign and signifier, aporia—it
takes so many forms) between correspondents. In letters we confront our ever-present awareness of that gap, and, while at times
using distance to protect ourselves, we usually struggle to overcome
it. Most of the time, as Virginia Woolf writes, we try to create "someone warm and breathing on the other side of the page" (5).

Examining a genre that presents its protagonists in the midst of
discourse also enables us to understand the ways language and writing encode power. In a world where power has seldom been shared
equitably, relegation to silence, or as Mae Henderson puts it, having
"no say," has been a pervasive problem for many women, people of
color, and individuals shunned by the majority culture ("Speaking
in Tongues" 125). Marginalized characters in epistolary novels "act
out" a solution to that problem through their letter writing as they

take control of language in a particularly direct, personal, accessible form of communication.

Literary critics have borrowed the epistolary form, too, in what I see as a similar need for freshly personalized discourse, but also, perhaps, as a need to change the ethos surrounding literary critical work (including critics' relationships to each other and to their audience). As Fredric Jameson asserts throughout *The Political Unconscious*, a text's form results from ideological choices, so that the form and its application to the text's content will tell us much about the cultural and political conflicts perceived by, acting on, and reproduced by a writer.[2] In the choice of form, a writer participates in a set of values and beliefs: "It becomes possible to see narrative technique not simply as a product of ideology but as ideology itself" (Lanser, *Fictions of Authority* 5). Again, such formal and ideological choices affect both fiction and critical writing.

In the seven twentieth-century fictions central to this study— John Barth's *LETTERS*, Ana Castillo's *The Mixquiahuala Letters*, Upton Sinclair's *Another Pamela*, Lee Smith's *Fair and Tender Ladies*, John Updike's *S.*, Alice Walker's *The Color Purple*, and Jean Webster's *Daddy-Long-Legs*—women letter writers are my focus. We live in a society that espouses equal rights for women, but that still (often subtly) silences them in many spheres—social, economic, legislative, medical, educational, and more. Twentieth-century novelists, writing in a variety of styles, have depicted the resulting silences as well as the ways women break such silences. When authors choose the letter form they tacitly but necessarily take a stand on a woman's "right" to own her discourse and her story. Note, of course, that the author's stand need not fully grant that right. Historically, many an epistolary novel has depicted a heroine's eventual acceptance of prevailing conventions (as in Burney's *Evelina*) or punished the heroine for her transgressions—usually through death (as in Richardson's *Clarissa*).

In epistolary fiction, because of traditional social structures, the marginalized protagonist is frequently female, her primary antagonists (whether involved in the correspondence or not) usually male. When we move to epistolary critical works, positions and tactics do not sort out along gender lines. Male and female critics experiment with epistolarity. As the scholarly letters discussed in this book demonstrate, through examples from Gloria Anzaldúa, Jacques Derrida, Kady Daughter of Ann, Gerald MacLean, Douglas Robinson, Robert

Stepto, and Fay Weldon, the choice of form seems more about authority than anything else. Each letter writer interrogates, to some degree, however, some of the same issues found in epistolary fiction, such as public versus private discourse and the power of signature. Frequently, the critic-correspondent becomes involved with gender questions too, for whether male or female, the writer takes the "feminine" position, questioning, as Kauffman writes of Barthes and Derrida, "propriation, property, propriety, and paternity" (*Special Delivery* 106). Crossing from standard argumentative essay form to the letter not only encourages new responses to genre definitions; it often also carries implications for our responses to assumptions about gender in writing.

Epistolary critical work takes many forms and serves many needs. Like Fay Weldon's *Letters to Alice,* a text may adopt a private and digressive form to question the "objectivity" and authority of literary scholarship. Criticism presented in letters may also directly confront issues of a subjective shift from silence to power, as in Gloria Anzaldúa's "A Letter to 3rd World Women Writers." In addition, should the scholar take on fictional personae, writing letters in others' voices as Robert Stepto has, the letters become a phenomenological response to (rather than analysis of) the worlds of the texts under investigation. Then too, in the same way that the letter form provides epistolary characters with a mode of responding to others, with the chance to rewrite themselves and others, criticism in letter form helps us to rewrite our concepts of academic discourse, perhaps even our concepts of the academic self and academic institution. At the very least, letter-criticism can allow us "pleasure in a process rather than striving for an all-important ending" to any particular scholarly debate (MacArthur 28).

Personal as well as theoretical/political orientations nourish my interest in the epistolary genre. In my own life and the lives of friends and family members, I see that the ability or power to tell our own stories benefits teller and listener—writer and reader— in many ways. This ordinary thing, the letter, with its personal and sometimes plodding nature, can provide space in which to practice conversing privately or to bridge the gap between private and public. The letter can also provide a necessary affront to the anomie our highly technological society partners with speed and efficiency. For some of us letters' relative permanence and portability have particular appeal because of our very mobility, a mobility that easily leads to uprootedness, isolation, and alienation. In addition, twentieth-century epistolarians, whether writing criticism or fiction, derive power from the letter form's long tradition, whether parodying, paraphrasing, critiquing, augmenting, accepting, or rejecting that form's previous achievements and limitations.

Nowadays, telephones and electronic mail systems make letter writing a choice rather than a necessity in our communications, although one's income does influence such choices. The conditions of our social organizations frequently set up barriers to relationships, whether barriers of location, time, language, socioeconomic differences, prejudice, or personal history. We have tended to see those in our society who suffer such alienation as victims; I like the way the letter form positions the subject—whether fictional character or literary scholar—as one who, no matter how alienated and isolated, has found a tool with which to reclaim herself or himself as active respondent to and shaper of his or her past, present, and future.

2

Epistolary Fiction: Space to Respond

No student of literature can avoid letter fiction. Whether reading *The Sorrows of Young Werther, Pamela, Clarissa, Evelina, Frankenstein,* or *The Expedition of Humphry Clinker,* we absorb the form's eighteenth- or early nineteenth-century conventions,[1] consider its contributions to the evolution of "the novel," and then, usually, relegate epistolary texts to the past. Although once part of the literary norm (according to Robert Adams Day, between 1660 and 1740 forty percent of all published fiction was epistolary; between 1740 and 1800 about twenty percent [2]), twentieth-century epistolary work strikes many readers as an oddity, literature encumbered rather than enhanced by its structure. Nevertheless, it is for those encumbrances, and for other qualities, that modern authors come to the form, just as poets still work with the sonnet, finding productivity in responding to that form's poetic traditions and constraints.

Actually, one can find in the letter form features with special affinities to aesthetic, critical, and philosophical issues of our day, so it is not so surprising that authors continually turn to the epistolary. Given these affinities and the form's endurance, the surprise is that until recently so little critical work has been published on *current* letter novels. In the past fifteen years or so, only four important studies have devoted appreciable space to modern epistolary novels. Janet Altman's *Epistolarity: Approaches to a Form* analyzes earlier texts,

but also considers some present-day uses of the letter form, mention-
ing adaptations of the letter by Henry de Montherlant, Colette,
Gunther Grass, Saul Bellow, Natalia Ginzburg, Thornton Wilder,
Bob Randall, and the trio of Marias who authored *New Portuguese
Letters* in 1972 (3, 195). Although she does not devote major por-
tions of her discussion to these novels, Altman is keenly aware of the
epistolary form's possibilities for contemporary artists. A study that
does focus on modern fiction's use of epistolary elements is Linda
Kauffman's *Special Delivery;* the texts covered—some strictly in letter form, others using aspects of the "epistolary mode"—include
Shklovsky's *Zoo, or Letters Not about Love,* Nabakov's *Lolita,* Barthes's
A Lover's Discourse, Derrida's *The Post Card,* Lessing's *The Golden Notebook,* Walker's *The Color Purple,* and Atwood's *The Handmaid's Tale.*
Kauffman's earlier *Discourses of Desire* is devoted primarily to seven-
teenth- and eighteenth-century epistolary fictions, but does "explore
. . . the fluid boundaries between the letter as literature, literature
as a letter" (160), discovering, for example, that *Jane Eyre* and *The
Turn of the Screw* contain many characteristics of a letter novel. In
Discourses, Kauffman also applies her insights to both the epistolary and the nonepistolary sections of Faulkner's *Absalom, Absalom!*
A wide-ranging essay collection edited by Elizabeth Goldsmith, *Writing the Female Voice: Essays on Epistolary Literature,* contains three essays that discuss twentieth-century epistolarity: Linda Kauffman's insightful and creative reading of *The Handmaid's Tale,* Alicia
Borinsky's comparative analysis of Manuel Puig's *Heartbreak Tango*
and Jacques Derrida's *The Post Card,* and Carolyn Williams's helpful
study of *The Color Purple.* Besides these full-length studies, occasional articles and reviews about particular twentieth-century letter
novels can be found, but anyone fascinated by epistolary work in
its modern manifestations and in the letter as a particular ongoing
form of discourse will find only a short list of pertinent scholarship.
Even finding titles of twentieth-century letter novels is difficult because there are no current reference works devoted to tracking the
form.

   Perhaps it is because most scholars have associated the letter with
"traditional" literary forms that they ignore the experimental, postmodern, playful, feminist, and deconstructive possibilities of the
epistolary form. For instance, Raymond Federman, in his 1975 call
for avant-garde novels or "surfiction," seeks work that "tries to explore the possibilities of fiction; the kind of fiction that challenges

the tradition that governs it" and work that "exposes the fictionality of reality" as well (7). As have others, he stresses the notion that "no meaning pre-exists language" because "language creates meaning as it goes along" (8). Although this idea has great application for epistolary work, he never mentions the letter form. Modernist and postmodernist scholars focus on twentieth-century literature's self-consciousness, its use of montage or collage, its resistance to or submergence in fragmented values and life patterns, the always alreadiness of its language. All of these qualities seem germane to recent epistolary works. As Altman helps us recall, the letter form particularly encourages "elliptical narration, subjectivity and multiplicity of points of view, polyphony of voices, interior monologue, superimposition of voices, interior monologue, superimposition of time levels, [and] presentation of simultaneous action" (*Epistolarity* 195). Because of these characteristics, one would expect recent letter novels to attract greater critical attention. In addition, one might think letter fiction's frequent focus on restricted freedom to communicate (in spite of the supposed gains societies have made in granting individual rights) and on the difficulties of communication would encourage scholarly attention to contemporary epistolary fiction.

In the following chapters I will discuss seven novels-in-letters, some "literary" and some "popular," published in the United States between 1912 and 1988. In each work, a heroine, caught in situations that ask too much of her, reacting to people who seem to misunderstand or ignore her, puzzled by a changing self, uses letter writing to perceive and document her responses. Within the repeated rectangles of correspondence she finds a means to redefine herself and define others.

In epistolary novels published from the seventeenth century to the present, we often find women characters who increase their power or sense of self through the opportunity to write their own truths. Their material conditions may not change greatly (although sometimes what they write does affect their circumstances, directly or indirectly), but their words shape their own lives and the lives of others. Behind this transferred power, the novel's author still manipulates the letters' contents and form for particular ideological or entertainment purposes, but the letter form will constrain us to read those manipulations within the dynamic of the female character's agency, power, and discourse. The form itself will continually draw our attention to questions of language and representation. Thus, letters can fit into what Rachel Blau DuPlessis calls "writing beyond the ending," serving to "sever the narrative from formerly conventional structures of fiction and consciousness about women" (*Writing Beyond* x). Additionally, letters can encourage what Molly Hite calls "reading other-wise" (*Other Side of the Story* 3), a practice (in part) of concentrating on the genre innovations used by women to tell their stories effectively. Hite's concept extends, for me, to a more general appreciation of the formal devices used by previously silenced persons to tell their stories. The epistolary form serves political and aesthetic needs, as it so neatly packages for us issues of representation and interpretation, voice and authorization. The form itself authorizes the protagonist's subjective desires; the pen is in her own hand.

For male epistolary protagonists the issue of agency is usually about maintenance of power rather than its acquisition. For example, Thornton Wilder's 1948 *The Ides of March* allows the exiled Julius Caesar a space in which to explain himself and to maintain certain political and personal powers even in exile. As another character writes of Caesar, "He writes seventy letters and documents a day. They fall over Italy like snow, every day" (28). In Mark Harris's *Wake Up, Stupid,* an academic at crisis in his personal and professional life uses letters to retain his sense of self: "I must write a little something every night, as a fighter punches the bag a little every day" (7). John O'Hara's Pal Joey writes to his buddy Ted without introspection or self-development; the epistolary nature of *Pal Joey* humorously highlights how little Joey changes as he recounts his adventures (Ring Lardner's *You Know Me, Al* takes the same kind of ironic stance). Historically, the male voice dominates the epistolary novel of advice, such as Jack London and Anna Strunsky's *The Kempton-Wace Letters* (1903), in which an older and a younger man debate the benefits of companionate versus romantic marriage (unsurprisingly, London took the older character's role while Strunsky took that of the younger, gentler man). Likewise, Lee Harriman's *The Dublin Letters* (1931) presents an advertising executive who writes to his wife and nephew, advising the latter on how to succeed in business and informing the former of his agency's internecine plots and their nephew's ups and downs.

In order that the letter novel's form may be most fully investigated, I have chosen novels that contain little or no nonletter narrative, although in a few cases a bit of such material exists. *The Color Purple* opens with an italic line representing Celie's father's warning not to tell anyone of his abuse of her. *The Mixquiahuala Letters* offers us a table of contents and authorial advice about reading the forthcoming letters in various sequences. *Daddy-Long-Legs* begins with a few pages of third-person narrative. *Another Pamela*'s foreword asks us to believe that Upton Sinclair obtained permission from a "reincarnation" of Richardson's Pamela Andrews to publish her letters. Except for the introduction of these minimal narrative devices, the seven novels come to us as letters only. This being the case, meanings within them will derive significantly from their "epistolarity," that is, "the use of the letter's formal properties" (Altman 4). Those properties include salutations and closings, time lapses between letters, orthography and language style, the letters' lengths, and changes in addressees.

The essential situation of the letter novel, whether Samuel Richardson's *Clarissa* or Ana Castillo's recent *The Mixquiahuala Letters*, is the individual "alone in a room with some paper and a pen" (Perry 107). We can imagine a typewriter or computer instead of traditional writing instruments, and we can imagine that lonely writer as almost any literate individual of any background. Like the Portuguese Nun, she may write letters trying to persuade her lover to return; like Clarissa, she may attempt to convince family and friends of her virtue; like Evelina, she may try to define her role in a sophisticated, confusing society. Whether created by male or female authors, these epistolary heroines, suffering physical and/or emotional restrictions, use the letter-writing process to investigate and to confirm their responses to others and to themselves, as well as to encourage certain responses from others.

The letter-writing female protagonist uses the pen not only to affirm herself, not only to bridge the gap between self and other, but often to *rewrite* the self, presenting a personal self-definition that contradicts, supersedes, or supplements the identity others have assumed her to have. Her concerns and activities will necessarily echo one or more aspects of our century's feminism(s)—discovering and questioning her own voice and language; asserting her ownership of narrative, history, and property; perceiving the constructed nature of social and sexual roles; and taking part in the construction and/or deconstruction of those roles.[2] James Watson finds that "the self recorded in a letter is the contemplated invention of the Sender, a studied epistolary image shaped from materials selected and formally arranged for the Receiver" (1–2). "Invention" usefully captures the creative nature of the protagonist's task. I would also stress, however, that the invented self is usually a corrective to representations already in circulation. These letter novels present heroines who gain power over themselves and their circumstances not through another's intervention nor through luck, but through their own power to (re)write.

The letter fictions I discuss frequently put the external reader (along with the characters) in a situation to explore responses to representations of the self. Kauffman points out, from her experience working with the epistolary mode, that "identity, like meaning, is not intrinsic but situational and relational. . . . What we define as individual experience is shaped externally as well as internally. Subjectivity seems to arise solely from personal experience, but what one perceives as subjective are in fact material, economic, and historic interrelations" (*Special Delivery* xxi). She also points out that for many epistolary heroines "one must first have the opportunity to be constituted *as* a subject before one can endorse the 'death' of the author or the subject's decentering" (*Special Delivery* xxi).

Whatever has caused the letter writer's isolation or confusion, writing letters allows that character the opportunity to bespeak self in personal, self-selected terms. Of course, any first-person narrator has that privilege, and as Joanne Frye brings home in her study of contemporary novels by women, the first-person narrator has a "subversive capacity inherent in her subjectivity," along with agency lodged in the selection and sequencing she controls as she tells her own story—her "freedom of construction" (56). At the same time, the epistolary heroine also creates a material object—the letter— that not only speaks the self but, metonymically, is the self. The object-letter-self enters the world, directed to a particular recipient, who, ideally, will respond to the letter in the way its writer expects. Of course, the recipient can misinterpret or ignore the writer's message. The letter can also go astray, suffer destruction, or, worse, be read by someone for whom it was not intended. The attempt to present a redefined self does not necessarily succeed with her addressee. The constant threat of failure the letter writer endures becomes part of the appeal of the epistolary form. Still, whether the message received is the one the letter writer intends or some other message, the letter process itself will have engendered some level of change within the framework of the narrative. And all the while, the novel reader's perceptions of the power struggles set forth in the book act on his or her awareness of language's capacity to change or enforce existing relationships.

My view of the letter in fiction as a device that opens up response space for the protagonist's rewriting of self is affected by four theoretical interests, each of which is central to contemporary discourse analysis: absence/presence, gendered writing, intertextuality, and the semiotics of reading/writing. The main theoretical approach used with each novel seems immanently logical to me of course, yet I know that a certain arbitrary quality, call it quirkiness or individuality, informs the combinations and recombinations of argument, analytic tools, intertextual connections used by any reader/scholar. While one theoretical concern dominates the discussion of each novel, that concern will inevitably reappear as part of other chapters. In addition, although one issue or question frames each novel, other issues and a mixture of critical approaches appear too. Perhaps the letter form appeals to me because its emphasis on the personal makes present the subjectivity of our responses: that of the author, the letter-writing protagonists, the letter-reading characters, the novel's readers, and the novel's critics—those of us who add our own written responses.

What I call absence/presence resonates strongly in Lee Smith's *Fair and Tender Ladies* and John Barth's *LETTERS*. My analysis of twentieth-century American letter fiction begins with this concept and these novels because absence/presence is *so* essential to letters —an agonizing pull between here and there, intimacy and separation, bonds and barriers, time present and future (or past and present), the tangible and the intangible (Altman, *Epistolarity* 13–15). The letter writer, no matter how she may strive to make her correspondent present, no matter how she labors to be present to her correspondent, remains alone. At the same time, her writing may make both self and other more vivid than they seem in the flesh. The character may write to strengthen a relationship or prevent it, but for the novel reader the letters will stimulate ideas concerning how we are made present by language and how we present ourselves and our relationships through it. Letters force us to perceive the distressing gap that always exists between self and other, between articulation and feeling, and between our words and the things they "stand for." In *Fair and Tender Ladies*, letters negotiate the space— physical, emotional, and psychological—caused by the separation of Ivy Rowe from family and friends. The space of separation is a factor in *LETTERS* as well, but many of the barriers experienced by Germaine Pitt result from the nature of language itself. In both novels the letter-writing heroines redefine or rewrite themselves through negotiating absence and presence.

Even the nonverbal aspects of letters play with absence and presence. For instance, as James G. Watson points out, "even the time a letter writer permits to elapse after receiving mail is a significant commentary on the content of his [or her] letter" (53). The time lags incorporated into *Fair and Tender Ladies* create such a commentary. In John Updike's *S.*, the frequency and length of Sarah's letters become nonverbal messages that alter the balance between presence and absence, desired intimacy or separation. In *LETTERS*, verbosity also signals the futile effort to overcome a gap, although, as ever the case with Germaine, the novel's sole female writer, the effort itself must be commented on: "30 pages have not assuaged my misery, only lengthily recorded it" (390). The way a character thinks, her stops and starts, associations, understandings, and misunderstandings can be well documented through the letter's physical, nonverbal form. "Tears, handwriting, punctuation, and even spelling may be part of the message," revealing or making present what the correspondent's words leave out (Altman, *Epistolarity* 125). Clarissa's tears on her letters make her body present too; changing orthography, as in *Fair and Tender Ladies,* or missing punctuation, as in *S.*, demonstrates shifts in the writer's development or mental state. Blank spaces, rips, erasures, and mendings can signal the writer's own fragmented feelings and thought processes (Altman, *Epistolarity* 182; Castle 119–27; Kauffman, *Discourses of Desire* 141, 147), along with the indeterminacy of language.[3]

The second concept informing my response to these letter novels concerns the gendering of the writing style. In part this involves the rather large and difficult question of *l'écriture féminine:* what we term "feminine" in writing, regardless of the author's gender (or because of it), and how our reading processes, conditioned in part by gender, participate in the analysis of the "feminine." In addition, for reasons that may have a variety of sources—class, education, work background, and ethnicity, for example—external readers (a term I will often use to distinguish the person holding the book from the person within the fiction who holds the letter) will respond differently to the writing style invented for a particular character. What convinces us, as we read letters supposedly written by a

woman, that these letters do represent a woman's writing? What
convinces us that *this* woman would write *these* letters?

Most women authors of letter novels stay with a female voice.
How they then attach the "feminine" to the writing, or if they present various versions of the feminine, has much to tell us about the
concept of writing as a woman. Alice Walker's *The Color Purple* jux-
taposes two letter writers responding differently to the harshness of
their society: Nettie's unemotional, flat tone demonstrates her pain
and need just as the emotional, direct tone of Celie demonstrates
hers. Walker creates two distinctive styles to project the different
ways two women write and rewrite the self. Having two letter writers
and two writing styles allows Walker to argue against any kind of
essentialism in defining woman's writing. More specifically, her format forbids essentializing black women's writing.

In *S.*, Updike's Sarah is the sole writer, although she writes over
a number of different signatures and in a variety of styles. In spite
of her language facility, however, she denigrates her own writing,
which implies serious limitations on what she can learn from her
own written explorations. She seems unable to trust or value fully
the responses she records. Consequently, although she can write the
self, she cannot rewrite it. Responding to *S.*, I find Updike's exploration of writing as a woman a disturbing although often entertain-
ing exploitation of the female voice. It is difficult to decide whether
his sometimes stereotyping presentation of the character is sympathetically comedic or misogynistic.

The third theoretical element influencing my study of epistolary
novels, not surprisingly, is intertextuality, because each of the seven
novels discussed here portrays powerful relationships among texts.
Letter fiction characteristically questions its own uniqueness. As
Kauffman states, although we may initially react to letters as containing "unique, transcendent passion," embedded in the writerly role is
the readerly one, which leads us to perceive that letter fiction becomes "a compendium of the already read, the already said" (*Special
Delivery* xxii). Naturally, letter novels commonly include references
to previous letters by the epistolary heroine and her correspondents.
At times a fictional letter becomes a palimpsest of previously written
letters, so that a 1950s letter can carry traces of sentiments and
phrases from centuries past. Some novelists working in this form
find useful doublings and layerings provided by explicit references
to earlier letter novels. Barth's *LETTERS* figures numerous allusions

of this kind and also introduces a self-referential form of intertextuality by recycling characters and events from the author's own earlier novels.

Although these various forms of intertextuality influence our readings of letter novels, two particular intertextual modes especially fascinate me: what I call *relettering* and *delettering*. In relettering, intertextuality functions as an overtly empowering medium, an earlier text repeatedly or extensively entering a novel to broaden the context of a protagonist's experience. In *Another Pamela,* Upton Sinclair provides his innocent, Bible-studying heroine with an alternate text—Richardson's *Pamela*—that becomes as vital a part of her education as the scriptures. Sinclair's 1950 novel contains components of parody, but his imitation of the earlier novel and his incorporation of long excerpts from it force both the heroine and the novel's reader into constant comparisons of texts and contexts. What I am calling *relettering* resembles the "bibliofables" of Jorge Luis Borges; as a stylistic technique it harbors interesting possibilities for "parricide" (Edward Said's term, 209) as an author repeats but undoes an earlier text.[4]

Working with the motif of intertextuality, I also investigate one letter novel's career as the intertext for a series of dramatic and cinematic productions; I term this adaptive process *delettering* because the adaptations remove the letters' primacy. In a once-popular novel by Jean Webster, *Daddy-Long-Legs,* words and drawings become the seductive, enchanting means through which a young girl turns an anonymous benefactor into a father figure and, eventually, a lover. When Webster's novel is adapted for the stage and then for various movies, where does the protagonist's power reside?[5] The delettering process, which begins with Webster's own stage version of her book and continues through various films, betrays this novel's heroine. Delettering the text robs the heroine of considerable personal power and reconceives how she defines and redefines herself and world.

The last response area basic to my study of epistolary fiction concerns the letter form's concentrated metaphorical use or semiotics of the reading and writing acts. Especially in the chapter on *The Mixquiahuala Letters,* one can see that depictions of a character's reading and writing acts theorize, in narrative form, how we read and write our world and selves. Letter fiction also asks us to undertake new consideration of the reading (and sometimes writing) responses of the external reader. An epistolary confrontation encourages that external reader to new awareness of his or her investments in reading and writing acts. As we encode and decode texts and intertexts, we play various roles; when we are reading others' encodings and decodings we cannot escape admitting that such actions are metaphorically laden. It seems to me then that reading letter novels returns us to other texts with heightened consciousness of what we do as we read and write. One can say that a letter novel has the capacity to serve as a kind of arch-novel. Although I do not totally agree that "the epistle . . . is not a genre but all genres, literature itself" (Derrida, "Envois" 48), I have certainly found that investigating the processes at work in letter novels enlarges or changes my readings of all fiction.[6]

Ana Castillo's postmodern *The Mixquiahuala Letters* highlights metaphors of reading and writing. With its multiple table of contents, this text asks us to choose our own reading strategy, calling into question the notions of letters' verisimilitude and of authorial control. The letter-writing heroine, Teresa, writes to an artist friend who seldom replies, yet words (and by implication drawings) offer chances to create new patterns rather than retrace patterns of the past. Castillo wants us to explore alternate ways of reading a text. This leads me to look at her novel and at the other six in my study in terms of what Janet Altman calls the "pragmatics" of all reading (*Epistolarity* 192). We need to ask whether "epistolary narratives have particular ways of playing to (or against) the reader's desire for mastery, his [or her] creative pleasure in coordinating fragments, his [or her] voyeurism?" (Altman, *Epistolarity* 183).

In a move to incorporate some of the qualities that the correspondence form brings to texts, I asked various authors and critics to contribute letters to the seven chapters of *Epistolary Responses* that concern fiction. Happily, all sent "real" letters. Although the novelists and critics sometimes answer questions I ask, in no instance does the book's text "answer" the letter; my hope is that the interpolated letters add additional perspectives, questions, and possibilities to the discussion, not that they or my responses to them yield closure. In the case of the participating novelists—John Barth, Ana Castillo, and John Updike—the letters respond to, but do not necessarily "answer," specific questions I posed. In the chapters on Upton Sinclair's *Another Pamela* and Jean Webster's *Daddy-Long-Legs,* I selected archival letters that, although written to other people, still permitted these novelists to respond to my text or my assertions in some way. The scholars who participated—Linda Kauffman, Dorothy Hill, and Jim Schiff—reacted either to particular questions or to sections of the book I asked them to read.

3

Fair and Tender Ladies:
Letters as a Response to
Absence, Presence, and Property

In *Fair and Tender Ladies* Lee Smith gives her heroine powerful tools with which to overcome loss and silence, hold onto the culture from which she comes, and, finally, establish herself as a force in her society, even a respected property owner: Smith gives Ivy the pen and the letter. With these tools the protagonist masterfully documents her efforts to create and declare her own place in the world. As we read Ivy's letters, we see an individual woman's growing verbal power and her shift from displacement to placement, from isolation to integration.

With the use of a fairly traditional epistolary format, Smith tacitly establishes the idea that the narrator's own control of her discourse can lead to her developing selfhood or self-presence. At the same time, these letters have a material reality that, combined with certain story elements involving physical possessions, connects the issue of selfhood or self-ownership to that of property ownership. In addition, *Fair and Tender Ladies'* particular way of using the epistolary form leads the external reader to a deeper awareness that, in the "real world" and in the world of the novel, the isolated, private work of one woman writer, once collected and published, can be a precious resource serving many others.

At the most apparent level, the epistolarity of *Fair and Tender Ladies* effectively presents an Appalachian voice and a sense of narra-

tive immediacy, but the form also substantiates the interrelated issues with which this protagonist must struggle. Just as in *Clarissa,*
where a heroine's speech has been silenced by her family, here too
writing becomes a way to claim a space and place of one's own. In
both novels, when others attempt to create the heroine's absence
and lack of subjectivity, she responds by declaring her presence and
subject power. Nevertheless, Ivy Rowe's situation is in many ways different from Clarissa Harlowe's. Clarissa's written messages are often
misread or destroyed by others; Clarissa's missives exist along with
those of others; and Richardson's novel records the slippage between Clarissa's intentions and her correspondents' deliberate or
accidental misreading of her words. In Smith's novel, Ivy Rowe is the
only writer; others' reactions to her words, if they come to us at all,
come to us only as she records them in subsequent letters. This ar-
rangement focuses the novel less on others' interpretations of Ivy
and more on her own interpretive acts, less on the heroine's victimization and more on her growing strengths.[1]

Ivy Rowe, born in the coal country of Virginia at the turn of the
century, writes from the time she is ten until age seventy-five. As one
reviewer succinctly puts it: "Poverty and early motherhood destroy
her dream of writing professionally, but write she does, scores of
letters from girlhood until death" (Starr Smith 95). These letters
contain a highly individualized, often nonstandard style, creating
a voice the *Times Literary Supplement*'s reviewer called "credible"
and "sonorous" (Kaveney 803). The sonority derives from individualized orthography, syntax, and vocabulary and the inclusion of Appalachian stories, food ways, songs, history, and customs; the credibility not only derives from these authentic-seeming details but also
springs from the novel's situation—its focus on isolation and loss
and the logic of the heroine's attempt to overcome those negative
forces through writing.

Her father's death is but the first of Ivy's losses. The family
moves from their original small farmstead; the mother dies and is
buried away from her home and husband; siblings die or drift away
to pursue their own lives. Ivy's closest sister is institutionalized and
later dies of influenza; Ivy and her illegitimate child are sent to live
with a sister in a coal camp; and eventually, after marriage and return to the farm, Ivy loses her energy and joy in life, beaten down
by poverty and hard work. An exhilarating but destructive love affair ends in further loss, the discovery that one of her children has

died during her absence. Later, her husband dies, widowing her at a relatively early age. Finally, after her children move away, she remains alone in her mountain home, proprietor and protector of the family farmstead.

Only at the end of her life is Ivy physically alone, although she is often separated from particular family members. Oddly enough, it is this character's keen intelligence, combined with her potent emotional and physical desires and her pleasure in the details of events and objects, that frequently alienates her from those around her. Writing has two benefits for Ivy: it overcomes her sense of isolation as she makes connections to herself and to others who might understand her better than those with whom she lives, and it becomes a method of documenting and validating her responses to events, people, and a changing self.

At first it may seem, as Willard Spiegelman writes, that Ivy's primary motive for writing is simply "to keep in touch" with friends and overcome the loneliness she feels even when in company, as if letter communication could solve the problem of absence. "To keep in touch" assumes that one unitary, stable, known being contacts another such being. Now, although Smith creates Ivy Rowe as an "innocent" in some ways, the character has insight into the fact that her letters can neither contain all of her nor always contain the same her; writing seldom fully satisfies the desires of writer or reader. Nevertheless, the epistolary protagonist perseveres.

In *Fair and Tender Ladies,* as in most other epistolary novels, space separates the letter-writing character from her correspondents, so writing remains a means of demonstrating to the letter recipient the particular self-definition the writer has undertaken. The letter's content will spell out ideas, events, and feelings, but the letter itself is the medium of enactment.[2] Its paper and ink make those changes real. One could say then, adopting J. L. Austin's well-known terminology, that much of the letter is performative: the writing does not stand for but *is* the action of making value judgments, exercising power, making commitments, taking a social posture, establishing relationships. As Ivy puts it later in life, writing to her grown-up daughter, Joli, things become real to her when she writes them. Her husband's death, for instance, was an abstraction before she took pen to paper: "We bureid him yesterday. but somehow it did not seem real to me, not even then. It does now, for I am writing you this letter" (274).[3] When Ivy relates an event or tells a story, she is not just passing information along—she is positioning herself as an agent of her own experience. When she writes she moves toward or away from others: she forestalls loss; declares her relationship to others, ideas, and events; and situates herself in mental and physical space.

Yet the writing act always lacks full presence: when the letter is being written the reader is absent, and when the letter is being read the writer is absent. When Altman writes that "the letter contains within itself its own negation" (*Epistolarity* 43), she points to the fragmented, gap-ridden "différance" that makes the epistolary form so modern, or shall we say postmodern, and a quality that makes the epistolary character's longing for closeness so poignant.[4] Ivy's letters to friends do seek to initiate a level of intimacy missing in her daily life, but, as she herself eventually realizes, the other benefit of letter writing is that it makes the writer more present to herself. Smith herself has stated that "Ivy was writing (letters) as a way to comprehend her life. And I was writing the novel for the same reason" (qtd. in Romine, 5C). Whether Smith was writing *Fair and Tender Ladies* to comprehend her character's or her own life, the letters of the novel served as sites of response, where therapeutic, aesthetic, and intellectual self-knowledge and self-presence could be achieved.

Ivy's alienation and losses fuel her enormous desire for intimate friendship, as the first letter of the novel demonstrates well. Smith has her write to a Dutch girl (whose name has been given her by her schoolteacher), with Ivy hoping desperately that this girl will become her pen pal. The letter is long and incredibly detailed, recounting not only the history of her mother and father's romance but also her own ambitions about becoming a writer, her impressions of the rest of her family, and descriptions of her home and of the surrounding area. This desperate ten-year-old attempts to recreate her whole physical and emotional world on paper, to make this world and self fully present to the foreigner. When the schoolteacher rejects Ivy's letter as too long, too open, and too detailed, we as readers can predict that Ivy's verbal *jouissance*, her great joy in and attention to sensual details, voice, and words, and the strength of her own vision will frequently create a gap between her and others. Indeed, her communicative skill and her pleasure in making imaginatively present that which is physically absent even contribute to her separation from those among whom she lives. For example, when very young, she and various siblings create fantasy parties in the woods, but by the time Ivy is ten, one sister is more interested in courting than in imaginative play, another wants to use only real names and rejects Ivy's playfulness, one brother wants only to play at imitating actual religious services, and another will only watch. Ivy's closest sister, Silvaney, often becomes confused by the games, and Ivy's mother says Silvaney is "too old to play" (11). Smith demonstrates that no one in the family has time for any of Ivy's oral elaboration, for she has Ivy write that "it seems like I can not talk to my Family they is so many of us here in the house" (24).

Fortunately, the family and neighbors do enjoy one form of imaginative verbal play—telling folk stories. These stories cement intergenerational bonds, provide entertainment, and pass along embedded values concerning loyalty to family, private property rights, and the transformative power of love. These oral stories, whether real or fictional, are a valued part of Ivy's heritage, but she wants more. Inspired by a few books from the school she has attended on and off, she longs to *write* her own poems and stories. In addition, although the frustration of not being heard may fuel her desire to write, I believe much of her motive for writing comes from her need for physical presence, material reality, for something that will last and counter her many loses. Social and economic deprivations within her world, however, leave Ivy no time or quiet to develop as a literary artist or professional, no way to take seriously such possibilities; letters are her only creative space.

Even in a second letter to the Dutch pen pal, when Ivy attempts brevity and concision, she finds herself lapsing into a long story of chestnut hunting. Action, description, and dialogue all embellish the letter until she brings herself up short with "I see I have writ so long agin" (15). Ivy's continuing use of physical detail, while verifying her potential as an artist and her interest in documentation of the material world, also reminds us of her need to offer herself in full friendship. Louise Bernikow explains that "in our various incarnations as characters in other people's stories we [women] have had little to give aside from our bodies and an occasional act of devotion. In fact, we have been given" (115). Because from the start of *Fair and Tender Ladies* Smith establishes Ivy as author of her own story, the book presents the female writing self as an active participant attempting to construct and contribute to her world: a giver, not only an object given. Bernikow also finds that women's exchange of gifts symbolizes intimacy: for women, physical gifts are representations of the self, offered to cement or represent a relationship (115). Thus, we could say that Ivy offers her detailed stories and descriptions not only as a way to communicate particulars to her correspondents but also as metonymic representations of her very self.[5] Furthermore, as she gives to another, she gives to herself. This idea is confirmed when we read letters she writes to her pen pal even after she has realized that she cannot send them.

In the pen pal letters and many others, we find Ivy working against loss by holding onto fading traditions, history, and relationships. Although often emotionally alienated within her family, Ivy is nourished by ancestral traditions—folkways, family stories, farming customs, the homestead itself. Just as various cultures use writing to transmit the record of history, Ivy uses letters to chronicle her own family's history and to maintain for herself and others a record of connection to the past.[6] Through the bridging created by her narratives of past and present, this writer fights loss. She sees herself as maintainer of whatever family connections can survive, joiner of time and space, preserver of memories. As she laments, at age forty-two, to her brother Garnie, begging him to get in touch, "We are the only ones that remember the same things" (250). In the same way, Smith has the child Ivy write to her dead father, not only trying to make him present but also trying to compensate for her lack of connection to her work-hardened and distracted mother. From the same impulse for connection teenager Ivy writes to her family, during a stay in town at her teacher's home, sharing with the family the new town life she is enjoying, but assuring them that she is not becoming spoiled or too separate from them.

Letters to family also solidify Ivy's role as family chronicler.[7] As chronicler, she "records" history: W. P. Kinsella stresses this aspect of Ivy's missives, finding that "through Ivy's letters we watch the advent of change."[8] To absent family members she writes of the mother's sale of mineral rights under the farm, a younger brother's turn to religion, and the mother's death and strange burial. The chronicler not only records history, however; she creates it. For instance, when Ivy writes to her sister Beulah of their mother's death, the discourse functions to control and shape that event, not simply record it. Her account stresses the mother's smallness at death and Ivy's awareness of the large spirit within the corpse, the mystery of this woman's great love for her husband, a "great and strange" love, and the agreement among family members that the mother should be buried beside him. Then, using descriptive terms to set her stage (including stormy weather and people's ways of moving, looking, and talking), Ivy dramatically recounts how her grandfather came and stole away the mother's body to bury her back where she was born: "She is mine now, he said. She will go with me" (121). Finally, Ivy links what has happened to her mother's body to her own mind-state: "I feel so bad now, like I too have been berried in a strange town among strangers" (123). Although Ivy cannot control the disposition of her mother's corpse, her epistolary account attempts control of both body and history through narrative technique.

Placing herself in the role of family chronicler brings Ivy some possibility of therapeutic pay-off, for she is installing herself in the mothering role—she can create and nurture her writing as a surrogate for the missing body of the mother. Subsequent letters to family continue to create a body of information and relationships that substitute for her mother or that put her, as provider of information, in the role of mother. In addition, her letters document and materialize experience. The letters then serve as what Homer Brown, in an article about the different functions of letters and gossip in literature, terms "memorial." The letter "establishes authority of the person, of the *moment,* a text part of the meaning of which is that it can be read later" (581–82). Ivy's literacy provides for others as well as for herself a much needed sense of permanence, for her letters not only shape their collective memory, they do so in a form that has an enduring physical nature.

A subset of Ivy's connective, chronicling, anti-loss letters to family strives to chronicle not the family's changes and traditions but her own most private feelings and ideas. Almost all of these letters, written to her sister Silvaney, desperately claim this sister's confidence, her nonjudgmental acceptance of some aspect of Ivy that she cannot write (or tell) anyone else: "I feel I am bursting with news but I can not tell it to a sole, I have no one to talk to. . . . Oh Silvaney my love and my hart, I can talk to you for you do *not* understand" (emphasis added, 96–97). These letters are addressed to the barely verbal Silvaney, an older sibling damaged by brain fever when a child, who eventually grew so wild that she spent almost all her time wandering the woods and was finally institutionalized. Silvaney's wildness seems related to her inability to verbalize, a terrible limitation but emblematic here also of a certain freedom for Ivy.[9]

Adapting Altman's terminology, one can term Silvaney a "zero-degree confidante," for she passively receives confessions and sto-ries. Normally even the passive confidante has some force; at the least, some of such a letter recipient's words are occasionally quoted or paraphrased (*Epistolarity* 50–51), indicating that the recipient has interacted with the protagonist. The speaking done by the mentally damaged Silvaney was always minimal, so the only "quotes" from her are Ivy's recollections about the things she and Ivy shared: guessing where babies came from, playing statues, listening to sto-ries on Christmas Eve. Also recalled are Silvaney's past wild actions. Ivy "paraphrases" her sister's wanderings, refusals of food, sleepless-ness (208). Ivy's quotations and paraphrases of Silvaney's past ac-tions make her "present," and this sympathetic "presence" allows Ivy to confide feelings and actions that the people around her would judge aberrant. Only when writing to Silvaney can Ivy reflect on her own wildness, a wildness whose reality may be destructive but which she must nonetheless know.[10]

Silvaney can be seen as a projection of Ivy that she cannot show to the rest of the world. This part of herself, her heart, does not censor her, but allows her to be totally herself: "you are my soul" (271). This inner self is externalized, made real to her, by the pro-cess of writing. The letters to the sister who cannot understand help Ivy to understand herself, to get below the surface of things and words. As the teenager writes: "I feel that things are happening two times allways, there is the thing that is happening, which you can say, and see, and there is another thing happening too inside it, and this is the most important thing but its so hard to say" (96). Smith's hero-ine has a growing reflexivity and depth of perception, but this con-tinually dooms her to a realization that, within the presence of each word and action, knowledge of another presence creates a sense of absence too. Silvaney here functions as what Derrida, exploring the fragmenting aspect of all representation, calls the "reflection, the image, the double" that "splits what it doubles" (*Grammatology* 36). Writing to her sister is both an effort to achieve a unified self (at one point she declares "we have all got a true nature and we cant hide it" [280]) and a realization of the self's nonunitary nature.

So far I have concentrated on the ways epistolarity functions in-*Fair and Tender Ladies* to document the values of writing for the main character's self-development, helping her overcome psychological and physical losses. I have seen the protagonist's efforts as useful expressions of feminine desire for selfhood and also touched on the complications to that desire created by separation of physical space and the space of individuality. Yet, even as Smith's novel celebrates Ivy's efforts at performative control of her own development, it reveals an odd, distracting slippage. Within this text's construction lie certain elements that ask us to question the protagonist's power as individual agent of her own destiny.

In standard epistolary works, such as *Letters of a Portuguese Nun, Pamela, Clarissa, Evelina,* or *The Expedition of Humphry Clinker,* an editor explains how the work's letters were collected, someone in the cast of characters evinces an interest in gathering the letters for posterity, or the characters have a continuing relationship or are limited in number; thus, there is an easily explained reason or stated possibility for the letters' collection. As Altman puts it, most epistolary novels "tell the story of their own publication" (*Epistolarity* 110),[11] and although Smith's narrative does not rule out the possibility of the letters' collection, the logic of that collection is never overtly confronted. Thus, for the external reader the problem of the letters' reproduction becomes an enticing, provocative element within the reading process.

Smith draws attention to the framework of her novel in various ways. One perceives immediately that Ivy Rowe is the only writer of these letters, so their destinations seem determined solely by her. As an older woman, Ivy exerts further control: she burns some of the most confidential letters, those written to her sister Silvaney but never mailed because Silvaney had died. For me, the impossibility of full congruence between language and deed, thought and expression, and past and present is symbolized by the appearance in the collected letters of particular missives Ivy actually destroyed. Ivy's other letters, ones actually sent to family and friends, are dispersed among numerous recipients over a period of six decades, so the possibility of their collection would be highly unlikely. In addition, Ivy herself never evinces any interest in calling back her letters. Still, the letters are collected, and, given the realistic style within which Smith presents the fiction, one asks: by whom? The only logical guess is that Ivy's daughter, Joli, who becomes the professional author Ivy never could, undertakes the arduous task of finding and preserving her mother's letters. Are we to imagine that, as a professional writer and loving daughter, she also "invents" the letters Ivy burned, in a caring effort to share her mother's experience and tell her mother's story?

Why does Smith structure her epistolary novel to raise the question of who collects and who owns these letters? Why, when she focuses so vividly on the experiences of one poor, undereducated, Appalachian woman born at the turn of the century, does Smith simultaneously draw attention *away* from that character and toward the necessity for another character to take a hand in gathering the letters? Is it to mark the postmodern dislocation writers and critics know so well, disclaiming unitary character or continuity between language and experience? I cannot deny those possibilities. In many recent letter novels formal dislocations serve just such a function; I think particularly of Ana Castillo's *The Mixquiahuala Letters* and Gilbert Sorrentino's *Mulligan Stew* (which combines epistolary and nonepistolary genres).

More intriguing to me, however, is the idea that Smith's technique draws attention to the letters as inheritance or collection to raise the issue of women's relationship to various kinds of property. Just as one of Ivy's motives for writing has been to forestall loss, her daughter Joli's work as collector/editor will provide a physical negation of absence, loss, and emptiness. The words of her mother can endure. At a more abstract level, the collection of her mother's letters represents the connection between one writer and another, the valuation by a woman of writing work performed by another, the prizing of archival documents that tell a woman's history. If we think of Ivy's writing as a form of "feminist critique," or "feminist reading," a "mode of interpretation" that is often "revisionist," to adopt Elaine Showalter's terms, we can see Joli's collecting/editing as a form of "gynocritics." By bringing together and thereby permitting reproduction of the letters, the daughter enacts and encourages others to adopt a deeply positive responsiveness to women's writing ("Feminist Criticism" 245–46).

"Gynocritics," according to Showalter, includes studying "the psychodynamics of female creativity; the trajectory of the individual or collective female career; and the evolution and laws of a female literary tradition" ("Feminist Criticism" 248). Imagining Joli as "editor" of her mother's letters, I also see her making available to future readers knowledge of the conditions that affected or discouraged women artists of the past.[12] In particular, one might see the fictional Joli as a participant in the feminist effort to recover literature produced by women and either ignored or quickly forgotten. As an author in her own right, Joli claims her biological mother as literary mother too, in an act of ownership that places women's private discourse in the public realm. The letters become a valued asset— property that can pass to future generations.

Ivy Rowe never owns much physical property. Her marginal existence is typical of that depicted in many recent works about women. As Linda Wagner-Martin points out, concerning this novel and others by contemporary southern women, "the marginality of the poor, the child, the wife, the slave is a pervasive theme" (19). Smith's novel details Ivy's deprivations and her resulting attitudes toward both tangible and intangible property.

Notably, however, Ivy does actually own a small property as an older woman, and in her old age she is sole controller of that property. It is so precious to her, and she so much wants it to remain intact for her grandson who loves it, that she physically wards off coal strippers who attempt to cross her land. The land is the only property she truly values. Her valuation is within what we might call a feminine or even ecofeminine system, for she loves the land not for its economic exploitability, but in terms of its natural beauty. Early on she announces, "It is the prettest place in the world" (6). This place is sympathetic to her spirit. Her very name and that of her retarded sister Silvaney form a tie to this natural world (Wagner-Martin 23).

The fact that Ivy eventually owns and controls this small homestead might seem to indicate a possible power base for her in society. As Karen Sacks has remarked, however, the owning of property by women may accrue them power "vis-à-vis a husband," but will not yield them power in the larger society until that society grants women status as full-fledged adults (218–19). In addition, given the farm's marginally productive capacity, it cannot count much as an economic force. The kind of recognition Sacks discusses emerges for the women in Ivy's world gradually, over the time period covered in the novel. In her world, women must still work very hard to achieve any such recognition, but the possibility is definitely emerging: Geneva, a friend of Ivy, owns and manages a boarding house; Violet, another friend, becomes an active union organizer; Ivy's childhood friend, Molly, runs a school; her sister Ethel comes to own and run the general store her husband started; one daughter-in-law becomes an effective real estate agent; and her daughter, Joli, becomes a professional writer. The marginalized Ivy becomes a full-fledged adult and force within her community's economy at the novel's end when she thwarts the coal company's efforts to seize her mineral rights. This new level of force and *public* action parallels the personal force and *private* action Ivy has exerted to create her own story by writing letters.

Economic power based on market exploitation is portrayed mostly as a negative force in this novel; timbering and mining destroy the land. For much of her life Ivy exists at the margin of the political and economic forces of the larger society, and so she neither receives recognition for her contribution nor often even realizes she is being deprived of something she deserves. Like many women, her "participation in social production" has been largely ignored (Sacks 222). By the time Ivy is sole owner of her property, after the death of her husband, she is beyond desiring participation in the exploitive market economy that has destroyed so much of Appalachia; she is not about to use the land for petty gains. She may grow a few vegetables, she may even be tempted, under financial duress, to sell a small piece of the acreage to survive, but finally she resists the economic exploitation of the land. She wants to protect it, regretting that "everybody has took everything out of here now—first the trees, then the coal, then the children" (296). In her role as property owner, Ivy does not want to master or control or shape the land, but instead wants to identify with it and share it with those who will also care for it.

Just as central to Ivy Rowe as the farm on which she begins and ends her life is the founding romance of her family, the story of John Rowe's courting of Maude Castle and carrying his love off against her father's wishes in the dark of the night. Although, as the young Ivy admits, "they did not live haply ever after as in Mrs. Browns [her schoolteacher's] book" (6), their story has some power to sustain the couple's reality against the deadening circumstances of illness and poverty. Certainly the story is important to Ivy, giving her a sense of her parents' original love for each other, a love that daily life has all but deadened. In none of her letters does Ivy ever dissect this particular romance or speculate on the incompatibility of romantic passion and marriage. Other incidents in the novel, however, make clear that Ivy perceives the flaws in popular notions of romantic love. In various letters she relates the hardships of her mother and considers the destruction caused to marriage when passion leads couples into affairs. Her own affair with the beekeeper, Honey Breeding, almost kills her. But Ivy can never deny the wildness in her own nature or in any one else's—in spite of its potential to destroy, she honors it as part of the human condition. By maintaining intact the story of her parents' passion she keeps that notion of wildness alive. This is another kind of property—a piece of her genealogy, a piece of oral history that she records to give it permanence.

The old folk tales told by her father or by neighbor women are also powerful narratives for Ivy. The stories draw power not only from their themes of passion and trickery but also, of more importance, from their actual existence. The stories create a sense of continuity and tradition, their very transmittal working to forestall loss. Within this novel, it is not surprising that Ivy turns to narrative as a way to partake of that continuity. To make narratives of her own becomes, for Ivy, a way to create control; her letters frame and hold onto a world that otherwise is mostly characterized by loss.

Thus, besides the physical property that comes to mean so much to her, the other property Ivy owns is the intangible legacy of stories passed on to her by family and neighbors, along with the versions of experience she creates. Transmitting others' stories, chronicling family events and myths, and detailing her own experiences become forms of "social production," but without attached dollar signs. Ivy gives the stories enduring materiality for, as Hill perceives, "Ivy *writes* in mountain dialect, thus providing a bridge between the lyrical oral and the codified written" (*Lee Smith* 107). Stories and language that might otherwise disappear receive added presence within Ivy's letters, which in turn become artifacts, with their own physical reality, and can then become (for an individual or group of individuals) tangible property. The fact that Ivy herself does not collect the letters or value them as objects, but that *someone* does, brings our attention squarely to the question of property—tangible and intangible—and the problematic situation of property for women in our society. More specifically, Smith's tactic focuses attention on the economy of woman's narrative itself: who tells it, who recovers it, and how it is transmitted.

Smith has had a continuing interest in the question of who owns whose story, in particular, how a woman's story gets told, and has experimented with genres that can underscore this issue. Her fictions often establish tension between the stories others write about an individual and the stories the individual writes of herself. In *Oral History* (1983), young Jennifer undertakes a class project that will engage her in tracking her past. This genealogical work inspires her deeply; she avers that before the experience she "was nothing . . . she didn't know a thing" (16). Jennifer's story is only a small section of the novel, framing the main text. That text consists of impossible oral histories, told to undesignated listeners. These "spoken" narratives combine with journal extracts to move between past and present. Could they be collected? Could Jennifer come back and somehow gather this material? Is she telling the story we hear in others' voices? Who is? To whom? Who owns this oral history?

In *Family Linen* (1985) Smith invents third- and first-person accounts by or about various members of a southern family drawn together by the death of their matriarch and the possibility that the matriarch may have murdered her first husband. An omniscient author creates this Faulkner-like story structure, but never reveals her gathering hand. As in *Oral History*, the reader knows more than the characters, and there is no logical explanation for the collection of the various narratives. Individuals, Smith seems to say here, own their snippets of experience: author and reader play god and see the whole picture. In this form of novel, the author practices what Wayne Booth calls "omniscience with teeth in it" (161). The reader shares with the narrator more knowledge than the characters ever have.

In *Fair and Tender Ladies* Ivy Rowe is given the central role of creating her own story. We never know more about her than she reveals, although we may guess at the disillusionments and sufferings that will come to her. Ivy's voice dominates the novel—her peculiar choices of words and phrases, her elaborations or deletions, her responses to others and to herself. The illusion Smith creates is that it is up to Ivy to select and order information so that she truly speaks for herself. Through the fictional ceding of control to her protagonist, Smith implies a theoretical stance concerning voice and appropriation of voice. This theoretical position is one she has also articulated, explaining that "the story—no matter what it is—is finally the storyteller's story" (qtd. in Hill, "An Interview" 18). Although Smith herself is not an outspoken proselytizer for feminist politics or theories, her work is deeply committed to exploring, through its content *and* its form, women's roles and experiences. As Dorothy Hill puts it, Smith "is neither political by nature nor polemical by predisposition. . . . She is, however, interested in the female experience. . . . For her, female self-expression is where healing lies, and she is interested herself in writing as self-repair" (Hill, "An Interview" 5).

At this moment, when feminists are so focused on issues of gendered writing, the female tradition in literature and the arts, and questions of feminine voice and writing styles, Smith presents Ivy writing herself in a nonhierarchical form, defining herself through her own creation of narratives of various kinds. By putting her narrative in the epistolary form, Smith gives her protagonist control of the evolving story. Nonetheless, because the letters are collected and organized by another hand, Smith must be valuing the role of that collector too. With Ivy's distinctive voice and her clearly articulated need to write, we have no doubt that the letters affirm Ivy's right to herself; she owns herself even when she owns nothing else. She owns her own versions of the truth. She determines what level of public exposure to give her experience, writing to one family member or more of certain events, only writing to the dead Silvaney of others. As the imagined recoverer (and inventor?) of what would otherwise be lost, however, Ivy's daughter, Joli, also enters the story process. She becomes the inheritor of her mother's legacy, but only because she makes that effort, not because of Ivy's willing it to her deliberately.

In spite of all I have said about Ivy's privileged role, the fact is that we as readers still know that the letters are a fiction and that Lee Smith is the one who created them. Chapter headings are an element of the work that force us to remember the constructed nature of the fiction. The novel's physical form works to focus attention again on questions of ownership and collectibility. Five sections, with headings such as "Letters from Sugar Fork," beg the question of where the letters came from and who arranged them. For the character Ivy, the letters' durability is not what matters. For her daughter, Joli, the letters could have sentimental, historical, and/or material value. For Lee Smith, an artist creating a publishable commodity, the letters, in addition to yielding artistic and personal satisfaction, *are* property.[13]

Although I have stressed the connection in *Fair and Tender Ladies* between intangible and tangible property, I think other readers see the novel's handling of material property functioning more symbolically. In her letter to me about the novel, Dorothy Hill, author of the Twayne volume on Lee Smith and a good friend of Smith, takes issue with my approach (but in a helpful way) and questions my implicit and explicit privileging of writing over other creative acts. Yet I find that in her expression of appreciation and longing for the kind of connection that writing and receiving letters can accomplish, Hill echoes sentiments I have expressed.

----

12 September 1994

Dear Anne,

For starters, I have to pick a bone with you. You start out your chapter talking about either Lee's or Ivy's "mastery" (words from the male domain sneaking in? taking over the old thought-process?), and you get so subsumed by that seductive masculinity infecting our language that you even say that Lee gives Ivy a "powerful tool" (Hello, Freud!), the pen. Lee is the last person in the world who would privilege the pen over any other connector. And she for sure thinks baking cakes, say, is as important as writing, that overvalued act. (Did you read *Tristes Tropiques* by Claude Levi-Strauss? He says that, if you ask what writing was for, it wasn't for making civilization possible. Civilization shaped right up centuries before writing. No, what it was for, was, to record—make a record of—how many hours that slave dragged that stone each day across the sand to make those pyramids and that what writing did was make possible a master class and a slave class.) And Lee is the last person in the world to think she *gave* Ivy anything. No, Ivy gave *her* the letters and the book. Remember how Lee started this epistolary novel? She bought a packet of letters at a yard sale for 75¢. When she sat down and opened them, she found that the letters contained a woman's whole life, told in letters to her sister. For Lee, who—like Little Sister Death—never had a sister, the letters gave her the book. I guess they finally gave her a sister. Lee is all about Connection, that is just what she is all about. Remember E. M. Forster's "only connect"? Lee says that she just writes books to give her an excuse to go out on tour and talk to people. And do you remember all those letters Ivy keeps writing to Silvaney even after Silvaney's dead? Remember what Ivy eventually does with them? She burns them! She says they don't matter, that it was the writing of them that mattered. The process, not the product! It's the opposite of commodification, the opposite of materialism. One of the themes that runs throughout Lee's fiction is her own struggle with what art *is*. Claiming Virginia Woolf's influence, Lee says that she thinks the things women have traditionally done—setting a table with flowers, giving a birthday party for a child, fixing hair, and, yes, writing letters purely out of love—are art. But they aren't thought of as art because you can't sign your name to them and hang them in some museum. She loves the process, not the product. I think this is true of most artists. *They* are not the ones paying bluebillion bucks to *own* the things they make. Have you read (this title contains one of my very favorite post-colonic surges) *The Gift:* (here it comes) *Imagination and the Erotic Life of Property*? It's about artists, about people who are gifted (I think it focuses on Walt Whitman) and how they need to be in a culture where gifts circulate freely and thus don't do very well under capitalism. Lots of Lee's characters you can see she loves most give things away freely—like Ivy and her letters.

It is amazing how deeply this book touches people. I spoke at a conference on Lee's work at Methodist College in Fayetteville, South Carolina. The thing I remember most vividly is the urgency with which several people tried to make me understand their experience of seeing the off-Broadway play based on *Fair and Tender Ladies*. The play is called, I believe, "Sincerely, Ivy Rowe." No, I just checked my book on Lee and there I have the title as "Ivy Rowe," written and produced by Barbara Smith and Mark Hunter. Anyway, several people spoke *urgently,* clinging to me for my full attention, of how whole audiences of middle-aged women would sit and weep throughout the whole play. Weeping and weeping, wiping and spilling tears. And I have thought about this. What is it that Ivy Rowe does? Well, it's more what she doesn't do. She doesn't buy into the dominant culture, not in any way. She doesn't go off to Baltimore with what's-her-name (Miss Torrington?)—I'm practicing my own little resistance here against academia by not going and looking everything up—I realize that can be used to completely discredit me, like when they all started whispering on the back row when I misquoted Dylan-for-heaven's-sakes-Thomas, but I'm trying to occupy a different persona here, the me before I got tooken by the dominant culture and quit writing letters altogether—anyway, Ivy doesn't go off with Miss Torrington to Boston or Baltimore or wherever to go to school. She doesn't take her big chance to GET OUT. She stays, right there in the underbelly of America (RAW). She doesn't accept the culture's definitions for her own self, either. When she gets pregnant, she's *glad* to be ruint. It frees her. She doesn't have to act any more like she's going by all the conventions. And by the book's end, she even stands up to her brother Garnie's typical Christian denunciations of women as whores of Babylon and so forth. What she is curious about from the time she is a little girl is the nature of love. She worries because she wants to experience everything about it and know everything about it but doesn't want to have loads of children and get "titties as big as the moon." Well, there's the female dilemma right there, isn't it? And I think as we get more and more institutionalized, we are losing even the memory of what that woman's loving was.

I personally miss women. I miss the women at church picnics when I was small, with their puffy ankles and varicose veins. I've often mused on how we made up a Father God that loved us and would die for us because we already knew that for sure about our mothers. Our mothers carried us in their bodies and their bodies were changed forever. They loved us that much, and did everything for us for love. Entertained us and sang to us and held us against their bodies and carried us out to show us the whole sweet world. All for love. My husband and I were just talking about great titles and I offered "Some Gave All" from Billy Ray Cyrus from my neck of the woods down there in Kentucky. He countered with *Everything We Had*, a book by a nurse who served in Vietnam. I started to write that typing that last title made me cry, and I remembered being cautioned by a writer not to reveal that, for it would allow THEM to cancel me out. Why are we living in a world where the emotional is unacceptable? Or, better still, *how* are we? But back to mothers and titles and sacrifice. (O, let me throw in one more thing. I'm glad I threw in my home boy Billy Ray back there because whenever I get very far down this road I have to back up and say something. When we talk about the feminine and the masculine, I often think what we are really talking about is the creative and the analytical. Then, because we arc materialists, we completely collapse the categories of feminine and creative because, by golly, we know those little babies pop out right between their legs and it's how we all got here, so they must be creative. Right? And I think creativity is generous by nature, freely giving. And we all have that streak. We *all* have a creative unconscious and we all have analytic capability. So let me try to find a way out of these parentheses and reenter the flow *without* anyone thinking when I say female I mean embodied by the female or when I say male I mean embodied by the male. I think we've literalized and concretized our own metaphors and that all our problems stem from that. I think because men have to get hard for the sex act to occur and human life to continue that we come to think of men as "hard." He says "I'm getting hard" or she says "Are you hard yet?" and they both put into the air the idea that he's hard, whether anyone is aware of it or not. Same with softness and so on.) So we were swimming around, or thought we were, in a sea of unconditional maternal love. And I find I miss it. My own mother has had a stroke now, and I moved back in with my parents for the first year of enormous, profound change and real trauma. And I felt so alone. The women in the houses on either side were gone to work all day, too. And we rarely ever see neighbors in this typical suburban neighborhood anyway. I began to long for the days when women talked over back fences, out hanging up clothes, or dropping by with a pie wrapped in a dish towel. I know we can hire help, but I'm talking about love, freely given. I got much closer to my parents during this time, of course, and one day I happened to think to ask my mother how she felt about television when it dropped like a bomb into our living room and everyone else's. She was a bit reluctant, and I asked her directly how it made her feel for us to turn from her and fixate on the box. Her eyes filled with tears and her head went down— it's so hard for her to believe she has a right to ask for anything —and she whispered, "I didn't want to lose you." And Ivy didn't want to lose Silvaney. And we don't want to lose Lee. And she doesn't want to lose us, either. A woman writing for the *London Times* wrote that Lee writes at her best when she writes out of love. So do we all.

True Confession

I used to write out of love. I used to write letters all the time and there are people still waiting for them. That is one way women used to keep connections alive between people who mattered to each other, through letters. Then I went back to school and got my Ph.D. and I wrote a dissertation and then a book and I never write letters anymore and there is a huge loss, in my world and that of people who've loved me. My mother's brother writes her all the time, and he is always apologizing that he didn't get more schooling so he could write better. And my father's sister and brother have college degrees and never write. My husband's mother, with a third grade education, writes more than he does. Look how long it's taken me to get this letter to you. Somehow, every time I've thought of writing it, I've remembered something. When I was a teenaged girl, my sister and her boyfriend found a letter in an old house. It had been preserved in a magazine from about 1905, I believe. It was on blue paper and dated *during* the Civil War. It was a woman writing her sister, and in the letter she told about another woman dying in childbirth. But then she reminisced about the days before her father went off to war. She remembered how he would work in the fields and when it got near sundown the children would string out along the road looking for him to come in, hollering "Yonder comes Pap" and running around his legs, to touch him. We didn't know how to preserve the letter and it lost its color and crumbled in no time flat. But you made me remember it, and a whole gone world, by waiting for my letter.

Thank you,

Dorothy Hill

———————————

4

"Help! Love me! I grow old!": The Central Role of Germaine Pitt in John Barth's *LETTERS*

In *Fair and Tender Ladies*, I looked at ways Ivy Rowe emerges, through her letters, from silence to selfhood and from loss to ownership—of self, of story, of property tangible and intangible. In John Barth's *LETTERS* I also look at a female character struggling with possibilities of loss, yet I can hardly call Germaine Pitt, the novel's only female letter writer, a silenced or deprived woman. Her fluency, verbosity, and established position as a scholar would seem to guarantee that Germaine Necker-Gordon Pitt, Lady Amherst, Acting Provost of Marshyhope State University, will have no difficulty in making known to others her thoughts, feelings, and desires.

Circumstances undermine the self this protagonist has taken for granted, however, and she finds herself deeply questioning her assumptions about sexuality, intimacy, and all her most important relationships. Particular situations leave her "thoroughly alarmed, confused, distressed" (361) at times, but, fortunately, her confessional missives to "John Barth" allow her space to sort out her multiple responses. In many-paged letters Germaine therapeutically attempts to "smother" a "funk"(376), relieve "misery" (390), or aggressively use pen as weapon as she reveals to one man what she suffers because of another. The letters to "John Barth" afford Germaine new opportunities for presenting and then re-presenting herself to an absent other and to herself.[1] Of most importance, writing becomes a way to compose her life as she converts her self-image from that of a cynical menopausal literary historian to that of a mid-life woman contemplating childbirth, new intellectual projects, and an energized, serene acceptance of the future.

In *LETTERS* seven correspondents (six men and Germaine) write letters that are collected at first hand or second hand by the "John Barth" character to make a novel. The component writings, dated from March 2 through September 26, 1969, range in subject from recountings of intimate lovemaking to personal histories, from philosophical discussions of art to quirky disquisitions on insect life to accounts of historical battles. Some commentators have found the book's expansive nature "wasteful" and even "boring" (Edwards 33, Schmitz 321). John W. Aldridge, focusing only on the five characters resurrected from earlier fictions, asserts that in this novel Barth's "vision has indeed become bottled and he voiceless in the wash of his previous vision, an amphora whose only function is to be a surviving artifact of a function he himself has rendered obsolete" (126). Such a reaction ignores the presence of the novel's newly cre-ated female character—Germaine Pitt, Lady Amherst—and the way her presence comments not only on what Aldridge calls "fictional reality" but also on "extra-fictional reality" (126).[2]

More positive reviews of *LETTERS* have often focused on the ways Barth's seven writers collectively and effectively investigate the necessity for and impossibility of bridging the distances and strangeness (in time, space, and culture) that keep us from feeling truly present to ourselves and others. The seven writers experience alienation and absence differently and use different strategies to overcome them. Placing the characters in relationship to one an-other, Barth creates an exhaustive study of the permutations of ab-sence and presence. Exhaustive indeed. One's awareness of the con-structed nature of this thing, a 772-page novel, heightens the sense that constructs are all we have. According to Patrick O'Donnell, the novel's very complexity, "with its many hidden keys and references to some master plot that underlies the divagations of its eighty-eight letters . . . encourages and, in the end, frustrates [the] readerly quest for expressive causality" (*Passionate Doubts* 49).

The dominant language through which Barth highlights his constructions of absence and presence is one that speaks of reen-actment, recycling, and revolution, the making or remaking of his-tories, public and private. Nevertheless, each character has his or her own obsession and task at hand. My focus is on Germaine Pitt's efforts at midlife to regenerate herself and others, particularly her use of the epistolary space to engage heart and mind in those efforts. Already a writer at ease with public discourse, Germaine requires a different discourse form to explore and analyze her responses to the confusing people and events around her. Barth provides her with a privileged locus for self-regeneration through seven months' worth of "Saturday epistolary fix[es]" (450).

Given John Barth's own passion for recycling of literary form and content, and given his own commentary in 1967 and 1980 essays, respectively, on "The Literature of Exhaustion" and "The Literature of Replenishment," Germaine's personal efforts at regeneration can be read as an echo of his own artistic striving. The regenerative theme percolates through the six male writers' letters also, but receives a special force in Germaine's contributions: as the only woman writer in this novel, her comments foreground the necessity of including the particulars of woman's experience (reproductive, relational, artistic, historic, economic, and political) in any discussion of social and personal renewal. Germaine's epistolary efforts respond primarily to her own assumptions about what it is to be a woman at midlife, but at the same time she responds to experiences of the two "authors" in the novel—"John Barth," who invites her participation in his novel-in-letters, and Ambrose Mensch, who invites her participation in his personal and artistic rejuvenation. In industrialized Western culture at least, women usually lose status and sexual recognition as they lose youth. Menopause traditionally has been associated with the exhaustion of women's generative powers, but Germaine replenishes herself (and perhaps others) as she writes and rewrites her past, present, and future.

Barth's characters, like Lee Smith's, work against transience and loss. All seven writers, as they attempt connection with each other, unborn children, dead fathers, or even themselves, struggle to create anew—whether to create a new generation, a new work of art, a new sense of self, or a new understanding of history. Each of the characters "asked" by "John Barth" to participate in the novel is at some kind of midpoint: "All six fictive letter writers measure their ongoing development by addressing their old selves at some point in the novel in a résumé of the first half of their lives" (Schulz 40). In the correspondence of Germaine, her desire to become pregnant with the child of her lover, Ambrose, becomes a strong source of narrative drive—can she and Ambrose conceive, given her age (fifty) and his "low motile" sperm? The desire to conceive a child demonstrates both individuals' need to overcome various losses in their lives. Parallel to the lovers' efforts to create a child we have the author-character's regenerative endeavor to create a novel that will combine realist and modernist modes into his own brand of post-modernist fiction.[3] Max Schulz perceives that " 'the Author'/Barth is regenerating a new novel, *LETTERS,* which is the child of the second half of his literary career. Thus does 'the Author'/Barth also engage, like his six fictive correspondents, in self-recreation in the changing form of his fiction, which is the only 'life' finally important to a writer" (42).

Following Barth's own formulation of his female character, many discussions of *LETTERS* "read" Germaine almost exclusively in the symbolic roles of "Fair Embodiment of the Great Tradition" or "Literature Incarnate" or "The Story Thus Far" (39–40), roles that the two professional authors in the novel ("John Barth" and Ambrose Mensch) initially ask her to play. For example, Heide Ziegler defines Germaine as "the personification of modernist literature or . . . the personification of the history of that literary movement" (67). But the character herself refuses to be defined solely by those roles, even though at times she willingly and self-knowingly plays with them. That is, she will not enter the text as muse or symbol, although once in it as a complex "living" participant-character-correspondent she does not seem to mind representing "Literature" in a film or serving temporarily in an inspirational capacity to "Barth" or Ambrose. Readings that overemphasize the character's symbolic aspect reinscribe her as woman into the traditional modernist functions of muse, comforter, dark continent, inspiration, and object.

Barth himself provides some information about this character; his pleasure in his invention's refusal to serve only as a symbol is evident.

4/12/92

Dear Professor Bower:

Your letter of March 18 mentions that *your* concern, in the novel *LETTERS,* is "mostly with [my] invention of and reaction to

Germaine Pitt, Lady Amherst, the only 'novel' protagonist in [my] novel," and you thoughtfully supply me with an itemization of that concern. I'll address those items in order—although my own chief concerns in the novel and in the character of Ms. Pitt are not necessarily these.

Q: What, as far as you're concerned, are the distinctive qualities of Lady Amherst's voice, as against the six male letter writers' voices?

A: She's British and female. More particularly, she's a well educated, independent-spirited British woman, no longer in her first youth, with a fair amount of mileage on her experiential odometer and of literature under her belt, stuck in a third-rate American university with a somewhat exploitative American lover, younger than herself, who inclines to cast her in the role of Mother English, or the Great Tradition—a role that she spiritedly and eloquently resists. My designs upon her, as author, were similar to her lover's, with the difference that I intend her eloquence (i.e., my ventriloquism) both to echo the tradition she resists and to express her resistance to it. I hasten to add that the six male correspondents have voices about as different from one another's as from Germaine Pitt's.

Q: How much consideration did you give to the feminist need to reclaim "herstory"?

A: Little or none—but the pliability of History is a main theme of the novel.

Q: Did you give Germaine Pitt British nationality not only so that she could so amusingly represent English (Literature) but also so that a small, provocative distance would exist between her language and that of her correspondents?

A: No doubt.

Q: Did it "feel" different to write as a woman?

A: Not so different as it felt to write as that particular woman—whose voice and person I found as agreeable to inhabit as Scheherazade's, in other of my fiction. Among the satisfactions of the trade is that sort of ventriloquism: the inhabitation of invented persons very other than oneself. It was equally agreeable to speak in *LETTERS* for the aging bachelor lawyer Todd Andrews, the psychocripple Jacob Horner, the vaguely sinister and protean A. B. Cook, the human-mimicking insect Jerome Bonaparte Bray, the failed avant-gardist Ambrose Mensch, and that personage of few words, the Author. But I maintain a particular affection for my beleaguered and valorous Lady Amherst.

The present Earl of Amherst, by the way—a lineal descendant of Lord Jeffrey Amherst of French-and-Indian War fame—was shown the novel by my British editor before UK publication, and graciously gave his imprimatur to my invention of Lady A.

Cordially,

J. B.

By creating a new character who writes herself through letters, a female whose vitality "is a particular triumph[—] . . . printed word . . . indeed become flesh" (Charles Harris 168), postmodernist Barth pushes against the poststructuralist decision that unitary character is impossible and allows his female character to assert her own subjectivity. All the while he simultaneously foregrounds the character's constructed nature and her own awareness of the many ways her world constructs her plus her own participation in that construction. "I know (so far as I know) that I am real, and I beseech you not to play tired Modernist tricks with real (and equally tired) people," Barth has Germaine plead ironically (199).

In spite of her entreaty and Barth's partial disavowal, one cannot simply gloss over this character's symbolic functions. As past consort of many modernist novelists, as a literary critic in her own right, and as the most effusive epistolarian in the novel, Germaine does function as a representative of traditions in fiction. Richard Bradbury proposes that in *LETTERS* "Barth returned to the idea that the way forward in narrative was to go backwards in search of an 'old' form which could be rejuvenated" (61). Bradbury sees clearly the way in which for the author (Barth himself and the Barth character in the novel) the epistolary genre provides an amalgamation and thereby a resolution to problems in all the major literary traditions that attract him. In the complex structure of *LETTERS*, realism, modernism, and postmodernism overlap and intertwine, as if they critiqued each other through the novel's epistolary play.

Bradbury, like many others who concentrate on the novel's structure and metanarrative content, gives no particular weight to any one of the various letter writers. In contrast, E. P. Walkiewicz is among those who find that Germaine's "voice is raised for us above the others[;] her final acceptance of her lover's proposal ends the book on a note of promise that resonates with the possibility that

future recombinations will lead not to mere replication or reen-
actment but to the replenishment of life, language, and fiction"
(138). I too give Germaine symbolic primacy because, given the artistic "mid-life crisis" experienced by the author-character who is
constructing the novel before our eyes (Charles Harris notes that
the novel was composed during the actual author's forties [159]),
the problem of artistic regeneration is most vividly bodied forth in
the situation of a character who, while seemingly past the time for
birth can still bring forth new life. Germaine's letters to the novel's
"author" character provide a fascinating gloss, in the flesh, on the
author's effort to attempt literary conversion or rejuvenation. Although the male author (and his double, Ambrose Mensch), originally wants to exploit the female as muse, inspiration, and source of
sexual energy in all the ways that have been fully detailed by feminist critics of patriarchal methodologies, this female character also
puts "John Barth" and Ambrose Mensch to use for her own self-
transformative purposes. Bradbury's statement that the novel's de-
sign questions "the place of an author as a structuring mechanism
within the text" (62) concentrates on Barth-as-author, but that statement could also apply to the individual writer-character and *her*
work as a structuring agent of her text.

Kim McMullen helpfully extends Bradbury's statement about
authorial roles by examining the juxtaposition of the various
authors at work—the novel's multiple letter writers. She finds that
Barth is as interested in the ways *each* individual constructs the self
as in the product created by their interwoven writings, what she
terms "the collective narratives of nations," for he "exposes the self-
engendering act of 'lettering' by which each individual correspondent constitutes text, self, and world" (416). Indeed, each of the six
correspondents called on by the author to participate has a different
relationship to writing, and each character's discourse represents a
different aspect of the postmodern perplex Barth is attempting to
deconstruct.

Jerome Bray's numeric encodings question possibilities of any
verbal meaning; Jacob Horner's self-addressed deconstructive mis-
siles, where alphabetic order replaces chronology, also lead him to
abandon letters but not verbal activity; Todd Andrews's "inquiry"
features formalist synchronics and diachronics; and A. B. Cook's manipulative letters stress writing as a mode of power over others—
in times past, present, and future. Ambrose Mensch, a novelist of

modernist, formalist metafiction seeks some new way to enliven his writing and, in his efforts to direct a movie based on the works of John Barth, must question the relative powers of images and words. I see Ambrose as a kind of shadow figure for the author; Ambrose's needs and history are clearer to the external reader than are those of the author-character ("John Barth"). Ambrose's love relationship with Germaine does yield commentary on the author-character's correspondence with and related need for her. Germaine must be won if Ambrose is to survive as man and as author; his textual and sexual conflicts run parallel: "I see my own dispute with letters to have been a lover's quarrel. Sweet Short Story! Noble Novel! precious squiggles on the pristine page! Dear Germaine" (333).

The intertwining letters of this novel can be read as a complex detective story and a detailed analysis of history-as-narrative[4] but certainly contain a fulsome reflection on the situation of the late twentieth-century novel as an art form. "What emerges more clearly in this work than in any of Barth's previous fiction is the extent to which these letters are an attempt to make one's peace with generational conflict" explains Marjorie Roemer (43). She finds that Barth has experienced an "anguished need to define his place as artist, to achieve his postmodernist rapprochement with his nineteenth-century grandparents and twentieth-century parents" (44). If we accept this motive for the content and structure of *LETTERS,* then it would seem that the one female character in the work is, in a sense, being asked to serve as surrogate mother to the new novel (and possibly, incestuously, to the new novelist) Barth wants to bring forth. Given her middle age, given that she has, as scholar and woman, consorted with realists and modernists both, it seems Germaine is also being asked to serve as grandmother.

Germaine's existence in the novel would seem then to depend on a prior force—the invitation of "John Barth." However, initiation of their contact actually comes from Germaine, who as acting provost invites him to accept an honorary degree from the university that employs her. Her rambling postscript to that letter intrigues him so much that he invites her into his novel-in-the-making. The letters she then cooperatively sends permit her to say whatever she wants and to tell her own story her own way. The Author/John Barth persona neither edits nor comments on her letters. He does not even reply to them. Thus, as Bradbury points out, "the author's position as omniscient presence within the text is called into question; an

interrogation which allows the voices of the text to speak" (63).
"Your silence has drawn so many words from this pen," Germaine
comments (449). By repeatedly stressing that Germaine writes to a
nonresponding, silent confidant, Barth underscores the female character's need for an autonomous space of self-authority. She may occasionally long for a more responsive addressee, even at one point
driving to "the Author's" house and seeing her own letter to him in
his mailbox, but she concludes that his silence has been his greatest
gift to her. The formal decision for epistolarity allows Barth (and the
external reader) to explore the literary and philosophical questioning of voice and its expropriation, as well as character and its appropriation.

Barth stated in a 1988 interview that "a well-constructed, artisti-
cally successful work of fiction has its formal interests as well as its
substantial interests, and each becomes a metaphor for the other"
(Lampkin 488). Accepting then the "formal" or symbolic functions
of Germaine within Barth's metanarrative scheme, I will now focus
on the character's "substantial interests"—character qua character,
if you will.

During the course of her seven months' correspondence,
Germaine recounts her own eventful history and the ongoing confusing events of the present. Narration becomes a way to settle the
past and clarify the present; in some cases this means coming to
terms with people and events, and in others it means allowing those
people and events to fade away. Germaine's lettered responses to life
events—sexual, social, administrative—are as central to her process
of development as the events themselves. During the process of writing itself, change occurs. For instance, dropping a customary sarcas-
tic and ironic epithet ("dear, damaged daughter") from her written
discourse solidifies a changing attitude toward her lover's retarded
child.[5]

Participation in the confessional mode and in the sentimental
tradition (both such integral parts of the letter novel tradition) assist
the character to confirm her distaste for high modernist detach-
ment and elitism, giving her a new way into the dailiness and egali-
tarianism she will have to embrace if she is to marry Ambrose and
settle in Dorchester, Maryland. As we learn from her letters, in the
past she took pride in writing a highly literary prose (and still does);
even now she is willing to be a character in the author's novel and
to inspire her own author-husband-to-be's writing. Nevertheless, in

her letters this character becomes open to a broad range of discourse: pop, kitsch, digressiveness, the sentimental, the nearly pornographic, all fit easily into the epistolary space (yes, how very postmodern!). Simultaneously, Germaine attempts to incorporate old
and new literary styles and to incorporate old and new personal attitudes and behaviors.

Each chapter of *LETTERS* opens with letters from Germaine
Pitt (Lady Amherst) to "John Barth," giving the female character a
repeated primacy of place. ("John Barth" does retain the last word,
however; his letters close each chapter.) Besides her privileged writing location as initiator or generator of each chapter, Germaine has
other distinctions: she is also the only female letter writer, the only
non-American participant in the novel, the only person to write exclusively to but one addressee, and the only writer whose correspondent is of the opposite sex. No surprise then to find that even
though other characters in this novel sometimes write in a confessional manner, none presents material so unremittingly and com-
plexly eroticized.

The character's self-conscious enjoyment of her own sexuality
and humor about past sexual encounters keeps the external reader
from viewing her as merely the object of others' sexual/emotional
needs and desires. Germaine Pitt, Lady Amherst—her name is instructive here: she may be a lady and a literary one at that, but she
is neither afraid to pit herself against others nor fears life's psychological pits and oddities; she is pithy too. She is most germane to
Barth's whole literary project, perhaps the germ of his regenerative
effort. While Barth often portrays Germaine as object (requested
to participate in a kind of literary copulation in which she will
not only become a character in his text but also symbolize for him
the belletrist tradition that can fructify modernist and postmodernist aridity), he also portrays her as subject. Within the protected
space of letters, Germaine explores her responses to her changing
circumstances and self. She has initiated their correspondence and
continues it out of her own desire for confession/scriptotherapy.

Germaine's first letter brings up a multiplicity of duplicities and
doublings, absences and presences. (To use the otherwise innocent
phrase "brings up" has here a sexual connotation, for Germaine's
sexual consciousness is always raised and always pertinent.[6]) She is
writing to "John Barth," someone she has never met but knows indirectly because he is a friend of her friend Ambrose Mensch. The first

section of the letter is a formal two-paragraph invitation to accept an honorary degree; the letter is typed by a secretary and provided with conventional closing and the secretary's indication of her work ("GGP[A]/ss"). This part of the letter inscribes a certain distance, through its public style. However, the eight-page, hand-written postscript Germaine appends immediately reveals an effusive, lonely, self-mocking, literary writer, comfortable revealing a private, idiosyncratic self and style.[7] She exclaims: "But see how in the initial sentence (*my* initial sentence) I transgress my vow not to go on about myself, like those dotty women 'of a certain age' who burden the patience of novelists and doctors—their circumstantial ramblings all reducible, I daresay, to one cry: "Help! Love me! I grow old!" (4). Thus, Barth situates Germaine "deconstructing in her handwritten postscript what she has just articulated in the official typescript" (McMullen 411). This letter and later ones will depict a woman capable of vital emotional, sexual, intellectual, and social experiences. Yet she is somewhat a stranger to her setting and to the experiences of her love affair with Ambrose, so she has a need to understand and be understood. This need prompts her into a confessional correspondence.

The letter's last paragraph stresses the physical nature of texts. Here, as often, Germaine's correspondence partakes of what Linda Kauffman and others identify as particularly "feminine" approaches to letter writing: its physicality and emotionalism, a "discourse . . . based on the integrity of the body and the supremacy of the heart, which is antithetical to the logic enforced by men" (Kauffman, *Discourses* 133). When Germaine writes, "I hold your first novel in my hand, eager to embark upon it," she makes the author himself present through the metonymic presence of his book. When she writes, "in your own hand you may hold some measure of our future here," she is making the author aware, through the metaphor of holding, that his presence at Marshyhope could have a major effect on that institution's future and on Germaine's. Finally, in a wonderful theft of male sexual imagery, this character pictures her letter as a "spermatozoon." Her metaphor aptly depicts how its "tail . . . far outmeasures its body," and she then turns the male letter recipient into a Molly Bloom who will, she hopes, say "*yes* to the Litt. D., *yes* to MSU, and *yes* Dorchester, *yes* Tidewater, Maryland *yes yes yes*" (11–12). Thus, as McMullen points out, from the beginning of this novel, language is demonstrated as central to the "struggle for social and political power." Language is not only produced by one authority or one institution but also proceeds from each individual. Germaine's letters will "demonstrate how particular discursive practices inscribe institutions, behaviors, values, and histories" (McMullen 413), but the letters from different characters will perform these tasks differently.

Although the author-character refuses the honorary degree, he offers something that turns out to be much more valuable: he asks Germaine to participate in the novel he is writing. After initially rejecting the author's invitation, Germaine concedes because she has "much to tell, no one to tell it to" (59). Germaine-as-realistic-character needs these sites of response—spaces in which to record, confess, cogitate to a receptive, interested, but nonintrusive addressee. This form of writing puts her in charge of herself at a particularly tumultuous time in her life and provides the sense that she is "a writer writing first person fiction, an epistolary novelist composing" (378).[8] The nonresponsive author-character (as opposed to all those talky modernist lovers of her past who offered her their wisdom in exchange for comfort and sexual favors) never sends return letters. Germaine, however, values her nonresponsive recipient, finding "scriptotherapy" more effective when one-sided (72). The author-character's passivity helps her, frees her. "John Barth" then would seem to be a "passive confidant" (to use Altman's term) because he serves as "listener" or "sounding board" primarily (*Epistolarity* 50).

Nonetheless, as we cannot help recalling, Germaine's letters become a character in this epistolary novel. "The Author" persona of *LETTERS* is not really passive, for his collecting, arranging, and publishing functions are important activities. Such work within a letter novel can change the seemingly passive character. Although a passive confidant is usually "fundamentally an archivist" he can become "a protagonist or antagonist in his own right"—the latter activity moving him into the "active confidant" role (Altman, *Epistolarity* 52–53). Perhaps "the author" provides a validating function, his interest and acceptance of Germaine's private and public life providing a catalyst to her own analyzing and synthesizing. Of much importance, within the fictional artifice of his novel, the author-character will not appropriate or rewrite Germaine, but will instead permit her own voice and style to body her forth.

Yet, disturbingly, the confessional form, the giving of one's secrets to another, still seems to indicate the giving away of oneself.

"The impulse to confess is strong," explains Mary Lydon. "To claim essential womanhood, to assert oneself as subject, to demand the freedom to write 'like a woman,' to reclaim women's history, to speak [one's] own sexuality is a powerful temptation" (138). If women are not to be essentialized into stereotypes (in Germaine's case slippage into "the Great Tradition" or motherhood or muse), Lydon cautions, they will need irony and humor and Foucauldian strategies of avoiding self-entrapping definitions (139).[9] Barth instills these qualities into Germaine's writings and in addition allows her insights into authorial expropriation and questioning of narrativity. To a large extent, this female character has the freedom to thrive as an idiosyncratic, stimulating, unessentialized personality within the novel.

Confessing private feelings and reactions allows Germaine self-presence in a way similar to that achieved by Ivy in her letters to the silent Silvaney. Ivy wrote to an absent sister, really an absent aspect of herself. Like Ivy, Germaine most values the process of letter writing, not the product. She expresses no interest in seeing the Barth character's finished novel. Germaine writes to an absent author, but perhaps we need to see that authorial self as an absent part of herself. After all, she too is a published scholar. Her previous writing had been fairly standard stuff, but I begin to wonder whether Barth is hinting that as a scholar and as someone working through personal experiences, the letter-writing process will affect her future. Writing to the Barth character regularly and extensively makes her see that "to put things into words works changes, not only upon the events narrated, but upon their narrator" (80). At the book's end this character contemplates not only the birth of a child but also a return to scholarly writing. One senses that the character's writing projects may be different in form and subject; at least her attitude toward that work has undergone a transformation toward greater commitment.

In spite of all I have said here about the usefulness of the writing process to *LETTERS'* one female epistolarian, one could still query why a persona whose life embraces a vigorous love relationship (her affair with Ambrose) would still need regular self-revelations to another "other" on paper. Barth provides various reasons for the external reader to accept Germaine's epistolary urge. One imagines Germaine's ego has been stroked by the author-character's invitation to participate in his project; one postulates that, especially for an administrator who prefers writing and literature to executive work, it is amusing and productive to have a captive audience on whom to try out ideas. However, Germaine not only creates a character for "Barth's" novel and enjoys sounding off to a receptive reader, she also discovers that the correspondence can allow her to develop a redefined self. The text here asks us to assume that having an interested, noncontrolling, noncensoring recipient in whom to confide her confusions opens up a special space of self-authorization.[10]

As she writes, Germaine reconstructs her past for "the Author," detailing a difficult on-again, off-again love affair with one André Castine, the birth of a child by him, and the disappearance of both lover and child. She recounts her marriage to Lord Amherst and at times high-flown life style in Europe, love affairs with famous literary men, and her own publishing of articles on Germaine de Staël and on Héloise's letters to Abelard. She indicates that by middle age she had accepted her single life (though with prospects of some lusty affairs). However, the events of the novel change her, as does her own writing about them and about her past: her life and her letters have been, she decides, "digression and recapitulation," and now "it is time to rearrive at the present, to move into a future unsullied by the past" (224). Her letter writing has helped her give up (or over) her long-time fascination with and sense of ties to André. She acknowledges her son (who has become someone she does not respect), but realizes the futility of attempting a reconciliation with him. She accepts a modest lifestyle as wife to Ambrose Mensch and becomes comfortable, at least for the time being, seeing herself as a professor at Marshyhope, a third-rate college. She surprises herself by looking forward (with sensible trepidation) to being a mother again. Although this rundown of plot presents Germaine accepting the fairly conventional roles of mother, wife, and teacher, those roles deconstruct quickly. At age fifty the chances of her pregnancy miscarrying or ending in the birth of a damaged child are high (and never does she seem to look forward to the raising of a child). Happiness in marriage may not last: she is marrying a man whose family has a high incidence of cancer—one who may already have signs of that disease. Then too, given her opinion of Marshyhope State University and its administration, the chances of a durable teaching post and good working conditions are low.

In the drama of the novel, Germaine enacts the possibility of

transforming both the personal past and the present. As one facet
of the novel's discussion of literature, she encodes the possibility
of crossing boundaries among categories of literature to generate
something new. Her comments on writing supplement those of the
author-character and Ambrose Mensch and question/theorize the
very process in which she engages. When a carbon copy of a letter
gets her in major trouble (revealing to her boss her real feelings on
various issues and her sexual relationship with Ambrose), the presence and durability of written language, possibilities of misdirected
information, and roles of unintended readers become central. At
the same time, we find that written materials can also lack the documentary power we wish them to have. Germaine worries that the
author will think she is inventing certain events she relates (378).
Then too, she knows there is nothing "natural" about writing: in
an early letter, Germaine writes of a moment when "our alphabet
looked alien as Arabic; the string of letters were a code I'd lost the
key to; I found more sense in the empty spaces, in the margins, between the lines" (74). This protagonist never forgets that writing is
a highly uncertain system for presenting (which is, of course, always
a *re*presenting) any kind of "truth." Even so, she does not want her
doubts about writing to keep it from having substance. She worries
about her husband-to-be's preference for centering his own novel-
writing efforts on "avant-garde games" to the exclusion of passions.
Although she wants his work to contain feelings, he seems to want
their absence, preferring the formal distances of modernist or postmodernist games (348).

Through her many references to other texts—others' letters,
epistolary and nonepistolary novels of the past, the writings of her
lover and of the author to whom she writes—we know Barth's female character as a sophisticated reader capable of learning much
about writing and its possibilities from writers themselves and from
their works. As we learn of Germaine's long-term involvement
with literature, we are also surrounded by her words, her private-
audience literature-cum-part-of-a-novel-in-the-making, and find that
her own prose has such immediacy and vitality that it overpowers
the texts to which she refers. In part this is because she is such
a physical writer. Her confessional writings inscribe sexual activity
and the body more forcefully than do any of the male-authored
letters in the novel and make other referenced novels and letters
seem pallid.

In connecting letter writing with the physical body Germaine contributes an important factor to Barth's collective dialogue on the future of the novel. When Germaine parodies *Pamela, Clarissa,* and *Les Liaisons dangereuses* by combining writing and sexual activity, she is trying to make the action of the pen as vital as the experience of sex: "My left hand creeps sleeping-himward as the right writes on; now I've an instrument in each, poor swollen darling that I must have again. He groans, he stirs, he rises; my faithful English Parker pen . . . must yield to his poky pencil pencel pincel penicellus penicillus *peeee*" (70–71). The phenomenological experience of the word gives way to the sensory experience of flesh—the pen is dropped.

Germaine's gutsy or perhaps old-fashioned approach to writing opposes the methods of her modernist lover. Although her own discussions of writing reveal she values the abstract along with the concrete, she wants writing that is also intimate, "composed in private, to be read in private, at least in silence and virtual immobility, author and reader one to one like lovers" (393).[11] Writing is not a formal game. It is crucially important, for she believes that the written word can "say the unseeable, declare the impossible" (393).

As a character, Germaine arrives, through the scriptotherapeutic process of letters, at a regenerated self. Writing allows her to say confessionally things she can then go on to say or do (or not say or do!) within her actual relationships. At the end of the novel, she has reached a point of serenity that will allow her to accept whatever the future brings. Her child, if she really is pregnant, may be born handicapped or deformed; her husband, with his family history of cancer, may die young; her retarded stepdaughter will undoubtedly present many difficulties; her teaching post at the university may turn out unsatisfactorily; her own writing projects may fail; and even the "serene, serene" state she claims at novel's end may not endure (691).

Within the format of the novel, other letters portend changes of fortune that will indeed shake Germaine anew. In spite of its double wrap-up, consisting of an "alphabetical wedding toast" letter from the author-character to Germaine and Ambrose plus "the Author's" letter to the Reader declaring the novel ended, many strings are left untied. One easily agrees with Marjorie Roemer that "Barth is very much in the mainstream of current critical theory when he opens within his texts a space for claims and counterclaims and sets free before us a dialogized world without any attempt at reductive closure" (47).

Roemer's comment might seem contradicted by Charles Harris's idea that Barth's novel works toward "synthesis and transcension" (161). Nevertheless, Harris usefully sees that Barth's special achievement in this novel is to portray unity not as something imposed by the artist's individual effect on his world, but as something that resides "in the reciprocal, dialogic interchange between self and other" (194). This fructifying and responsive process is exemplified in the sexual, confessional, self-reflexive, self-composing, self-regenerating letters of Germaine Pitt.

5

Restoration and In-gathering
—*The Color Purple*

Alice Walker's *The Color Purple* is primarily the victory story of silenced, brutalized Celie, told through her letters first to God and then to her younger sister Nettie. It is also the story of Nettie, better educated, much more verbally adept, in easier circumstances, but equally estranged. Celie's letters cannot elicit concrete responses: God, after all, is an intangible addressee, and Nettie, in far-off Africa, receives few of Celie's communications (most are returned by the postal service). Nettie's letters to Celie also go undelivered for years, until discovered tucked away in a trunk where Celie's oppressive, abusive husband has hidden them. Neither sister, then, really responds to the other, which places a subtle obligation on the novel's external reader to fulfill the role of respondent.

In this novel, "Dear God," "Dear Celie," "Dear Nettie," is always also "Dear Reader," and to the extent that we enter the text our names are written into it too. *The Color Purple* foregrounds questions of address and signature and repeatedly brings up the issue of who is being addressed and who is doing the addressing. As a result, this novel functions to stimulate consideration of how we experience what we read and write. To some extent, one serves as the missing internal reader for the letters directed to either sister, reading through the eyes of Nettie or Celie. All the while, of course, one also knows oneself the external reader, just a person holding a book. Is it because neither writer's letters can be answered that many of us more willingly become involved with this text, reaching for our pens, pencils, and keyboards to write down our responses? Does this unusual reading situation begin to explain why *The Color Purple* has elicited such a tremendous outpouring of critical reactions?

After reading many of the rich multidimensional responses to Walker's novel, I find myself affirming the idea of book-as-letter, in this case with readers and critics of *The Color Purple* transformed into Walker's correspondents.[1] Indeed, taking into account the book's dedication—"To the Spirit: / Without whose assistance / Neither this book / Nor I / Would have been / Written," and signature-like closing—"I thank everybody in this book for coming. / A. W., author and medium," Carolyn Williams terms *The Color Purple* "one long letter" (283). Thus, in this chapter it seems appropriate to incorporate much of this larger correspondence, creating a sort of in-gathering. Such a format will echo the in-gathering within the novel itself that brings to Celie, at story's end, all that is rightfully hers.

Williams explores the letter aspect of Walker's novel by showing parallels between the characters' and author's spiritual and writerly activities (284). Wendy Wall also sees a link between the author and Celie, explaining that both writers "invoke an ethereal, invisible audience" (92). Walker writes "To the Spirit" just as Celie, her main protagonist, at first writes to "Dear God." Walker addresses both a transcendent and a superhuman spirit that is composed of and yet is more than the spirits of individual beings or ancestors or "old ones,"[2] and she addresses the *reader's* spirit—that willingness in the external reader to open himself or herself up to fictional realities, travel to impossible and unknown places, phenomenologically "believe" in and respond to the presented fiction: to correspond with the author in some way. In a similar two-layered form of address, Celie writes to a conventional God, but her diary-like letters simultaneously address herself and document the existence of a self.[3]

Henry Louis Gates identifies yet another addressee for the novel, terming it "a letter of love" addressed to Zora Neale Hurston, the literary ancestor Alice Walker has publicly claimed. Hurston's best known novel, *Their Eyes Were Watching God*, provides, in Gates's eyes, the base for *The Color Purple* ("Color Me Zora" 244). But he too takes seriously Walker's dedication to a more generalized spirit, identifying it with the same transcendent power that allowed one Rebecca

Cox Jackson to learn writing not under human tutelage but through inspiration. As Gates explains, Jackson was a free black who began a Shaker sisterhood and wrote extensively about her life and religious struggles from 1830 to 1864; these writings were not collected and put in book form until 1981. Walker wrote a review of Jackson's autobiographical writings that same year, just one year before *The Color Purple* was published, and so Gates supposes that "when Walker dedicates *The Color Purple* 'To the Spirit,' it is to this spirit which taught Rebecca Jackson to read" (243). Furthermore, Gates relates Celie's addressing God to W. E. B. Dubois's "After-Thought" to *The Souls of Black Folk*—"Hear my cry, O God the Reader" (qtd. in Gates 243). Walker's doubly double-voiced address[4] insists that we consider the multiple possibilities of epistolary salutation—to self, to the spirit within, to the spirits of one's ancestors, to a conventional God (as in Celie's first letters) or a redefined nontraditional God (as in Celie's closing letter), to previous texts and their authors, and to the spirit of God the Reader or to the Reader who is, after all, in some ways the author's God.

Within the polyphony of voices "answering" Walker's novel-letter, the majority respond to Walker's use of the epistolary form positively, finding it produces new insights about issues of reading, writing and voice, race, gender, class, and genre. Many also praise the complementary nature of the two sisters' letters. Such critics must find especially true Mikhail Bakhtin's notion that all novels contain "a *system of languages* that mutually and ideologically interanimate each other" (47). Nevertheless, some readers find the novel's epistolarity (or aspects of it) problematic or ineffective. The discussion that follows takes off from these negative readings, readings that I have found especially stimulating because they encourage me to explore my assumptions about how we read letter fiction.

bell hooks objects to Walker's use of the epistolary form because it places readers in the role of "voyeurs who witness Celie's torment as victim of incest-rape, as victim of sexual violence in a sadistic master-slave relationship; who watch her sexual exploration of her body and experience vicarious pleasure at her sexual awakening as she experiences her first sexual encounter with Shug" (458). Are we more voyeuristic here, however, than we would be were the novel in some other form? Does not all fiction about private life put us in that role? The third-person, omnisciently narrated novel lifts doors and walls so that we gaze on characters freely, lets us roam in and out of various characters' thoughts; the first-person novel puts us inside the thinking/observing protagonist whose sights, experiences, and thrills unroll before us.

Reading is always a metaphoric uncovering—titillating as well as intellectually and emotionally stimulating—that seeks some climax or naked answer. The epistolary form forces the external reader into deeper awareness of this condition. It creates, to an even greater extent than the formal aspects of other narrative forms, those juxtapositions and selections that Wolfgang Iser finds necessitate any fiction reader's interaction, his or her consequent involvement in a "performative action" (61). Iser states that "the involvement of the reader is essential to the fulfillment of the text" (66). If this is true for a standard narrative, how much truer it must be for novels in letters, with their special discontinuities and time gaps, closings, openings, and, when more than one correspondent is involved, sharp changes of viewpoint. In addition, with heightened self-referentiality, either to the texts of other letters in the novel or, intertextually, to other novels in the epistolary tradition, the letter novel's "repertoire" of cultural and social norms encourages the external reader's active synthesis of textual and extratextual elements. With Iser's functionalist incentive, much of reading becomes a "recodification of social and historical norms" (74). (In "Writing *The Color Purple*," Walker proposes that her novel is "historical" [355].)

Particular features of particular letter novels force us into awareness of particular components of reading. In *The Color Purple*, at least for hooks, voyeurism is such a component. Now, Roland Barthes confronts texts, regardless of their form, with pleasure in the voyeur's act (I hear a voice whisper, "surprise, surprise"). Barthes finds the true "pleasure of the text" is not a simple "striptease" in which the "end of the story" fulfills the "hope of seeing the sexual organ"; rather, for him, the truly erotic text is the one that through "intermittence" entices us: "it is this flash itself which seduces, or rather: the staging of an appearance-as-disappearance" (10). Whether one finds that the excitement of the text derives from those glimpses of nakedness or from the slow, methodical undressing of the text, one can see that the epistolary form, with its emphasis on a private mode of communication and its placement of the reader gazing on the writer (metonymically speaking), will necessarily put the external reader in the role of prier, snoop, ravisher, or voyeur. "The epistolary form complicates the notion of audience, making the reader a

voyeur (like Albert [Celie's husband]) to a private and intimate confession. This is an unsettling position; reading is portrayed as an act
of intrusion, of violation" (Wall 94–95). An eighteenth-century
reader looks over the shoulder of that rogue, Lovelace, participating
in his interception of Clarissa's letters and his plots to take her virtue, or looks over the shoulder of the caring confidante Anna Howe,
participating in her intimacy but also her curiosity about Clarissa. A
twentieth-century reader becomes complicit with epistolary characters of the rogue or spy ilk who revel in the self-exposures of their
correspondents. Reading Mark Harris's *Wake Up, Stupid* the reader
shadows Youngdahl as he dallies with fantasies of Gabriella Bodeen;
reading Thornton Wilder's *The Ides of March* the reader participates
as Caesar imagines the pleasures of seeing Cleopatra again; to some
extent, in reading *LETTERS* one may feel a discomforting awareness that one is receiving confessional secrets as the "John Barth"
character welcomes Germaine's weekly revelations.

To the extent that all novel reading capitalizes on our desire to
know what is hidden and that, furthermore, epistolary novels take
advantage of our desires to intrude on the private worlds of others,
The Color Purple does place us in the voyeur situation: Celie writes
to God, confessing intimate details of her life and experience, and
we gaze on those pages. While we are voyeurs, Walker works *against*
voyeurism in at least two ways. First, the voice presenting information that might otherwise be titillating is not one of a person taking
pleasure in extended description of sexual acts; the language used
is simple, matter-of-fact, without exaggeration. Then too (and this is
true in much epistolary fiction), what we read are Celie's own accounts of experiences. Although one cannot deny the realistic convention that permits one, painfully, to "see" the events Celie's letters
re-create, in one sense *no* actual activity exists for us to spy on. If we
were peeping through a keyhole, all we would see would be a person
writing. In fact, the real voyeurism here, always a factor in letter
fiction, occurs not because of particular sexual content but because
we read someone else's mail.[5] We read what we were not meant to
see—an individual's account of her inner, private self. To investigate
this voyeurism is to investigate reading itself, a subject to which I
will return in discussing *The Mixquiahuala Letters*.

hooks's objections to Walker's choice of form extend beyond the
voyeurism I have so far discussed; she also dislikes the narrow focus
of Celie's letters, finding that this protagonist's exploration of her

own needs and troubles ignores consideration of "the collective plight of black people" (465). hooks generally finds Celie's character unbelievable (this response assumes that the work is solely mimetic). She also objects that "there is no description of Celie with pen in hand, no discussion of where and when she writes"; this, for hooks, removes credibility from the act of writing (466). Finally, this critic finds that Walker's "didactic voice" dominates the characters so strongly that they are "the mediums" for Walker and not, as Walker has claimed, she the medium giving voice to her characters (467).

Trudier Harris has related difficulties because she cannot accept that a young black woman would or could be as passive as Celie. Harris objects to Celie's inability to fight against her male oppressors, reminding us that even slave women often ran away, harmed or fought off their owners, or poisoned or adulterated their masters' food (157). What Harris ignores or wants to forget is that many slaves did not have the self-confidence or bravery for such aggression; perhaps they lacked living examples of other women who had survived such acts. What she also ignores is that writing itself is a form of action, akin to other verbal practices of resistance that go back to antebellum days, when spirituals, folk tales, and talk helped slaves protect their sense of themselves (Awkward 204–5). Slaves who struggled to learn writing and reading did so not only to gain access to wider communication but also to defy their masters and to declare their humanity. Still, Celie's choice of writing troubles Harris: "I can imagine a black woman of Celie's background and education talking with God . . . but writing letters to God is altogether another matter" (156).

Accepting, for the moment, the notion that the novel is within the "realistic" convention and that therefore what we know and expect of our own experience should help us understand what takes place within the novel framework, is it impossible that a fourteen-year-old southern black woman would, under injunction from her rapist-father never to tell anyone but God of the sexual abuse he has inflicted on her, turn to paper and pen? Improbable, perhaps; impossible, no. Celie communicates with God because she can reach out to no one else. Perhaps Celie *writes* to God as an act of rebellion against her "pa" who gave her permission to "tell" God, but never would imagine she could write to Him. In her letters, Celie can choose her words, slowly build her own sentences, pick her own subject matter. As Deborah McDowell notices, the epistolary style not only emphasizes Celie's isolation and desperation, it also validates Celie's autonomous voice. Stripped of everything else, she still has and attempts to affirm self in the act of writing: "Everything we learn about Celie is filtered through her own consciousness and rendered in her own voice" (McDowell 289).

Perhaps Harris would expect a desperate and isolated woman to reach out to other women in times of trouble, rather than look to an abstract, patriarchal God. Celie's world, however, does not include women who can help her. Her mother dies; her female schoolteacher, a possible confidante, becomes unavailable when Celie's father withdraws her from school; her sister must leave home to avoid sexual abuse; and the sisters-in-law who urge Celie to fight her husband and his children are cowed by their brother and desert Celie. Celie's marginalization and extreme need leave only one available confidant—God. Not until Sofia (her daughter-in-law) and Shug (her husband's mistress) come into her life does Celie begin to gain some confidence; yet it still takes a while before she can turn to the female she has trusted most deeply and adopt her absent sister as addressee.

Valerie Babb discovers that letters serve Celie in two ways: they enable her to "fix the events of her life, thereby lending them coherence," and they put the protagonist in a position to "review" and reflect on those events (109). Wendy Wall also suggests that writing has more than one function for Celie—it is a symbolic as well as literal rewriting: she can "define herself against the patriarchy and thus . . . 'reinscribe' those traces and wounds upon her body inflicted and imprinted by others" (83). The act of reinscription works two ways. First, although Celie does not have the power in writing to remove what has been done to her, she can take some control of various painful acts as she puts them into her own words. Second, as she recounts her experience she creates a physical entity that gives body to her "suppressed 'self'" and that protects and preserves her. The letters, as Wall observes, "act as a second memory, a projected body that precariously holds [a] hidden self" (84).

Building on the insights of Babb and Wall, I find that the material reality of letters becomes a critical element of this novel. Celie's experiences of abuse have all but eradicated her; in her first letter to God she puts a line through the second word of "I am a good girl" and replaces it with "have been." Prayers to God might serve such a person's need for contact, and they might even contain within themselves the possibility of response. The problem is that prayers are ethereal. Even words spoken to another (particularly if that other goes away or dies) seem transient. Letters document. They document not only the events they recount; they also document the existence of the recounter. At no time in the text, however, does Walker picture Celie rereading her letters to God or rereading the letters she had sent to Nettie that were returned to her. In addition, Celie never even mentions the scene of her own writing. Certainly it is traditional that epistolary heroines describe the scene of their own writing (from the Portuguese Nun on), and a heroine such as Clarissa dwells on her writing because it is her only means of action. Nevertheless, cannot that formula be revised? My own reading methodology enjoys gaps and implications that I am left to fill or fulfill, and enjoys seeing a break from or change in an old tradition.[6] Why not imagine that Celie, although *needing* to write, has no interest in or context within which to comment on herself as a writer? Nettie, who has maintained a greater interest in writing and reading, does comment on her own writing.

Because the letters have material reality, they can function metonymically to mark loss and restoration of creativity, self, and community to Celie. Because no person receives Celie's letters, no one knows of her creative effort—she leaves no mark on the outside world. Within her first three letters we learn that she has given birth twice and that twice her "father" has taken her babies from her. She is convinced that he killed the first and sold the second to a couple in a nearby town. After her children are removed, Celie's normal biological processes alter. She ceases to menstruate, and even after she marries Mr._____ she never becomes pregnant. Effectively, then, the man Celie thinks is her father has stolen her children and her childbearing abilities. He has taken away her ability to procreate, and by removing her power to communicate with others, he attempts to seal off another potentially creative activity. Walker shows us that not only social functions but also the most biological functions of a woman's life can be shaped by forces outside her body.

In "Creativity and the Childbirth Metaphor," Susan Stanford Friedman details the different ways that male and female authors have used the childbirth metaphor to describe their own and others' writing. Friedman points out that language that refers to writing as giving birth, while connecting "mind and body, word and womb, . . . also evokes the sexual division of labor upon which Western patriarchy is founded" (51). Usually the "masculine appropriation of the creative Word attempts to reduce women to the processes of their body," Friedman continues (53), and so women are essential-ized around their procreative functions. What is so startling about the situation depicted at the beginning of *The Color Purple* is that Celie's pa attempted to rob her of both her children and her words.

During the course of this letter novel, however, Celie is able to recover her creativity, and with the return of her children at the end of the novel, children who are now grown into young adults, she also gains a link to the procreative line. The creativity that Celie dis-covers involves sewing, for under the encouragement of Shug Avery, Celie transforms her basic seamstress skills and begins designing pants that please both women and men. Her creativity also involves her work as a letter writer. The two ways of creating tie together beautifully. They form what Nancy K. Miller terms an "arachnology": a specialized "catachresis" or self-referential metaphor in which the textual and textural come together, increasing our awareness of the female as maker of both cloth and text and of the power of these artifacts to stand for her and mark her absence/presence ("Arach-nologies" 270–72).

Just as her supposed father (in fact, her stepfather) had prohib-ited Celie from communicating with people about his sexual abuse, so her husband prevents her receiving communication from Nettie by intercepting the younger sister's letters. Not hearing from her sister, Celie presumes her dead, but Shug Avery (the husband's mis-tress and eventually Celie's lover) discovers the letters, and together the two women read them. Having these actual letters gives Celie back some of herself even as it gives her back some of her sister. Nettie's messages include valuable information about their common past, including the truth that their real father had been lynched and that the man they had accepted as their father was in fact their step-father. That Celie can hold these letters in her hand gives the new truths potency. Walker marks the materiality of Nettie's letters by having Celie introduce the first few recovered works with her own sentences: "This the letter I been holding in my hand" (112); "*the first letter say*" (119); or "*Next one, fat, dated two months later, say*" (122). Nettie in her own body is still absent, but the body of her letters has great value for Celie.

Although writing may not initially seem a natural act for this character, when placed within (or against) various literary traditions, Walker's creation of Celie as a letter writer becomes more understandable. First, as I have mentioned earlier, we can comprehend her as one in a series of epistolary heroines who write to break an imposed silence. Carolyn Williams takes an interesting approach here, perceiving the writing as a way to maintain oral silence and strength. As she puts it, the protagonist's writing "must be seen to represent both the resignation of Celie's silence and its implicit strength: her silent refusal to lose her identity, despite her isolation" (276). Second, we can think about the novel in terms of other African American novels. For instance, remarking that *The Color Purple* is the first black epistolary novel, Gates elaborates the ways Walker's choice of form incorporates and signifies on the work previously performed by Zora Neale Hurston to proclaim the legitimacy of the black voice. Whereas Hurston's Janie and her narrator "speak themselves into being . . . Celie, in her letters, *writes* herself into being" (Gates, "Color Me Zora" 243, emphasis added). Third, we can, as Gates also suggests, consider *The Color Purple*'s resonance within the slave narrative tradition. Gates remarks that Celie's letters detail "her bondage and her freedom" ("Color Me Zora" 247), thus reminding us of the title of a Frederick Douglass autobiography.[7] Just as the individual writers of slave narratives had to prove themselves literate to claim full humanity and so always featured the stories of their own coming to letters, Walker's Celie writes letters to demonstrate the legitimacy, literacy, and humanity of herself and her vernacular.

Because Celie herself "does not understand writing as an act of power, or self-legitimation" (466), a reader such as hooks still does not see the protagonist's writing as a true means of self-development or empowerment, although she grants it gives Celie some "distance, objectification." hooks's reading divests Celie of will in her initial turn to God: because the man she thinks is her father has told her "never to tell nobody but God" about his raping her, it is his agency that turns her toward this particular addressee (458, 466). hooks here ignores that logically such a command would force the obedient respondent merely to "tell" God, i.e., to pray, or the command would cut off all communication; given these logical alternatives, Celie's choice of writing becomes an especially forceful self-exertion. In his psychoanalytic approach to the novel, Daniel W. Ross explains that an essential issue in the novel is that before Celie can enter the discourse of her community she must first discover

"desire—for selfhood, for other, for community, and for a mean-
ingful place in the Creation" (70). That desire is formalized in the
letters. Celie acts. Her hands hold and use pencil and paper.

Within the writing act various elements signal agency beyond
the essential fact of picking up and using writing instruments. Two
epistolary acts that mark a protagonist's emotional shifts are naming
a given addressee (picking and changing the terms) and changing
addressee altogether. In *The Color Purple* the most obvious instance
of changing a correspondent's name occurs in the last letter, when
Celie changes from the "Dear God" of her initial letter to an amal-
gamated "Dear God. Dear stars, dear trees, dear sky, dear peoples.
Dear Everything. Dear God" (249). Lindsey Tucker identifies the importance of naming to gain power and "establish selfhood," point-
ing out that within the body of her letters, Celie is at first inadequate
to this task: her father is "him," Samuel is Rev. Mr. _____, her husband Mr. _____. Perhaps because she is concentrating on the heroine's struggle against "patriarchal culture," Tucker overlooks the fact
that, within the protected space of letters, Celie does have some
naming power: she names women. Eventually, she will also learn to
name males: Albert, Samuel, and so on. In addition, by the writing
of her last letter, her concept of God is inclusive of male and female
and all elements on earth; the form of her address indicates not only
a shift in concept but also her newfound power to create a name for
that concept.

In *The Color Purple* another important shift in self-empowerment and self-consciousness is signaled through the change of addressee—the turn away from God to Nettie. Molly Hite explains that
"the drama of Celie's epistolary self-creation revolves around the discovery of a female audience that finally fulfills the ideal of correspondence. Celie initially writes to God as an alternative to speech.
The process of finding her speaking voice is a process of finding her
audience, first in Sofia, then in Shug. But she is not able to deliver
the Old Testament–style curse that in turn delivers her from bondage until she is assured of the existence of Nettie, her ideal audience" (*Other Side* 445–46). Nevertheless, when Celie first writes to
Nettie, there is no assurance the letters will reach their destination.
Celie wills the possibility of reaching her sister; her change of addressee marks belief in change, growth, *co*rrespondence.

Emphasizing the significance of Celie's epistolary change of direction, Williams finds that "the shift in Celie's address from God to

Nettie, divinity to humanity, figurative to real family, 'father' to sister, male to female, white to black, turns the novel in a new direction, toward the affirmative 'Amen' of its closure" (274). God as addressee was selected by "Pa" after all, and that God (i.e., that concept of God that Celie's stepfather would have held) is identified by Williams as part and parcel of the same abusive patriarchal system (275). Williams points out that the first addressee continues the isolation from women that Celie has experienced growing up; the turn to Nettie confirms her acceptance of a woman-centered community. "Celie's turn toward women overturns her earlier implication in the patriarchal network, and the revision in her epistolary address is the most graphic reminder of this shift" (278).[8]

In spite of what might be construed as epistolarity's appropriateness as a vehicle for female self-development and agency, Mae G. Henderson considers that, "as a genre, the epistolary novel, a form invented by men writing about women, embodies male control of the literary images of women" (*"The Color Purple:* Revisions" 14). It may not quite be true that the form was "invented by men," given that no one has really pinned down the sex of the author of *Letters of a Portuguese Nun*[9] and given that Aphra Behn's *Love-Letters Between a Nobleman and his Sister* precedes Richardson's *Pamela* by almost sixty years. Still, many of us learn about the development of the novel form and the novel-as-letters from books such as Ian Watt's *The Rise of the Novel* that claim Samuel Richardson as father of the epistolary novel. Assuming such a background, Henderson interprets Walker's choice of form as a move to claim "her authority, or right to authorship" and her right to "give voice and representation to these same women who have been silenced and confined in life as well as literature" so that Walker "creates a new literary space for the Black and female idiom within the traditionally Eurocentric form of the epistolary novel" (18). Among Walker's rhetorical manipulations of the form, Henderson most praises the way this author combines black vernacular and the "Western epistolary tradition," and she admires Walker's transformation of the sentimental novel tradition. In eighteenth- and early nineteenth-century epistolary novels, protagonists come to accept the society's norms or die; in *The Color Purple* the protagonists make their own norms and prosper (14, 15).

Henderson's positioning is echoed by Wendy Wall, Deborah McDowell, and Valerie Babb, who also enter into the novel's epistolary experience most openly. Perhaps Henderson, Wall, McDowell, Babb, and others accept the novel's form because they operate within interpretive communities that theorize reading from a feminist perspective that includes Jameson's ideas about the "ideology of form" and a strong sense of intertextuality. Trudier Harris and bell hooks read as feminists too, but measure the text mimetically against personal experience and judge the book in part for its efficacy as a cultural tool. The epistolary form has an intriguing power to bring out a variety of strong responses, engendering reactions that make us newly aware of our reading standards and methods.

Some of the early reviews of *The Color Purple* had particular difficulty with the letters written by Nettie, finding they lacked the power of Celie's writings. Dinitra Smith, for example, evaluated the first half (Celie's half) of the book as "superb," but read Nettie's letters as "Walker's didacticism" (183). Mel Watkins termed Nettie's letters "lackluster and intrusive" after Celie's "intensely subjective voice" (7). Smith's and Watkins's judgments about tonal shift may be a result of overlooking the text's epistolary nature. The "didacticism" of Nettie's letters is Nettie's; her "lackluster" style and lack of vivid subjectivity are not errors in Walker's writing but qualities the author has created that tell us much about Nettie and her particular deprivations. Nettie's immaculate discourse has been purchased at a cost—she has been robbed of her traditional vernacular and its energy. Nettie's very lack of zest effectively communicates the personal losses imposed on her by her society. As Williams puts it, "In relation to Celie's voice, the lack of 'color' in Nettie's voice may be seen as its point, spelling the losses as well as the gains of education, uplift, universalism" (285).

Looking at letter content, Adam Gussow writes that Nettie's information about the past she and her sister share makes us "rethink the meaning of Celie's shattered personal history," but, more crucially, Nettie's African material makes us "rethink the history of Black Americans as a group" (125). The responsive reader can see many parallels between the sources of oppression these two women document. In addition, as Elizabeth Fifer maintains, "the development of two distinctly different narrative voices" helps readers "to understand Celie's plight within a larger cultural context" (155).

Babb stresses the importance of having two letter writers so that we see how "black *women* take a form traditionally inhospitable to oral cultures, the written word, and transform it, making it, too, responsive to their needs" (207, emphasis added.) That Celie and Nettie both write testifies to their ability to "modify" the written word "so that they, as black women, are no longer victims of the racial and sexual oppression a white, theocentric use of writing can dictate" (108).

Although Nettie's letters lack the immediacy of style characteristic of Celie's writing, as Wall perceives, Nettie's letters also have a bodied quality; Mr_____ hides them in anger at Nettie's original rejection of his sexual advances: "he rapes her language because he is denied her body." He hides her letters in the same trunk where he has collected underwear from Shug Avery, his mistress, along with pornographic pictures. This placement, Wall finds, "links them with the body" (87). She elaborates: "Both the female body and their texts become subject to violation by the male, who retains the power to encroach upon these private spheres" (87).

With the help of Shug, these letters finally come into Celie's hands. With a new sense of her sister (alive, writing to her), her new sewing ability, and the love of Shug Avery, Celie is able to leave her husband and move to Tennessee with Shug, where she begins her own business, designing and manufacturing pants for women and men. She is now more able to communicate freely, speaking her mind to her husband and his children and writing not to God but to her flesh-and-blood sister, Nettie. The letters to Nettie are, compared with the letters to God, "longer, more exuberant, and more dramatic" (Cheung 166). Eventually all these letters are returned to Celie, at the same time as she receives a telegram from the Department of Defense stating that the ship Nettie was sailing home on was sunk. Celie's own words come back to her, but this is a sad occasion. The novel contains no scene of rereading, no reflection from Celie as to what it means to have these letters back. Eventually, however, Nettie and her husband and Celie's grown children return from Africa. The plot device of the letters preceding their addressee "home" assures that Celie has gathered up her words as well as her family.

Various critics, including hooks, have commented on the way the novel's plot restores so much to Celie—"everything her oppressor has wanted and more—relationships with chosen loved ones; land ownership; material wealth; control over the labor of others" (hooks 468). Looking at the in-gathering ending, Wall notices too that ano-

nymity disappears. Mr_____ becomes Albert, and another character, known as Squeak, takes back her real name—Mary Agnes. Celie,
whose letters to God had no signature, moves to closing her letters
to Nettie with "Your Sister, Celie" (92). The final barbecue also
links these family members in the United States to their African
roots.[10] In "Romance, Marginality, and Matrilineage" Hite looks at
the novel's concluding events as "magical" and "miraculous": and it
is easy to agree with her that the novel's ending is more romance
than realism when it yields the quick success of Celie's business, inheritance of a house and store, discovery of her true lineage, a new
agreeable (nonsexual) relationship with her husband Albert, along
with the return of first her lesbian lover, Shug, and then, from Africa, her sister and children and even new people to enrich the fold
(Samuel, her brother-in-law, and Tashi, her daughter-in-law) (436).

What usually goes unnoticed is that Celie also has all the letters
she wrote or that were written to her.[11] In *The Color Purple,* then, the
gathering up of these letters represents Celie's possession of her full
birthright. Through this aspect of the letter device, Walker highlights Celie's discovery of her right to use and own language—
to speak and write, hear and be heard, read and be read—and her
right to the physical control of these elements.

Now, although readers such as Harris and hooks decry the
novel's lack of realism, with its miraculous, Cinderella-like ending,
more than one critic finds in the example of Celie a "program," if
you will, with practical application. For M. Teresa Tavormina, an attractive aspect of this novel is that it offers its tools to others: "Taking
up a hem or writing a note to a friend are everyday, practical activities that can be practiced by people of almost any economic or social
class, given access to a relatively small amount of instruction and
practice" (227). Tavormina continues, "To take needle or pen in
hand, for man or woman, is to place oneself on a spectrum of creative possibility that stretches ultimately to the splendid art of experienced and inspired weavers, writers, web-workers of all kinds" (228).
Indeed. And that is why it is so important to remember that seeing
herself writing or reading her own writing would be acts assisting
Celie to know herself. In addition, Tavormina points out that part of
this book is about learning; if we are to grow in understanding ourselves and others, then "we must actively 'address' the Spirit within
ourselves and within others" (228).

As soon as Celie picks up a pencil she begins to act on her own behalf. I also find it intriguing that in this novel Alice Walker both heeds and critiques Audre Lorde's caution that one cannot take down the master's house using the master's tools. Celie does not have standard English—the master's tool—yet in and through her own language, her own tools, she reclaims herself and takes over his house. Nettie does have standard English. In some ways it is useless, for it cannot save her beloved Olinka from capitalist-imperialist encroachment and eventual destruction at the hands of Europeans, but in other ways it is powerful. Although imposition of a language's standard form is usually a mark of dominance by the hegemonic power, Babb finds that Nettie's use of standard English incorporates the survival of information about an oral culture, the Olinka, and she therefore sees Nettie's language use as somewhat subversive (113–14). "Nettie has thus used writing to do exactly what it has not done in the past, preserve rather than destroy oral culture" (115). Similarly "Celie transforms [writing] into the instrument that will end the male-oppressiveness of her world" (115). Fifer believes that "how we tell the stories of our lives determines the significance and outcome of the narratives that are our lives" (165). In *The Color Purple* letter discourse "between" two sisters provides the vital connection that eventually allows each sister to own a full life.

As I wrote at the beginning of this chapter, both the content and form of *The Color Purple* have stimulated so much discussion that it is almost as if all of us writing about it form a pool of correspondents, our articles and presentations going out to a silent addressee (Walker) and to critic-addressees who then respond with other articles and presentations. In the spirit of this correspondence, and because she and I often have different approaches to letter novels and critical work, I sent off sections of *Epistolary Responses* to Linda Kauffman, author of *Discourses of Desire* and *Special Delivery*, with a letter asking her to respond with a letter. For months, incidents of lost or misdirected mail seemed to parody the frustrated correspondence of Celie and Nettie, but finally our attempts were successful. The letter I received from Linda combines personal reactions and scholarship; with that dual approach she responds to me and my work and the texts I discuss—not only *The Color Purple*, but *Fair and Tender Ladies* (chapter 3) and letter-form criticism (chapter 10).

30 May 1993

Dear Anne,

As I read your work, I found myself mentally composing two different letters simultaneously: one for you privately, and one for public consumption in *Epistolary Responses*. What strikes me most, after twelve years of work on epistolarity, is the inevitable *artifice* involved in its creation; nothing is more difficult to manufacture than spontaneity! The strange adventure of our own correspondence (in which letters were circuitously routed from Washington, D.C.-Berkeley-Washington-Irvine-Santa Monica-Santa Barbara-Washington, with gaps & lost packages along the way) is symptomatic of the circuitous routing of the entire genre, from Ovid to Aphra Behn to Barthesian (Roland *and* John) word-play. I envy you the opportunity to tackle the topic again, because there is so much more to say, so many other writers and texts I would have liked to have discussed: not just Aphra, but Laclos, Ana Castillo, John Barth, *The White Hotel, Griffin & Sabine,* Bram Stoker's *Dracula!*

Reading your work was like visiting a former self, for each text you cite sparked flashes of memory of a mood, a place, a "spot of time":

May, 1983: sitting on the lawn in front of my home in the country in Ithaca, New York, reading *The Color Purple,* surrounded by lilacs, a flower which, as a Southern Californian, I'd never seen before.

Fast-forward to Chapel Hill in 1984: Trudier Harris and I spoke in tandem at a symposium on the novel, subverting the binary division between white-liberal-feminist vs. African-American-feminist. As you know, Trudier dislikes the novel and is suspicious of its canonization. Some white feminists, she told me, not only used the novel as a badge of liberal righteousness, but confessed their own histories as incest victims to her. Justifiably indignant, she asked, "What do I look like—their mammy?" White feminist literary critics still have a great deal to learn from their feminist colleagues of color: it seems remarkable to me that a decade later, so little has been done to theorize about *whiteness* itself as a racial category, as if it were still the invisible universal, the unquestioned order of nature against which all other categories had to be measured. It's interesting that what theorizing does exist is especially prevalent in film theory, like the special issue of *Screen* on "Race." In my new book, *Bad Girls and Sick Boys: Inside the Body in Fiction, Film, Performance,* I'm

writing on Ngozi Onwurah's *The Body Beautiful,* an astonishingly un-
sentimental film about the conflicts between a white British mother
and her half-Nigerian daughter in England that makes one rethink
one's formulations about mothers and daughters, sexuality, nation
and race.

I was moved by your conclusion to this chapter, where you say
that letters provide the vital connection that eventually allows each
sister "to own a full life." I saw so much wish-fulfillment in that sentence; so much desire for fiction to set things right, to resolve. (The
novel's fairy-tale qualities reveal its own investments in wish-fulfillment.) Your faith made me wistful, for all I could think was, "Yes,
the sisters gain much, *but at what cost?*" So many scars remain irre-
mediable—not just metaphorically, but literally. Walker herself
seems to agree, since she returns to Tashi and the subject of female
circumcision in *Possessing the Secret of Joy.* I'll always be grateful to *The
Color Purple:* it was the catalyst for my research into slave narratives
and African-American literary criticism and theory, areas that have
not only remained "of interest," but which have moved into the fore-
front of my current work.

What might it mean "to own a full life"? It makes me think of
Gus Van Sant's film *My own Private Idaho,* which I'm also writing on
now, the very title of which is a deprecatory allusion to living in
one's own private world (a line from a B-52's song). The narcoleptic
hero, Mike Waters (played by River Phoenix), cannot "own" his
world. Moreover, it isn't even *private*: he lives on the streets, among
the other gay prostitutes, homeless, and disenfranchised. The culture wars really heated up after Walker's novel was published; increasingly it seems to me that those who oppose obscenity have
nothing to say about *the obscenity of everyday life—The Color Purple* was
among the first attempts amid the boom years of the 1980s to expose that obscenity.

More and more I think about how experience circles back on
itself, revealing how inadequate one's grasp of it was at the moment.
As Faulkner says, "The tragedy of life is that it's always premature."
Alice Walker hadn't yet written *The Color Purple* when I heard her
speak at Spelman College in Atlanta in 1981.

I didn't much care for Lee Smith's *Fair and Tender Ladies.*
Having spent eight years in the South, I'm irritated with "hick
chic"—the regurgitation of certain myths of the South that are utterly at odds with the reality of Burger Kings, shopping malls, af-
fluent planned neighborhoods that have covered the place like
mould on cheese. The only sure thing about all idylls is that they're
always gone. The South has just been a little more recalcitrant in

reconciling itself to suburban homogenization, though it capitalizes on it eagerly whenever it can (like the ads urging Fortune 500 companies to move south because they won't be bothered by those pesky unions). By the time I escaped in 1988, my nickname was Quentin Kauffman: (*"Why do you hate the South?"*).

There's a weird disjunction between postmodern epistolary fiction vs. literary criticism that exploits the personal: while the fiction has moved *away* from the personal and instead has become obsessed with global politics (*The Golden Notebook, The Handmaid's Tale*), critics wallowing in personal criticism seem to be saying, "The world's problems are all a muddle. I just wanna talk about ME!" Feminist critics aren't the only ones guilty of such wretched excesses; male academics are indulging too. I marvel at their faith that they are unique and interesting individuals. (Are they sure that interest extends outside academia?) As you can see from my own life-and-hard-times-essay,* I can't understand why anyone would want to take a bad trip down memory lane. It's interesting that you [in chapter ten of *Epistolary Responses*] and I both revisit Jane Tompkins' "Me and My Shadow" and Gerald MacLean's response to her. These essays seem to have taken on a life of their own. Until I became an editor (of *Gender and Theory*, in which these essays appear), I didn't realize how much editing and epistolarity have in common. The cunning manufacture of spontaneity, through rewrite after rewrite. The hard-won appearance of seamlessness within and among essays in a volume. Establishing a community of readers and provoking further responses—as you say in your conclusion. I think of Rilke: "live the questions now. Perhaps you will then gradually, without noticing it, live along some distant day into an answer." AN answer—not THE answer.

With best wishes,

Linda

---

*Linda S. Kauffman, "The Long Goodbye: Against Personal Testimony or, An Infant Grifter Grows Up," in *American Feminist Thought at Century's End,* ed. Linda S. Kauffman (Oxford and Cambridge, MA: Blackwell, 1993), 258–78.

6

John Updike's *S.*: Gender Play

Letter fiction provides a site of response in which authors and readers can explore some of the complexities involved in writing as a woman. In my reading of *Fair and Tender Ladies,* this issue was touched on relative to the link Lee Smith forges between women's ownership of property and of their own stories. In *LETTERS,* one aspect of the novel discussed was Barth's creation of a female whose writing negotiates between subjective self-inscription and objectified symbolic function. In considering *The Color Purple,* certainly I and many of the other scholars mentioned were conscious of Walker's attempt to create two different female writers, each with a distinctive writing style that reflected her particular difficult experience as a woman.

In John Updike's *S.,* writing as a woman becomes a central issue. In Sarah's first letter, she expresses envy of her husband's "illegible male authority" and admits having felt "wonderful" when she forged his signature to release stock accounts (6); in her last she emphasizes how much the pleasure of writing to him depends on his "silence" (261). Given this frame, along with the character's recurring references to her own writing, signature, and language, I find *S.* a logical space, if you will, for discussing the difficult issue of gendered writing.

As male and female authors fabricate female epistolary characters they publicize their own theories of writing as a woman.[1] This is especially true because the letter form "draws attention to the ambiguous implications of signature, and exposes the artifice involved in critical perceptions of gender" (Kauffman, *Discourses* 21). Thus, through their characters' reflections on writing and uses of imagery, and through the novel's plot events (the fate of the writing, how others receive it, for example), novelists elaborate their ideas about why a woman writes the way she does and what that writing means to her and those around her. Each novel (and this seems especially clear in *S.*) incorporates the biological, psychological, and cultural factors that the author believes make the women characters turn to writing and write in particular ways.

The question of *character* complicates our perception of these theoretical issues, however. We may assume that authors such as Alice Walker, John Barth, Lee Smith, and John Updike are exploring and generalizing about women's writing practices. However, that author may be more interested in elaborating an individual character's personality and situation rather than universalizing from this protagonist to other women. Still, most readers will find that the epistolary heroine, whatever her personality and circumstances, enacts at least some theoretical concepts of the relationship between women and writing. (Similarly, when the epistolary heroine devotes considerable space in her letters to questions about women's roles, women's situations, and women's work, we perceive that part of her function as a narrative construct is to posit theories about gender; simultaneously we perceive that she voices her own personality and individuality.) Consequently, as external readers, we can never say with certitude who owns the theories detailed in a novel: the character, the author, the author-as-this-character? Further complicating matters, each external reader brings to the situation past readings and experiences that shape responses to the character, her situation, and the theories that underpin how she "lives" and "acts."

Susan Lanser offers some clarification about our varying reactions to protagonists and why we do or do not accept "the authority of personal voice." She explains that "the autodiegetic 'I' "—that is, the narrating and interacting protagonist—derives standing with the external reader from "a reader's response not only to the narrator's acts but to the character's actions, just as the authority of the representation is dependent in turn on the successful construction of a credible voice" (*Fictions of Authority* 19). For us to accept the authenticity of a character, or maintain any ability to hear and value that character, her actions, others' actions in relationship to her, and her *voice* must all be credible. Lanser further points out that "a female personal narrator risks the reader's resistance if the act of telling, the story she tells, or the self she constructs through telling it transgresses the limits of the acceptably feminine" (19). What Lanser does not say, but implies, is that each reader's measures of the "acceptably feminine" will vary on the basis of that reader's background (literary and nonliterary). Thus, whereas Updike's Sarah may never take on full presence for me, for other readers she may have credibility. I may find that Updike creates a female writing protagonist only to undercut her power of "self-authorization" (Lanser's term), and that this constitutes a theoretical position about women's writing, but others may conclude that the character's inability to move beyond her society's stereotypes is an essential and well-drawn aspect of her existence.

By creating their female protagonists as letter writers, Smith, Barth, Walker, Updike, and others offer (or appear to offer) their characters opportunities, through *writing* itself, to respond to the difficulties of their lives. In the epistolary space, a measure of control can be achieved, language can be owned, a self and voice defined. As previous chapters demonstrate, Smith's Ivy, Barth's Germaine, and Walker's Celie write convincing selves, letters providing them a therapeutic, creative tool for self-preservation, discovery, and self-transformation. Updike's Sarah is more problematic. The wild variations in her self-expression at times break down her believability, and the novel's satiric tone can undercut the external reader's sympathy for the protagonist as easily as it can slice at social mores. Then, too, writing in *S.* is not necessarily figured as a means of self-knowledge or exploration: much of it is a seizing of the "master's tools" to gain that master's goods, rather than to question fully who owns what and why.

Some feminist scholars contend that certain discourse forms or styles arise more consistently within women and call on women authors to give free play to those qualities—to express, not suppress, the feminine. Meanwhile, what to say of Samuel Richardson writing Clarissa, John Barth writing Germaine Pitt, John Updike writing Sarah? Must one conclude that just because they were born biologically male these authors cannot create authentic female writing subjects? I want to believe that both sexes can avail themselves of "feminine" writing elements or qualities. Historically, however, most men have sought mastery, logic, unity, and hierarchical patterns in their own and others' writing, in conformity with the expectations and privileges commensurate with their social and economic status within the patriarchy. They have usually rejected the writing of women and rejected too the writing qualities associated with women, such as discursiveness, multiplicity, and emphasis on personal relations and community.[2]

When Carolyn Heilbrun advises women to "avoid the trap of depriving ourselves of male discourse altogether while we attempt to subvert it," she infers that we have two distinct kinds of writing. When she adds that "the discourse of males is not all 'male' discourse: much of it is human discourse that society has denied to women," she also implies that whatever 'female' discourse may be, it too is "human discourse" available to all (295) and that the terms "male discourse" and "female discourse" merely label tendencies or customs. When Hélène Cixous writes in "Sorties" of Kleist and Shakespeare, male poets "capable of becoming woman," she too seems to assume that verbal discourse of various kinds is equally available to both sexes—if, *based on sincere motivation,* individuals choose those discourse forms (98). Nevertheless, many feminists have concluded that males who choose to write in the female voice (whether in fiction that centers on a female's point of view or in critical work from a feminist viewpoint) are moved less by empathy and genuine desire to know the female than by a desire to encompass, contain, and control her.[3]

Luce Irigaray warns that men "prospect" women's sexual and theoretical beings (*Speculum* 145). Solipsistically, the male subject "plays at multiplying himself, even deforming himself, in this process. He is father, mother, and child(ren). And the relationships between them. He is masculine and feminine and the relationships between them" (145). In what seems a related move, Nancy K. Miller alerts feminist theorists to the dangers of reifying or packaging the "female writing subject" for the use of others. Rather than creating universal statements to define women's writing, Miller asks us to remain aware and accepting of the "ambiguities" and "contradictions" we will find among the writing of women ("Changing the Subject" 116–17). Perhaps defining or even describing this thing we are terming "feminine writing" is too prescriptive. Mary Jacobus encourages us, instead, to concentrate on the forces and processes that yield feminine writing; such an approach "frees woman's writing from the determinism of origin or essence" (6).

Updike adopted the female point of view somewhat in *The Witches of Eastwick,* but that novel's negative reception by feminist critics may have given him pause for thought. Between *Witches* and *S.* it would seem he took the time to familiarize himself with feminist theories about women's writing, language, and the cultural formation of gender, for some of that knowledge surfaces in *S.* As a feminist I still question how this novel's language and style transmit the woman character's experience. In addition, given the novel's epistolarity, written language becomes doubly central: Sarah's letters construct not only her character but also her concepts of writing as a woman.

S. entertains and amuses me; the satire often makes me smile. Nonetheless, my admiration for Updike's undertaking is dulled by seeing how unkind the overall plot of this book is to Sarah, for it keeps her entrapped in a traditional narrative—waiting for a man to make her life complete.[4] Alison Lurie thinks that *S.* is, in part, a response to feminist criticisms of Updike's earlier work, but she finds that the created female is "wholly hateful" in her snobbishness and insidious materialism, as well as pitiful in the humiliation she suffers in relationship to her guru (4). Michiko Kakutani regrets the way Sarah's letters use "the worst self justifying (and now dated) rhetoric of the woman's movement" (C29). Richard Gilman contends that the novel yields a "fixed sense of women" created as "projections of male sensibility" (39, 41).

Authors (male and female) have traditionally incorporated certain markers of female discourse in their epistolary novels, including biological, psychological, linguistic, and cultural characteristics. Such "female" aspects, of course, may be intimately tied to stereotypes of women in currency at the time of the novel's creation. Clarissa's sentimentality and the tears that fall on her prose, Evelina's uncertainties and lack of education, Germaine Pitt's rampant sexuality and sexual word play, and Ivy Rowe's youthful romanticism may tell us as much about their authors' acceptance of or portrayal of female stereotypes as they tell us about their authors' real desires to discover how women experience the world and write about it. In this sense, Patricia Spack's comments concerning letter novels' frequent complicity with the dominant culture prove insightful (69–75). Thus, whereas a novel such as *The Color Purple* may use women's writing to subvert clichéd assumptions about women and their discourse, giving them the power to restore themselves through writing, a novel such as *S.* may finally enforce conventional formulas. Updike's satirical novel features a protagonist who, in many ways, does "write like a woman," but her words create a stereotyped female self inscribed into a male-structured order.

That Updike's character can seem likable, distasteful, pitiable, or perhaps even enviable to different readers verifies the author's ability to produce a semblance of a woman who writes herself. Is semblance enough, however? Anatole Broyard points out that in an interview about *Witches of Eastwick* Updike averred he would like to be a woman, *temporarily,* to "investigate" the state of being female. As Broyard reminds us, however, to place such conditions on the imagination will diminish creative power: "For a man to write a profound book about a woman, it may be necessary for him to forget himself. There are no temporary women" (7). Whatever else it may be, *S.* is not a full exploration of writing as a woman; it is more like a short camping trip into that region. A further problem is that, given all his skill as a stylist, and presuming his awareness of feminist theory about the cultural construction of women's roles, Updike *chooses* still to portray his protagonist with so little insight into herself, so strong a belief in biological determinism, and so little ability for real change.

Because I found Sarah such a puzzling character, I wrote to Updike with some questions about inventing her. Reading his response helped me to realize that, for him, transformation or change in a character would be a fairly unrealistic idealization.

April 2, 1992

Dear Ms. Bower:

Thank you for your letter of March 18th, 1992—my 60th birthday, as it happens. I have been pondering your curious request, not quite able to ignore it, yet not able, either, to imagine exactly what you want. It has been a number of years now since I wrote *S.*, so my memory of my intentions may be inexact. You complain that you "think of the epistolary form as one that has the potential to empower change in its heroines, but didn't see that much change in Sarah." My goodness, how much change do you want? She begins as the cossetted wife of a New England doctor and ends as a refugee from justice on a remote Caribbean island. She has passed through a variety of lovers and a crash-course in Indian religion to achieve peace and, as a single woman, empowerment. Anyway, I don't generally think of my characters as being transformed, since our characters are about as hard to change as our faces. I think of them as passing through a number of adventures to a new, if momentary, state of resolution and suspended activity.

As to your question "did it 'feel' different to write as a woman?," I would say yes and no. Sarah has a personality that might be called "giving," "meddlesome," or "manipulative," depending on how sympathetically she is viewed, and from the standpoint of an author her wish to reach out and impress herself, whether on her husband and daughter or on Sheriff Yardley, is ideal. Her voice has what fiction requires, which is energy, and it was a pleasure, for this author, to dwell, during the months of composition, within such a center of energy.

I hope this satisfies your own mysterious need for a letter from me. Please do not expect to engage me in a long correspondence— I am *not* Sarah Worth. I take it this is for your book; use my letter entire, if you use it, and take care to reproduce it accurately. In preparation for writing *S.*, I looked into *Clarissa* and Upton Sinclair's *Another Pamela,* but didn't get very far in either. Ring Lardner's *You Know Me Al* and Thornton Wilder's *The Ides of March,* both read in adolescence, may have been the epistolary models in my mind.

With best wishes,

John Updike

While admitting the difficulties of the task, I still want to look at what Updike achieves in *S.* as he strives to put together a female persona, to prove himself aware of feminist cultural studies, to take advantage of and experiment with the epistolary form, and, furthermore, strives to situate his female character and her fate within the context of a major textual event: Hawthorne's *The Scarlet Letter.*

The two passages from *The Scarlet Letter* that serve as epigraphs to *S.* predict that Updike will work within and against Hawthorne's novel.[5] The first selection describes Hester Prynne's beauty and dignity as she leaves the prison; the second concerns her shift from "passion and feeling, to thought" and her discovery that "the world's law was no law for her mind." *S.* parallels *The Scarlet Letter* in that Sarah blooms through the experience of breaking away—she feels younger, more passionate, renewed, and more of an individual. Also, like Hester, she has an affair with a religious man (Broyard 7). Then too, Sarah, like Hester, discovers that some social conventions do not suit her. Unlike Hester, however, Sarah remains very much within the world's law, with her Swiss bank account, her desire to have her daughter Pearl succeed in some fairly conventional ways, and her continuing need for self-definition through a man. She is created *against* the Hester image also in that she is mobile; rejection by her immediate society does not mean as total a rejection as it does for the earlier character.

One of Hester Prynne's primary characteristics is her silence, and one can see her silence as a symbol for the generalized obliteration of woman's voice the patriarchy has imposed. (Another perspective takes the silence more as an act of will. To speak would be to cooperate with the patriarchal order.) In contrast to Hester, one of the qualities Updike gives Sarah is volubility. Whether donated with good or bad faith on her author's part, this profusion denies the long repression of the female voice; Sarah's letters and tapes are frequent and often lengthy. The length of Sarah's letters to her family and friend Midge are a seizing of the floor, a demonstration of her will to be heard and her pleasure, at least when writing to her husband, that he cannot interrupt her writing with carping and scolding (261).

Updike's writing as a female acknowledges the woman's need to be heard and specifically includes some feminist concerns with representation of women. In a letter to Pearl, Sarah compares the words "daughter" and "son," expressing fondness for the first with its "mysterious silent letters in the middle" (16). She explains that she honors that silent space as a valorization of her femininity and female power (genital/pleasurable and procreational), reacting against the notion somehow passed on to her of her genitals "as a kind of wound" (16).

Images of the body abound in Sarah's letters: she writes to her dentist about her teeth, her hairdresser about her hair, and her former yoga teacher about bodily sensations caused by various postures. At another level, woman's body and its relationship to writing are inscribed in Sarah's letters in a way that has strong intertextual echoes. Like Clarissa (and many other epistolary heroines) Sarah weeps onto her writing, and emotional distress causes orthographic disruption as well. For instance, she notes that "those round blurry spots . . . are tears, actual tears" (206), and "I must be tired all my commas are dropping away" (20). Then too, she writes of textures, smells, and appearance, and of her pleasure in her ex-husband's body and her interest in others' bodies—male and female. Updike enables Sarah to write easily about her body and feelings. Hélène Cixous characterizes such a practice as feminine; she finds that woman's writing incorporates "bodily functions," "erotogeneity," "the fantastic tumult of her drives," and "her goods, her pleasures, her organs" ("Laugh" 876, 880). All of these elements are part of Sarah's letters.[6]

Updike also works at stressing Sarah's preoccupation with physical connectedness. Bodies do not exist as mere objects for her, but in relationship to her. Thus, in writing to Charles of what they once had together, she describes body smells as "doorways into another being, another body like your own, helplessly a body" (8). Writing to Alinga, a woman who has been her lover at the ashram to which she fled after leaving her husband, Sarah remembers the pleasure of brushing Alinga's hair with the sparks of static electricity playing over them so that their bodies seemed to intermingle (168).

Sarah's longing for continuing connection to her mother and daughter permeates the entire novel. She writes to her daughter: "I must appeal to you as another woman to understand me, to simply *know*" (17) and is always writing to her mother with questions, advice, complaints, or requests. Updike takes special care to show Sarah's fierce attachment to her daughter. They are "women and on the same continuum" because, asserts Sarah, "I am her mother. I am she as she was once I" (63). This emphasis on woman-to-woman relationships often marks women's writing. Cixous, for instance, calls on women to capitalize on their strong ties to other women, asking them to write not for men or to please men, but to write for each other—for self, mother, daughter, sister, and, one supposes, friend, allowing woman to "rethink womankind" rather than continue to be "what men have made of her" ("Laugh" 882). Updike has worked hard to capture this aspect of women's writing.

Updike is partially successful in elaborating the idea of multiplicity as a dominant quality of woman's voice. One way he captures this element is through Sarah's varied signatures. From the novel's start, signatures are given special meaning. In her first letter to her husband, Sarah tells Charles that she forged his name on an order to sell stocks: "that signature, it's been branded into me, I wouldn't be surprised to see it burned into my flank" (6). She wants to have the power of the man's voice and position, something she only had in totem before as his named spouse. Forging his signature steals a sense of his authority along with securing some capital (6). (Her maiden name was Price, her married name Worth; both her price and her worth, to herself and her society thus figure in the novel's play with signatures.) In this and subsequent letters she tries on signatures, writing herself "physically" into different relationships. Updike may be trying to show a nonunitary character through this device, as Sarah is variously S., Mother, Sarah Worth, Sarah Worth (Mrs. Charles), Sally Worth, Sare, Sarah P. Worth, Sara (Worth), Sis, Mummy, Sara nee Price, #4723-9001-7469-8666 (for her Swiss bank account), Ma Prem Kundalini, or Kundalini, or signs the name of the ashram leader. On tape she exists without written signature.

The variety of signatures certainly works well to demonstrate that Sarah has many sides to her personality. She is conservative and authoritative with her daughter, rebellious and holier-than-thou with her mother, gossipy and yoga-happy with her friend Midge, self-righteous and sensible, but sometimes sentimental with her ex-husband, and manipulative in her official ashram correspondence. Explaining her many-sidedness, Sarah notes: "We all have a number of skins, especially women I think, because society makes us wriggle more" (236). Sarah's wriggling includes duplicity too. For instance, her last letter to her husband claims that "having known the Arhat's divine love I am not in the market (unlike needy old you) for any further attachments" (263), but a letter written within the same week to her first love, Myron Stern, reveals she *is* "in the market"; she communicates considerable interest in a renewal of their relationship, should Myron care to pursue it (240–49).

A part of Sarah's personality that emerges in her letters to women concerns conflicts about women's roles. To her daughter, Sarah expresses some resistance to woman's traditional homemaker role: she wants Pearl to complete college and not to marry early, as she did. Women, Sarah finds, have suffered "a million years of slavery" (15), and she perceives that the commodity exchange of women is continuing in her own family as Pearl's father (Sarah's ex-husband) encourages the daughter's early marriage, handing her

over "like a manacled slave to another *man*" (205). To Pearl and her
friend Midge, Sarah postulates theories about women's easily roused
jealousy, linking it to biological drives to protect babies (151), and
about women's generosity and subservience and the way men capitalize on both (55, 157). She comes to see psychotherapy as part of
the patriarchal power structure (103), and she critiques men's communication mode: "They're always trying to find *out*, they don't just
take things in" (137).

Furthermore, Updike's Sarah criticizes men's power plays
and demonstrates knowledge of ways in which women are sometimes complicit with the patriarchal culture in which they live. What
Updike does not allow his protagonist is any deep insight into
the forces that encourage that complicity. The explanations Sarah
is permitted to discover are based largely on biology. Only super-
ficially does she discuss the pressures created by the dominant culture. At one point she can tell Alinga, her temporary lesbian lover,
that she does not want Alinga to play the part of guardian as her
husband did. She feels that Charles (and, by extension, Alinga) attempted to protect her, but sees great limitations inherent in acceptance of that protection (166). To her friend Midge she writes of
"the conditioning that had us trained to keep quiet while all these
fathers and husbands and sons and lovers and lawyers and doctors
and Indian chiefs talked. All this trying to be not too smart, not
too loud, not too sexy, not too wonderful" (193). Sarah can see that
she has often acted in conjunction with the power structure of the
society, but Updike never has her truly analyze that society.

Whenever she pushes hard to explain things to herself, Updike
forces her to bring up motherhood, the "fascination" of heterosexuality, or woman's "natural selfishness" (166–67). It is no surprise
then that she describes her parents' condemnation of her youthful
romance with Myron Stern as stemming from their "creaturely nature" (212). Here again, Updike denies Sarah any power for deep
cultural critique. She tells her mother that the best that parents can
do is "follow the fashion and trust biology to override culture—if
we try to be better parents than our peers, our children will feel
uneasy" (216). In a similar dodge, Updike has her reflecting on the
women in Hollywood, who, she has heard, have power in the community but are conditioned to turn it back to their agents and husbands. When she wonders why this is, Updike has her conclude that

it comes from woman's biological role as child bearer and child protector (247).

Another feminist concern that Updike shows his heroine exploring, through her ashram experience, is language ownership. He has Sarah explain to Charles that one of the things she found when she took up yoga was that it "gave me a vocabulary" (11). To those not in power, the dominant culture's language can seem just another means of controlling, obfuscating, or limiting ideas and feelings. As Sarah explains concerning the language of her husband's lawyer, his "blustering" language, a fusillade of terms such as "prosecution," "extradition," "deposition," and "restitution" is meant to cover, not expose, meaning (139). Unfortunately, Sarah's criticism of the lawyer's discourse practice is undercut by her self-denigration when she states that his language makes her feel like she's back in Latin class (139), inadequate in intellectual ability.

Given the concentration of certain feminists on the difficulty of undoing patriarchal control while using the patriarchy's language, Updike's interest in his character's use of Sanskrit could be seen as an exploration of alternative language, words that might undercut what we have come to call the law of language and the law of the father. Sarah uses so much Sanskrit that the external reader can grow impatient with it. One begins to wonder whether Updike's use of Eastern terminology is in place as much to prove his cleverness as to demonstrate the need of women for a language that can disrupt the dominant culture's hold.[7] "Updike is wickedly impatient with the wisdom of the East," comments John Leonard (124), and that impatience undercuts Sarah's supposed discovery of language. His mockery erases any real concern he wants the protagonist to express about language trapping us in gender roles.

Eastern language and philosophy appeal to Sarah in part because they incorporate an emphasis on the body (104). Especially for French feminists, allowing the body to "speak" is a central language and writing issue. Nonetheless, Updike locates Sarah at an illegitimate ashram, where the organization's leaders are more interested in personal power than religious elevation, and the religious head of the group, the *Arhat*, uses Eastern language to manipulate others rather than enlighten them (he turns out to be from Massachusetts, not India as he has claimed). Is Updike trying to make the sincere point that, depending on power relations, any tongue can be

a master tongue? Or is Sarah's interest in the language just a flirtation with the exotic? (Or some of each?) Updike sends his heroine
off in search of self and religious values but then lets us see how
easily she has been duped. He makes fun of her, showing that she
is not finding the peace that surpasses any understanding (or even
much understanding). He has her writing that she moved past hat-
ing her husband, but then has her compare Charles to an annoying
insect in a most virulent way (116). In a similar ironic juxtaposition
he has her explain that the heavy security guard system is needed at
the ashram because "there is so much hatred in the world against
simple love and peace" (118).

Some reviewers of the novel find Updike in sympathy with his
letter-writing persona. Paul Gray, for instance, rejects the idea that
this novel mocks women. For Gray, Sarah's "pilgrimage" and self
are "serious, but her surroundings decidedly are not" (98). I wish I
could agree, but in my view Sarah's pilgrimage fails to change her
significantly. Evidently, Updike wants us to see that though she can
change her circumstances, Sarah cannot change her deepest self;
after all, his letter to me stresses the conviction that deep personality
change is immensely difficult and unlikely. We must recall, as James
Schiff reminded me in a letter, that Updike often treats his males
harshly too.

---

16 July 1991

Dear Anne:

   . . . Updike, I think, is certainly mocking Sarah, for her hypoc-
risy and self-deception; yet, he doesn't strike me (correct me if I'm
overstating your point) as misogynistic. As a male, I see Updike as
being rather impartial in exposing and satirizing all of his characters, male and female. Though readers may disapprove of and fail
to sympathize with Sarah Worth, I think the same can be said of
Rabbit Angstrom. Updike is clinically frank in revealing the worst
about his characters. There are probably few characters, male or
female, in Updike's writing with whom I would ever want to be on
intimate terms (yet I am intrigued by how Updike creates these fictional lives). For me, the major difference between Updike's attempt at writing from a male and from a female point of view isn't
that Updike denigrates women and empowers men, but that he is a

good deal more convincing and expert at telling Rabbit's story than Sarah's; as you say, a woman's point of view is sometimes a "foreign land" for Updike. . . .

Sincerely,

Jim

In measuring Sarah against Rabbit, Kakatuni finds the former given less serious consideration, with Rabbit (specifically in *Rabbit Run*) depicted in "a carefully shaded portrait of a difficult and incomplete man, torn between his yearning for freedom and his need for roots." In contrast, Sarah presents merely "a satiric picture of a careless woman, eager to shuck her family responsibilities for a fling with self-fulfillment" (C29). Yes, Sarah's circumstances change, and, yes, Updike is tough on all his protagonists, but still I find myself distressed that for all her situational shifts, Sarah's intellectual and emotional growth are minimal.

S. moves Sarah through her ashram adventures satirically. The net result of the often funny debunking, however, is to belittle the protagonist's attempt at change and to establish her essential, ongoing need to "come home" to a man. Her infatuation with the Arhat is linked to her first lost love, Myron Stern, the Jewish man her parents made her give up so that she could marry the upwardly mobile, Protestant Charles, who fit in with their social set. Sarah's pilgrimage turns out to have been an exercise in freeing herself of Charles so that she can seek Myron. Her letter to her old love apologizes for spinelessly allowing herself to be married off and is signed "Your unextinguished old flame, / Sarah nee Price" (249); it demonstrates her willingness to take up with Myron where they left off years before. It would seem that Updike wants to believe that such a romantic youth-love could survive. He has constructed Sarah's yogic ashram experience as a "phase" that, although it does put her through enough stress to reconcile her to mother, daughter, and ex-husband, does not really make her throw over any of the rather essentialist values with which Updike endows her.

What are these values? The first is that a real woman, even though she may experiment with an alternative, is heterosexual. Sarah explains to her onetime lesbian lover that their lovemaking lacked the "seriousness" that the possibility of procreation gives to heterosexual relations (167). A second value is that a woman's most divine purpose is to have children and grandchildren. Sarah does question this idea, asking her mother, "children aren't *entirely* the point of a woman's life, are they?" (215), but she has no idea of any other center for female existence. At another point she imagines that her body and spirit are but packaging for the all-important eggs her body produces (260). Although she is forty-two and healthy and has two years of college education and a large cash reserve to draw on, Sarah's horizons seem oddly limited; she has no self-directed plans (or even fantasies) for travel, education, or career.

The third value Sarah enacts through her writing is that without a man a woman is incomplete; this idea frames the novel. For Donald J. Greiner, Sarah is like her predecessor Hester because "both need a man in order to rebel successfully" (494). Hester turns to the Puritan minister, Dimmesdale, Sarah to the Buddhist/Hindu Arhat. Greiner thinks that, in "allowing Sarah to think that she is free of patriarchal clumsiness, be it bearded God or unfaithful husband," Updike both celebrates a modern woman's freedom and mocks her "extremes" (494). Nevertheless, Sarah's overriding need goes beyond a male helper or guide; she accepts the cliché that a woman cannot exist without a man. The strongest images Sarah creates reinforce this traditional view of the female; framing the novel, they occur in her first and last letters, both addressed to her ex-husband Charles. In the last paragraph of each of these letters she waxes nostalgic about waiting to hear the sound of the automatic garage door and the rumble of her husband's car as he returned to her (14, 264). Although both descriptions have a wonderful satiric edge, cleverly playing on sexual associations of women to houses and men to cars, the amusement is ours and Updike's; my sense is that for Sarah it is all quite serious.

In the early letter, written as she approaches Los Angeles by air, it is "our house" to which she refers, imagining Charles returning to it now that she has left—the garage door automatically opening to receive his Mercedes, followed by his "aggressive footsteps" and his discovery of the house's emptiness and darkness (14). In the last letter, written from a Bahamian island, Sarah still associates part of the house with herself. She admits that even on this island she finds herself "listening for the grinding sound of the garage door sliding up, in obedience to its own inner eye" (264). Through this framing imagery, Updike presents his heroine still waiting for a husband to bring her fulfillment, still listening for her own sexuality in terms of an automatically triggered response to a man.[8]

The novel's plot and imagery sabotage Sarah. Updike even has his heroine undercut her own writing potency. One thinks of the epistolary protagonist as seizing power when she holds the pen; Sarah, set off as she is against the silenced Hester Prynne, would seem deliberately created secure in her verbal powers. Sarah denigrates her words, however, writing to her daughter Pearl to "think of these letters as what I do now instead of embroidery" (158). Because Sarah never elaborates on her needlework as a creative or fulfilling occupation, the implication is that both writing and embroidery are trivial activities that fill up a woman's empty hours and that neither deserves serious consideration as art or craft. In the one letter to Myron (her old flame) this comparison returns, as Sarah again discounts her writing: "I sit inside and embroider my letters and read" (244).

In *The Scarlet Letter* Hester Prynne's needlework is a powerful tool of self-expression. Her elaborately embroidered decorations of the punitive "A" work to declare self-transformation through creativity. In contrast, Sarah Price Worth seems incapable, through needle or pen, of achieving the dignity, beauty, or rebirth of her distant textual ancestress.

With his plot devices, use of language, and use of the letter form, what is Updike conveying about woman's experience and writing? Is he saying that Sarah is a typical woman and that what is true for her is mostly true for all? That woman's private writing is insignificant embroidery, that biology explains woman's social acts, that a man and a child *are* woman's highest destiny? Or is he saying that Sarah is just one woman, an individual not yet able to overcome cultural constraints, whose struggles to break free are comically limited by her own complicity with the power structure? Or is he being duplicitous, so that, to use Richard Gilman's terms, Sarah is "simply a man in novelistic drag" (41)? Does this character deny herself insight, has society so conditioned her that she can see only so far, or has Updike brought her to life wearing blinders of his own devising?

Updike's appropriation of the female voice, although often clever and sometimes funny, strikes me finally as a belittling of woman's voice and intellect. I wish I could agree with Tom Wilhelmus, who postulates, excusing Updike from "solecism," that *S.* is a

genuine effort to explore a "witty and intelligent" woman and that
Updike's narrative effort is a sincere effort at "knowing" (550, 548).
Wilhelmus believes that narrative is a way the artist seeks knowledge
by questing within himself. Such an impulse is admirable, I would
certainly agree, but Updike's experiment with writing as a woman
disappoints me. Knowledge worth the seeking should change us,
shake us, move us into new country. Sarah is not allowed to get there.
At novel's end she *is* in the Bahamas, but only as a tourist. Updike
seems to have been a tourist, too, come to the shores of the feminist
country to play. For all his display of familiarity with some feminist
concerns, I am not convinced he has deep sympathy for those concerns. Like the tourist, he has taken snapshots to prove he has been
to a faraway land, but then he went home, never really learning the
deepest concerns of those who live in what to him will probably always remain a foreign land.

    Literary gender changes are no easy matter. The way a given
external reader responds to an author's effort to cross the sexual
borderline may say as much about the reader as about that author.
Given my own interests in the reading process and in epistolary novels as a means to raise our awareness of how we read, it is necessary
to look at the reader's role in gender creation. According to Jacobus:
"In constituting woman as our object when we read, we not only
read in gender, but constitute ourselves as readers. The stabilizing,
specular image of woman in the text makes reading possible by assuring us that we have women's faces too—or men's, for that matter,
since 'woman' serves also as a figure for a reflection of 'man.' " (4)
Thus, our own need to feel securely located in gender is a condition of reading. Derrida forces confrontation with this issue in his
epistolary "L'Envois" (part of the volume titled *The Post Card*), where
the reader's uncertainty about the sex of the beloved unsettles
the reading act. My discontent with Updike's Sarah reflects my own
desires as a feminist. My rejection of Sarah becomes also a rejection of the extent to which Western capitalist society has encultu-
rated Sarah's values in me. My criticism of the character and her
writing as depicted by Updike functions to reinforce my doubts
about our society's materialism and reliance on biological determinism and to help me question the ongoing popularity of the romance plot. This process allows me to confirm myself as a woman
different from the character and, of course, different from Updike.
Jacobus also brings our attention to the way that "reading woman

(reading) is surely nothing other than this disclosure, this discom-
position, which puts the institution of difference in question
without erasing the question of difference itself" (24). In spite
of whatever discomfort Updike's attempts at gender play may cause
me, *S.* productively focuses my attention on questions of difference,
its epistolary form heightening my sensitivity to the construction of
gender and gendered voice.

7

Delettering: Responses to Agency in Jean Webster's *Daddy-Long-Legs*

In *LETTERS*, Ambrose Mensch, the lover of Germaine, actively engages in a battle between image and word, attempting, as scriptwriter, to instill verbal force into a movie adaptation of John Barth's works. Germaine describes a moment when Ambrose's words are literally erased: the film's director manipulates the writer's carefully constructed scenario so that the actual written script is "washed away" in the ocean. Ambrose decides this is "brilliant" because the scene "was not only nonverbal, but *unwritable*" (235). Germaine herself has experienced moments of writer's block, but as an epistolarian she is endlessly devoted to words—in them she finds regenerative power and control.

Although Jean Webster's *Daddy-Long-Legs* is very different from *LETTERS*, it also features an epistolary heroine devoted to writing as a scene of discovery—a powerful, protected, personal site of agency. The kind of conflict between word and screen image set up in *LETTERS* does not occur between the covers of Webster's 1912 novel, yet it enters my discussion of the book as I trace the ways in which various film adaptations of *Daddy-Long-Legs* respond to the original text, removing power from the heroine. Pursuing this kind of intertextuality, which I term "delettering," helps me to consider twentieth-century popular culture attitudes toward the notion of woman's self-empowerment through writing.

The letters that compose Jean Webster's sentimental and once popular epistolary novel, *Daddy-Long-Legs,* recount the progress of an orphan girl who, partly through her own efforts, moves from rags to riches. Like many other popular novels of its time, Webster's text presents the "cheery view of life," and were it not for the mocking humor and feistiness of its letter-writing heroine and the effective use of the letter form itself, this fiction would slip into the "syrupy pathos, sentiment, and optimism" that James D. Hart characterizes as emblematic of late nineteenth- and early twentieth-century senti-mental novels about orphans and children, such as the Elsie Dins-more books, *Rebecca of Sunnybrook Farm, Mrs. Wiggs of the Cabbage Patch,* and *Pollyanna* (208–12).

The orphan status of *Daddy-Long-Legs*'s protagonist, Jerusha Abbott, would appeal to early twentieth-century readers; orphans were popular novel subjects, "for somehow orphans were considered purer in heart and nobler in spirit than children still burdened with parents" (Hart 213). Jacqueline Burke's study of late nine-teenth- and early twentieth-century fiction for young women de-monstrates that in such work, "mothers are conspicuous by their absence" (188). For the youthful female reader, the orphan hero-ine represents common fantasies of "the adolescent girl, eager to sally forth on her own . . . strongly impelled to reverse roles with her mother (vicariously through the stories she reads), to deactivate her mother if possible" (Burke 192). This is not a solely Freudian read-ing; Nancy Chodorow (among others) discusses the individuation anxieties of young women (133–140). Chodorow defines the separa-tion-individuation process as more about maintenance of relation-ship than did Freud. That redefinition does not reduce the amount of psychological work necessary for a girl's development, especially in a society that stresses individualism.

Alan and Mary Simpson speculate that the 1910 publication of Eleanor Hallowell Abbott's epistolary *Molly-Make-Believe* may have influenced Webster's creation of a pen-wielding orphan heroine. However, they point out that Webster had experimented with the letter form in an earlier story (148). That Webster's heroine shares the last name of *Molly-Make-Believe*'s author would seem to acknowl-edge a literary debt. However, if Webster was using Abbott's work as her most immediate model, she added some important elements that give her orphan special advantages.

Making her heroine an aspiring author and enthusiastic col-lege student makes it logical that the letters in *Daddy-Long-Legs* can contain not only news of studies and campus events but also reflections on women's suffrage and education, the class system, the pitfalls of fundamentalist religions, and the foolishness of overauthoritarian professors and administrators. Because these topics reflect questions first raised by (and still central to) feminists, we can conclude that Webster found the letter form congenial to opening up issues of particular concern to women. I imagine that Webster found her heroine's orphan state an appropriate representation of the isolated, unauthorized position of woman in a world still very much dominated by male authorities and systems. In addition, the orphan state may have represented for Webster the partial isolation in her own life caused by her long-term secret relationship to a married man.

Jerusha Abbott's letters, with their lively style, abundant quantity, illustrations, and inherent faith in words' power to make things happen, bear a strong resemblance to the correspondence of Webster herself. She was an inveterate letter writer. During the composition of the stage version of *Daddy-Long-Legs* her many letters to her lover, Glenn Ford McKinney, were a study of good cheer, chattiness, and constancy as she encouraged him to fight alcoholism and the frustration of work he did not enjoy.[1] Some letters, like those written by her character Jerusha, include amusing illustrations. Reading Webster's surviving letters, one senses her faith that her words could help steer McKinney along a safe path. Although the affair was known to certain friends and family members, McKinney and Webster maintained as much secrecy as possible because McKinney was married to an invalid he did not feel he could divorce. Letters were often their only contact; Webster at times wrote almost daily. For Webster, as for her most famous heroine, writing was a way to make things happen—to act, to change oneself and others.

To convey a sense of Webster's devotion to letter writing, I have extracted part of a letter to Glenn McKinney. The tone and content are typical of her communications to her lover.

10th St.

July 24. [1913]

Dear Glenn

I am afraid I was not very gracious about my birthday present— it was just that I thought such things between you and me were better ended. The pendant is very very lovely. I carried it to the bank this afternoon and tucked it into a corner of my safe deposit box— to be kept in trust till a happier time when I may wear it. The little leather box smelt so *tobaccoey* and like your pocket that I am keeping it in my travelling bag to hold the gold pins I use everyday. It has been with you so very recently that it seems to bring some of you to me!

I rose with the lark at six this morning, and packed and missed one train and sat outside the station for an hour writing Scene 1 of Act IV. You see with what up and coming bravery I am facing the future! To you the same. Our salvation is work and work and *more* work. Fortunately we both have some ready to our hands.

Set to work with all promptitude and cheerfulness at your farm and accomplish as much as possible against the time when I can look at it with you. I will be writing as good a play as may be. . . .

In Webster's own life, persistence and spirit won out over life difficulties; she and Glenn McKinney finally married in 1915. (Sadly, their happiness was short-lived; Webster died of childbirth complications in 1916.) *Daddy-Long-Legs* is also the story of female triumph over adversity. Webster's decision to present the novel in letters gives the protagonist extra power to shape her life and her chronicle. When the letter form is removed, self-empowerment goes with it, to a large extent. Thus, when Webster transforms her novel into a play, and when later it is transformed into a silent movie, two standard films, a musical, and finally a cartoon, the heroine loses much of her power to transform and shape her own fate.[2] I call this process delettering.

The letter convention can empower a protagonist in several ways. To start with, the letter gives some sense that the writer can reach beyond herself. In her discussion of earlier letter fictions, Ruth Perry asserts that a character's need to write, her isolation, and her uncertainty about her correspondent always reflect "the deeper truth that people are locked in their own skins, in their own consciousnesses." The letter, like all communication, is an imperfect solution, representing "the difficulties inherent in all human condition" (107). Thus, although the letter protagonist may wish to change another's image of herself or shift the relationship or elicit some understanding or action or gift from her addressee, failure or partial failure always threatens. When the letter writer is not only isolated and uncertain but also female (which seems the predominant case in letter fictions)[3] and her need is for love, her missives, from Ovid's *Heroides* on, become "discourses of desire" in which, as Linda S. Kauffman writes, "passion is transgressive, woman is disorder, and . . . writing is the revolution" against political or social constraints (*Discourses* 20).[4] The writer attempts, over and over, to create herself and her recipient in the images she desires. And, in spite of inherent possibilities of failure, it is in the nature of the epistolary form to emphasize the writing character's power and need to chart her own journey; she tries to "map [her] coordinates—temporal, spatial, emotional, intellectual" (Altman, *Epistolarity* 119). *She* maps them rather than giving that power over to someone else. The letter writer's insistent work demonstrates her belief that she can control or even change her picture of herself and another individual's reactions or actions or ideas or feelings if she will only write and write.

Jerusha Abbott, Webster's heroine, is the oldest orphan in the John Grier Home. An anonymous trustee, impressed with the humor in Jerusha's essay about trustee visiting day ("Blue Wednesday"), decides to send her to college so she can become a professional writer. Webster's stage adaptation of her novel retains Jerusha's writing as the impetus for the trustee's action. Later cinematic versions will convert this plot element so that instead of her intellect and writing activity it is mostly her attractive body and manner that motivate the trustee; at most, her ability to speak up or to weave a story out loud *may* earn admiration. In the novel, as in all dramatic adaptations, Jerusha's only obligation to her benefactor, other than applying herself to her studies, is to write a monthly letter to "Mr. John Smith" to report her progress. I take this situation to be Webster's representation of the male-female power relationships she saw still dominating her society: a man decides what opportunities a woman can have and how she is to use them and makes her accountable to him for any advances she may make. Nevertheless, at least in the novel, Webster, by using the epistolary form, hands over to her protagonist a way to participate actively in her own future.

In the book version of *Daddy-Long-Legs*, much of Jerusha's response to her subordinate situation involves naming herself and her benefactor. Through these Adamic acts the epistolary protagonist asserts self-authority and establishes a pattern of claiming herself and her desires through language. During the four years she writes to her sponsor, her discourse transgressively metamorphoses him from an abstraction into a creature and then into various family figures, including father, uncle, grandmother, and, finally, husband-to-be. With the salutation of each letter, she has the opportunity to name and rename her addressee; with each letter's closing she can name and rename herself.

Jerusha begins her transgressions by refusing the name she has been told to use when writing the trustee: she never writes to "Mr. John Smith." Instead she dubs him "Dear Kind-Trustee-Who-Sends-Orphans-to-College" in her first letter, emphasizing his connection to herself and all others he has helped or will help. Next she writes to him as "Dear Daddy-Long-Legs," a "private pet name" (23) she gives him, based on having seen his shadow, which appeared long and insect-like to her. Her language now embodies him and, although not imaging him in a particularly appealing or attractive form, does at least move him from an abstraction into an animal being.[5] In something as simple as naming her benefactor, the protagonist begins to gain some control over the relationship to him. Although regretting that she must also create a "pet name" for herself because no friends or family have marked her by that affectionate act (33), she designates herself "Judy" and instructs him to address her as such. Webster thus has the heroine subversively suggesting the possibility that the distant anonymous benefactor will at some time address her—and address her on her own terms. In the novel, Judy does receive letters from the trustee eventually, although we learn of them only by references in her letters. Thus we do not know his terms of address for her.

Subsequent letters in the 1912 text continue the protagonist's pattern of disruption: Judy writes more often than instructed to, about matters that go beyond those prescribed, and even signs "yours with love" (58). She continually plays with the boundaries of her relationship. When jealous of her college friends' cozy relationships with their grandmothers she asks her addressee "should you mind, just for a little while, pretending you're my grandmother" and closes that letter "Good night, Granny. / I love you dearly" (64–65). In a later note, having met a roommate's uncle, she asks her benefactor, "Do you mind pretending you're my uncle? I believe they're superior to grandmothers" (86–87). When angry she uses name change to reduce her addressee, abbreviating his pet name to "Mr. D. L. L. Smith." Webster then allows the character enough power to remove life: "I don't even know your name. It is very uninspiring writing to a Thing" (67). Still, the heroine is intelligent enough to know that her transformational efforts have limits: she fumes because she cannot make her benefactor "behave" the way she wants him to and because sometimes he seems "just an imaginary man" she has created (166–69). However, her despair is temporary, and she does not give up trying to control her sponsor. Finally, when she discovers that the man she has been falling in love with (her roommate's uncle, Jervis Pendleton) and the anonymous trustee are the same person, she amalgamates the various names she and others know him by into "My very dearest Master-Jervie-Daddy-Long-Legs-Pendleton-Smith," maintaining her power to name her lover and to display an allied power, the ability to recognize the various roles he has chosen for himself.

Judy's self-authored text, supplemented and further personalized by amusing drawings, includes not only the power to name her addressee and herself but also uninterrupted moments in which to declaim her opinions on issues of concern to a class-conscious, independent-minded, creative young woman, issues that (unsurprisingly) particularly concerned Webster. For instance, the protagonist discusses the ills of orphan asylums,[6] she wonders why no one worries about education harming a man's nature whereas so many people think it will harm a woman's, and she theorizes about male-female relationships. Judy also relates the events of her daily life at college, commenting on her own and others foibles, strengths, and ambitions. Last, she relates her progress as a writer, from rejection to acceptance and an income, and even encloses a check from her own earnings to repay the trustee, further asserting her selfhood. Declaring her world and self to another—and that other being an authority figure of sort—legitimizes her world view and view of herself.

When Webster turned her novel into a play, her heroine's independence and self-transformative powers were diminished. In the dramatic form, Judy no longer has as much control of her fate. The play, appearing first in 1914, packed houses in Chicago, Atlantic City, Washington, D.C., and New York City, and for two seasons was "the biggest dramatic hit in the country" (Simpson and Simpson 181).[7] Later it was made into a silent movie, starring Mary Pickford (1919); a talkie, starring Janet Gaynor (1931); a musical, starring Fred Astaire and Leslie Caron (1955); and finally a cartoon version for young children (1984). (*Curly Top*, a 1935 movie starring Shirley Temple, is obviously based on the same story, although the film credits make no mention of this.) Each of these responses to Webster's original text shifts the relationship between Judy and the forces that shape her life, for even as succeeding versions move into what might be considered more dialogic forms, they de-authorize the heroine, giving other people and events the powers previously lodged in Judy and her pen.

In Webster's stage version the heroine is known from the start as both Judy and Jerusha. We do not know the source of her nickname, but no hint is given that she picked it for herself. As in the novel, she sees her anonymous benefactor's shadow and therefore nicknames him Daddy Long-Legs. Because the audience sees from the start that Jervis Pendleton is the anonymous trustee, however, Judy's task, as far as the audience is concerned, becomes discovering and influencing the true nature of her benefactor, not transforming it based on her own internal needs and concepts. The roles of uncle and grandmother are not requested of an anonymous benefactor but of Jervis Pendleton, a roommate's uncle to whom she is attracted first as a friend and later as a romantic interest. Her requests that he take on family roles seem impossible whim, trivialized by the presence of the man standing before her. It is the absence of her addressee that makes this aspect of the story powerful in novel form, for her isolated state emphasizes her need for family. Then too, when we read her letters to the trustee she has never seen, we are struck by the poignancy of her imagining for him qualities she wishes an ideal relative to have, giving flesh and blood and emotions to such an absent other. Reading the novel-in-letters we are dependent on the writing protagonist to create trustee-father-friend-roommate's uncle-lover; the stage version removes that authority from the heroine. In addition, of course, we no longer intimately share Judy's private reflections.

Webster's dramatized version holds onto the idea that Judy writes letters to her benefactor; we learn secondhand that in her letters she exerts some power: she names the trustee "Daddy Long-Legs," writes more than she is supposed to, and makes her letters indecorously affectionate. Because she writes to and names him, the stage Judy retains some sense of control: for instance, echoing language of the novel, she tells Jervis Pendleton that her benefactor, whom she contacts only by letter, "belongs" to her (67). This works nicely against Jervis's own statement to another trustee that he feels "a proprietary interest" in this girl who "belongs" to him (50). In Webster's stage version, however, Judy's writerly transformation of the anonymous trustee is not *observed,* her letters do not finally call forth letters from him, and his final conversion to lover is stolen from Judy.

In the play it is the benefactor/lover who asks, in the last line: "Oh, Judy, couldn't you have guessed that *I was Daddy Long-Legs?*" (114). In the novel we realize that Judy has made this discovery when she conflates the names of Daddy-Long-Legs and Jervis Pendleton in the salutation of her last letter. For the external reader, the salutation necessarily precedes the account of discovery and thereby establishes and gives primacy to Judy's ability to know. In the body of the same letter she then recounts Jervis asking, "couldn't you guess that I was Daddy-Long-Legs?" (302), but through the epistolary format *her* words appropriate his. She could have left them out or not reported the question as a question. As recorder of her story she is allowed to be the creator of that story and of a document that carries the story into the future. Although we may not analyze this rhetorical empowerment as we read, I think we unconsciously realize that she who tells the tale does more than transparently pass along information; she participates fully in the creation of her world. Thus, the Judy of the novel owns information and maintains narrative power, making her more the agent of her own fate than is the stage Judy.

Further changes produced by film versions of *Daddy-Long-Legs* continue to rob Webster's heroine of power. Although, as Miriam Hansen explains in her study of the silent film era, "the cinema figures as the site of magical transformation—of things, people, settings and situations" (112), the power of transformation is not necessarily lodged within the characters themselves. More than half of Mary Pickford's 1919 version centers on Judy's life in the orphanage.[8] The hardships of the orphans are stressed much more than in the novel or stage versions. Judy's reflective and writerly strengths are downplayed. Pickford appears first as the twelve-year-old Judy (the novel presents the character as eighteen when the story begins and uses few flashbacks to childhood scenes), and, as the *Variety* reviewer put it, "The punch of the picture is not in the love story of Judy grown up falling in love with her guardian and eventually marrying him, but in the pathos of the wistful little Judy, with her heart full of love, being constantly misunderstood—extracting joy through the instructive 'mothering' of the other little orphans" (54)—a far cry from the original version. Pickford in previous roles had won popularity as the "embodiment of the eternal child/woman: lovable, spirited, whimsical and pure" (Hoffman and Bailey 235) and as "the somewhat sentimental spirit of the prize puppy as underdog [,] . . . a little girl with gumption and self-reliance" (Haskell 60), and Pickford's stock character, of course, shapes the portrayal of Jerusha Abbott.

Pickford's version of Judy Abbott retains some strong connections—at least in spirit—to the original text. Her protagonist contains rebellious elements—leads "The Great Prune Strike," shows anger at "charity without kindness," mistakenly gets a fellow orphan drunk, destroys a rich girl's doll, and draws insectlike caricatures of trustees—but the 1919 Judy has no opportunity for extended reflection about her own role or societal standards. Later, as a college student, she works at becoming a writer. Also, as in the novel, she overcomes initial rejection, meets with success, and sends her first earnings to her trustee in repayment. Authorial achievement gives the character some status in her society, offsetting her orphan origins, but the film emphasizes others' reactions to her changed fortunes rather than giving us her own reactions to them.

Pathos and sentimentality completely take over, leaving Judy little control of her world. A woman finding and transforming herself is diminished to a child or child/woman, receiving the good fortune her virtue deserves. We could say that the heroine is now at the mercy of fate rather than being the mistress of her fate. Magic and luck have the upper hand: for example, a child-cupid decides "It's time Judy Abbot fell in love." The silent movie format—scenarios interspersed with written text or "titles"—also exerts considerable control over audience perception. David Bordwell points out that "between 1917 and 1921, one-fifth to one-third of a film's intertitles would be expository," so that while many titles contained characters' dialogue or thoughts, many provided guiding commentary (27). In addition, other elements contribute to an "omniscient" presentation: the camera portends or gives away relationships and anticipates action; accompanying music predicts events (Bordwell 30).

The 1931 *Daddy Long Legs,* just as successful at the box office as its silent predecessor, also stressed the "kid angle," as it presented what *Variety*'s reviewer called the "sentiment of forlorn childhood" and a "Cinderella-like romance" (*Variety* review, 9 June 1931).[9] This Cinderella quality, evident in the original novel within the poor girl/rich man connection, is stressed in all the movie adaptations, with the female only fitfully the agent of her own transformation and predominantly the passive object of the male's action. As in the 1919 version, much of this "talkie" is devoted to orphanage tribulations, but here we meet the heroine at age eighteen (as in the novel), when she is articulate in voicing injustices promulgated on her and other orphans at the John Greer Home. Janet Gaynor's Judy, although more knowing than the character as portrayed by Mary Pickford, maintains much of the adolescent, silly, innocuous qualities of her predecessor. Warner Baxter is a younger Jervis Pendleton, whose point of view the camera takes as he admires the wit and talent orphan Judy brings to drawings and stories that spoof an older, pompous trustee. Once she goes to college, we learn from her roommates that she is an excellent student and later watch a scene in which she gives the graduation valedictory speech, but this movie never informs us of any particular academic or career goals the heroine holds. She paints, and there is some implication she might be able to illustrate a book, but this is a throwaway. Thus, in the 1931 version of Webster's story, the heroine has no vocational, artistic, or intellectual goals; no voiced interest in earning her own way; no pride in personal achievement; and hardly an opinion on any topic.

This version's Jervis Pendleton, although finding the teenage orphan appealing and worthy of his financial support, is not initially bowled over by her attractiveness. She does write him letters. The screen shows us files overflowing with her missives; reviewing them one day convinces Jervis to visit her at college. Thus the notion that her letters act on him to make her more intriguing is preserved. Nonetheless, once he falls in love with her (at a college dance), the letters serve mainly to remind him of her; they become more preservative than transformative.

The romance between Judy and Jervis (although, of course, Judy does not realize until story's end that Jervis is Daddy Long Legs) is much less the May-December romance than in Pickford's version. This Judy acknowledges her feelings for Pendleton and once "in love" seems to have love as her only goal. Although portrayed as a young adult, the heroine does not have the power to discover her own love, for again it is the male figure who comes first to this realization. As the *New York Times* reviewer, Mordaunt Hall, describes it:

"There is no little charm in those scenes where Pendleton finds that he has fallen in love with Judy, who, still unaware that Daddy Long Legs and Jervis Pendleton are one and the same, reciprocates the affection" (15). She can reciprocate, but she does not create.

In *Curly Top*, produced only four years later, the Judy character is further diminished through dissection, yielding two orphans: Elizabeth, the curly-headed, outspoken, bumptious orphan child (seven-year-old Shirley Temple), and Mary, her rather angelic, passive older sister (Rochelle Hudson). From the film's inception, young Elizabeth's high spirits lead her into trouble: she brings her pony indoors during a storm, makes fun of stuffed-shirt trustees, sings when silence has been ordered. The older sister has strength of character too, but her fire emerges only under great duress. When Elizabeth is roundly reprimanded, Mary stands up to a scolding trustee, calling him "a mean and hateful man"; this act earns her the admiration of the orphanage's newest trustee, Edward Morgan (John Boles). As someone interested in music, he also admires Mary's piano playing and song writing. Drawn to both the older sister's attractiveness and goodness and the younger sister's cuteness, open affection, and high spirits, Morgan creates the fiction that a wealthy friend is adopting them, but for the summer he (and his aunt) will take charge of them.

In this version of Webster's story, the young adult Mary has little agency in her relationship to her benefactor. Her "spunk" and piano playing are not the impetus for his adopting her; that comes about only because she is the sister of "Curly-Top" (Elizabeth), whom he is adopting (secretly) so she will not be sent away to a public institution. Mary plays the piano, and the songs she composes do increase Morgan's admiration of her; we learn matter-of-factly that plans are afloat to send her to a music school. Oddly, this training or identity does not seem of any central importance to her, and she never brings it up. In fact, her only consistent activity seems to be socializing and becoming involved with young Jimmy, Morgan's rival for her affections.

The powerful female in this movie is the child Elizabeth. It is she who openly shows affection for "Uncle Edward." She rides on his back, jumps on him in bed on Sunday morning, and when it looks like Mary is going to marry Jimmy and that she would therefore have to live at Jimmy's too, she tells Morgan, "I don't want to get married to Jimmy . . . because I want Mary and me to get married to you."[10]

Subversiveness is removed from the "woman" figure and lodged in the immature child.

The film's credits list Paterson McNut and Arthur Beckhard as writers of *Curly Top*'s screenplay, and Fox Studios gave no credit to Webster for the original model. This version is substantially different, with no letters and no use of the name "Daddy-Long-Legs," yet the story line is clearly a variation on Webster's original. In *Curly Top*, the ingénue has no particular identity beyond loyalty to her younger sister and endless sweetness, and she expresses almost no desire; all strong personality (if you want to call Curly-Top's endless cuteness that) and expression of desire are located in the child. The male benefactor is initially attracted to both females. Neither really has to DO anything to alter his action, although the child's statement that she wants Mary and herself to marry him encourages his step forward. (His matronly aunt also suggests he tell Mary he loves her.) *Curly Top*'s delettering of *Daddy-Long-Legs* is marked not only by eliminating the letters (and any credit for Webster!) but also by removing certain disruptive qualities from the sexual young woman heroine herself and placing them within the innocent child-sister.

The 1955 musical version of *Daddy-Long-Legs* deletters the story differently; it substitutes music and dance for dialogue, saps the orphan heroine of any personal goals as a writer (or anything else), and stresses the roles of mediators placed between the orphan and trustee. Judy—now Julie (Leslie Caron)—does not even name her anonymous sponsor; the other children in the French orphanage see the American benefactor's shadow and name him. Does she express excitement about receiving an education, becoming capable of supporting herself, learning about the world? No, she anticipates her future by singing, "Daddy Long Legs . . . make me pretty, witty, make me just as nice as a girl can be." In addition, in this version what appeals to the benefactor is, first, the young girl's physical attractiveness and, second, her charming way of instructing the younger children at the orphanage.

As in previous versions, Julie is instructed to write monthly progress letters to "John Smith," and, as with the original character, her desire is excessive. Impelled by loneliness, she writes frequently and "pours out her heart." The busy American industrialist (Fred Astaire) who sponsors Julie's college education ignores her letters until staff members insist he pay attention. The writing heroine has agency, but her words do not affect Jervis Pendleton. Only the intercession of his secretary and assistant force him to read the letters at all, and when he does, what he focuses on is her projections of *him*. For example, as he reads, a fantasy dance portrays him in the possible roles she imagines: Texas billionaire, international playboy, and guardian angel. The letters of this adaptation contain no stirring accounts of the girl's growth, ideas, or questions—their total focus is on the male's desirability as male. The letters' language also betrays whatever selfhood the character might conceivably possess. For instance, instead of taking pride in the fact that someone finally "belongs to her," as in earlier versions, this heroine is proud that "now I belong to somebody."

Throughout the film, the Astaire character calls the shots: in a guardian angel dance sequence, only his magic touch enables the female to dance skillfully. Each of Julie's manifestations in a later dream sequence of her own (performing ballerina, sleazily dressed vamp, Pierrot-like loner amidst carnival celebrants) seeks only Jervis Pendleton. Given Astaire's star status, the shift caused by concentrating on the musicality of the spectacle, the large gap in ages between Caron and Astaire, and the lack of verbal power allowed to the female (now she does not even speak the man's language well), it is no surprise that this 1950s version presents a woman whose fate is determined not by her own agency but purely by luck or that Hollywood fate that joins "truc" lovers.

The most recent addition to the *Daddy-Long-Legs* archives, a 1984 Japanese effort (with English soundtrack), is a poorly animated one-hour children's video. Although retaining many elements of Webster's original plot, this video's infantile, sentimental oversimplification removes any self-empowering, creative, or humorous aspects of the text. (This is not just the reaction of a finicky adult; the six-year-old with whom I watched the film was equally bored.) The heroine is still Judy Abbott (not Jerusha) and still writes an essay titled "Blue Wednesday," which is the basis for her scholarship award. However, this heroine fears college because, as she admits, "I have no confidence," and she lacks any convictions or complex notions about people or events. She works hard and does eventually publish a novel. Snippets of her letter writing are shown; the trustee's staff remark on their excessive quantity and "impudent" familiarity. To a large extent the letters' effects on these staff persons lead to Jervis Pendleton–Daddy-Long-Legs's realization that his beneficiary is an interesting individual. As in the other film versions of

Webster's story, Jervis is in charge of disclosing to Judy that he and her beloved Daddy-Long-Legs are one and the same.

Although somewhat faithful to the story elements of Webster's novel, this video, directed at very young children, achieves its delettering through dreary dialogue, unimaginative visuals, oversimplification of the characters, and the annoying insertion of giggles into almost every line uttered by a female. The protagonist's letters exist, but they, like the entire film, are unbelievable and uninteresting, and they play no direct transformative role.

We can account for the stage and film changes to the Judy character and her epistolary powers in various ways. Drama is a social form, stressing the interrelationships of characters, the interplay of the characters and the audience, and even the social interaction of audience members—the confirmation of values held by live people watching a live performance together. Film, although removing the live actors, reaches out to many people simultaneously and must "sell" to a wide audience. Both drama and film use more action than reflection to reveal their characters.

For the audience, receiving a play or film must always be at least a quasi-public affair. Reading, almost always, is solitary. Thus, Webster's epistolary novel puts each external reader in the role of the novel's internal reader, and the protagonist's writing always works to transform the reader's vision of her. (Simultaneously, of course, the external reader responds by "identifying" with the writer too.) In contrast, the stage and film versions of *Daddy-Long-Legs* give the audience a shared, social observation of transformations wrought on Judy by others along with some changes her presence brings to individuals.

Obviously, not all the differences in the novel and dramatic versions deal with the loss of epistolarity and change in audience structure. Stage and screen productions also involve collaborations of an author and other artists. In the case of Jean Webster's play, the producer/director, Henry Miller, had distinct ideas about scene divisions, settings, and character development; during tryouts of the play he ordered many rewrites (Simpson and Simpson 149–65). In the various film adaptations, Webster drops out of the process (she died in 1916); screenwriters, directors, and stars all influenced the reshaping of Webster's original tale. With the passage of time, different social climates encouraged different ways of presenting women, and these ideological forces too would influence the stars, directors, and producers of the various movie versions.

I cannot deny that market and media forces help account for different responses to the story of Jerusha Abbott, nor can I say that everything the original novel's heroine achieves is the result of her self-transformations, embodied in her letter-writing efforts. The romance plot of the novel is a strong force; the hero's wealth and benevolence must still be bestowed on her, and luck and coincidence must still be marshaled to place people in each others' paths. Seeing the changes that occur as Webster's story moves from letter novel to stage drama and then to cinema, however, helps one perceive just how effective the letter device can be in facilitating a character's ability to assert and create herself. Perry proposes that early women novelists and those novelists' characters and readers trusted the letter form because women were, in one way or another, so often isolated—"imprisoned, seduced, abducted, raped, abandoned"—and had little other release than through letters (22–23). From early times, girls were taught letter writing in school, and diaries were encouraged as a locus of self-investigation (64); "letters were the one sort of writing women were supposed to be able to do well" (68). From *Letters of a Portuguese Nun* on, authors have taken advantage of the private letter's long association with women. Writers of fiction have seen and used the letter's power, but few dramatists or filmmakers have been able to incorporate epistolarity into their works. Modern drama, especially in its cinematic mode, depends largely on the specular, not the verbal.

If we follow John Fiske's lead (in *Reading the Popular*) and look at popular culture as the site of subordinates' rebellions against their victimization within a capitalist system, we may gain new insights into some of the shifts and transformations *Daddy-Long-Legs* has undergone. We can read the original Jerusha as representing the "new woman," orphaned not only by circumstance but also by an ideology whose beliefs prevent easy acceptance of traditional female roles. She can symbolize the reformist female who wants to break down the patriarchal system. Her anonymous benefactor represents that system, a system that has the capacity to recognize women's abilities and provide education, but which seldom does (the orphanage matron tells Judy "heretofore his philanthropies have been directed solely toward the boys. . . . He does not, I may tell you, care for girls" [10]). Then we find that in the novel the patriarchal figure is forced to recognize the ideas and abilities of the subject female. He may marginalize her—think of her as just a child—but she has the power to change his mind. Through her writing she can convert him to a new understanding of her abilities, interests, and desires, and, let it be noted, she can also earn her own money.

Dickstein remarks that "the power of [popular fiction] seems capable of surviving an infinite range of adaptation, simplification, even betrayal" (47), and certainly the play and films made from Webster's novel, although undoing the heroine's forcefulness in many ways, have had great popular success. However, as the form of letters disappears, more than just the form vanishes. We lose the young woman's use of her own language and creative talent to create self-transformation, to own her viewpoint. The delettered female protagonist and text are put to various uses. The Pickford version could be seen as a response to World War I losses, with a longing to return to the innocence of childhood. If Jervis Pendleton represents establishment capitalist systems, does the orphan Judy represent all those without fiscal power or status? In addition, although she "needs" his help (as war-ravished Europe needed that of the United States?), does not the leader need the loyalty and admiration of the subordinate? Pickford's version also could be read as a retreat from the New Woman, a depiction that restores patriarchal power. The 1931 and 1935 versions could both be linked to the Depression, with Hollywood propagandizing that riches can come at any moment to those in rags. The 1955 musical version could also be placed within the political context of the Cold War (it certainly extols the lifestyle of private wealth) and of that era's elevation of a passive, conformist female. Of course, I am merely sketching in some possibilities, suggesting explorations that go beyond my own focus here on epistolary agency. In all film versions of Webster's story, the subordinate, represented by an orphaned young woman, depends on the "master" not only for recognition but also for every aspect of her life: financial, social, and emotional. Although Webster's original novel is no complex analysis of women's oppression or progress toward liberation, it does present a heroine whose capacities, determination, and work contribute to her self-transformation. Chiefly, the agency of that self-transformation is writing—letters to her trustee and her own short stories and novels. The stage and movie versions deletter *Daddy-Long-Legs*, cheating the heroine (and the viewer) by downplaying the power of female activity and agency.

8

Relettering: Upton Sinclair's *Another Pamela* Responds to Samuel Richardson's *Pamela*

More common than the process of delettering traced in the previous chapter is the kind of intertextuality that incorporates elements of earlier texts into an epistolary novel. Barth's reuse of characters from earlier novels, Walker's echo of Richardson in Celie's way of referring to her husband, and Updike's concern with various aspects of *The Scarlet Letter* fall within the traditional expectations most of us hold concerning creative responses to existing texts. Epistolary fiction normally contains considerable intertextuality, but when letters from another text form a major part of a letter novel, something distinctive occurs. I call this authorial response to a text and protagonist *relettering*.

In the relettering process, ongoing, pervasive, and explicit intertextual use of an earlier letter text provides the foundation on which an author builds the new epistolary work. The letter-writing protagonist in a relettered novel is able to use the preceding text to illuminate her own condition; the earlier text extends her own experience. The protagonist's comparisons of her own situation with that of persons in the intertext can produce new comprehension of herself and others in the present situation. Then too, working with a previously existing text—quoting it, analyzing its content and form, and discussing its relevance to other texts or to her own life—the epistolary protagonist comes to new understanding of the past (her own and that of the persons in the intertext).

The term *relettering* indicates a special interdependent textual relationship, including emphasis on a time gap (the time between the texts' productions), the later writer's conception of the previous text, or both. Relettering may be parodic, as in the case of the 1741 *Shamela*, Henry Fielding's spoof of Richardson's *Pamela*. It may be fantastic, as with Madelaine L'Engle's *The Love Letters,* a modern romance with integrated quotes, themes, and imagined episodes from *The Letters of a Portuguese Nun*. Relettering may take the form of a sequel, as in Jean Webster's *Dear Enemy,* which builds on her earlier *Daddy-Long-Legs,* or it may create extended reflection on social and political conditions, as with *Three Marias: New Portuguese Letters,* a 1972 elaboration of the seventeenth-century classic.[1]

Upton Sinclair's foundation for *Another Pamela, or Virtue Still Rewarded* is, predictably, Richardson's *Pamela, or Virtue Rewarded*. On this base, Sinclair builds, to play with Henry James's metaphor, not exactly a house, but perhaps a bungalow of fiction. We could think of one room containing religion: in that space we would see a Bible, waiting to add its textual substance to any conversation. Another room would contain feminism, or at least Sinclair's version of it; imagine a wedding cake here, but, beside it, a pile of our heroine's paycheck stubs. In a third room picture a pile of coins, some keys, and 1920s newspapers with disturbing headlines about unions, wars, and poverty, for here Sinclair's heroine will struggle with various issues regarding social justice and class.

Samuel Richardson's servant heroine confronted class barriers and struggled to maintain her integrity as a woman. As Richardson's subtitle relates, he expected his novel to "cultivate the Principles of Virtue and Religion," which he saw as essential weapons in the heroine's battles. The 1740 *Pamela* certainly addresses "conflicts between social classes and their different outlooks . . . and conflicts between the sexual instinct and the moral code" (Watt 138). In his response to Richardson's novel, published in 1950 but set just before the stock market crash of 1929, Sinclair's creative energy, as in his other fiction, was at the service of his economic, social, and political goals. His best known works—*The Jungle* (1906), *King Coal* (1917), *Oil!* (1927), and *Boston* (1928)—demonstrate his continuing concern for "social and economic injustice" (Bloodsworth, preface n.p.). His later works show some mellowing, with more emphasis on religious and family values, but he never lost his concern for the struggle between classes and his conviction that capitalism's failings affected all aspects of our lives, private and public. Even a work such as *Another Pamela,* written when Sinclair was in his seventies, maintains a didactic, reformist urge. He thought of himself as a "proletarian writer" whose purpose was not to create "art for art's sake" but to use literature for social reform, as a "soldier upon a hard campaign" (qtd. in Leon Harris 92–93).

These days, Upton Sinclair is out of fashion, his didactic brand of social realism seeming oversimplified to many a modern sensibility. This author is no modernist in style, and certainly no postmodern techniques hide in this text. In reading *Another Pamela,* however, one can turn up the kinds of unravelings, juxtapositions, intertextuality, and encoded class struggles (though encoded rather thinly) common to "high art" literature of the twentieth century's first half. This is no surprise really, for, as Harriet Hawkins reminds us, the history of literature is marked by "the continuing process of cross-fertilization between the highest of 'high art' and popular genres" (6).

Still, I have to admit that many of the criticisms of Sinclair's contemporaries seem logical. It may have been "reckless" of Sinclair to include so many long quotes from Richardson's *Pamela* (Hicks 30), and, yes, Sinclair's tone has an "archaic quality" one may not find inviting, lacking the "warmth and emotional fullness" that a less mannered approach might allow ("Virtue Still" 6). Perhaps only those of us fascinated by letters and by artists' reworkings of texts will disagree with the reviewer from the *New Yorker* who found this novel just plain "dull" (26). While *Another Pamela* may not be great literature, it does include intriguing representations of the ways we use texts to define and redefine ourselves.

Even in this lightweight novel, written, Sinclair said, to have "a little fun" tempting Richardson's virtuous character with modern sins (*Autobiography* 298), one can see the letter form's special affinity for exploration of an individual's engagement with self-definition. Sinclair makes issues of social justice and personal rights part of that exploration. In his dedication to class struggle, Sinclair uses the epistolary format and female voice to critique, through Pamela, her wealthy employers and many of their Jazz Age values, as she locates herself in a new world. Nevertheless, as the following excerpt from a letter to Ben Huebsch of the Viking Press demonstrates, although "manners and morals" were very much on Sinclair's mind, part of his interest in *Another Pamela* was the fun he could have manipulating Richardson's text, and part of his interest was clearly commercial.

October 25, 1949

Mr. B.W. Huebsch,
The Viking Press, Inc.,
18 East 48th Street,
New York, 17, N.Y.

Dear Ben:

I was glad indeed to hear from you after a long wait. I hope you had a successful trip and are well. And now as to business.

I am sending this letter with a typewritten signature as I only see my secretary once a week, and I want you to get it as quickly as possible. I am saddened indeed to be told that there is a possibility that Viking may not wish to publish "Pamela." I understand, of course, that you do not have the final say, and I am marking this letter "personal" so that I can tell you that I appreciate this and will not have my feelings hurt. . . .

Now regarding the details of the story. I am never stubborn about those as you know. I made the change of having Pamela marry Charles because after thinking it over I decided that I had made a mistake in not adhering to the old story. In the end I made one or two slight cuts to reduce the degree of Charles's misbehaviour so as to make the marriage more acceptable. I would be perfectly willing to make more changes along this line if you so advise. I kept the poet as you will see and used him as the means of making Charles jealous which I think is in line with the humor of the story.

In making the dramatic version [the stage version was not published or produced] I cut back to the England scenes; one scene in each of the three acts. This caused me to go over the old "Pamela" book more carefully, and I decided that some of the stuff was priceless, and I put two or three more scenes into the novel. These were sent to your office and presumably have been incorporated in the manuscript. Ratcliffe read them and thinks they are too long, and I would, of course, be perfectly willing to cut these. Ratcliffe says that one of the scenes is "too gross". As you know many of our recent fiction successes have had this quality, but I am not setting out to cater to that public. What I think is that "Pamela" is a classic, and that the contrast between the manners and morals of the two periods is an important part of my theme. But I should be very glad to have your advice on this point; and in coming to a decision on the novel please have in mind that I will be glad to take your advice on any such details, and would be still more grateful if you could find the time to edit the book yourself and cut out anything to which you object. I gather from your last letter that the problem has to do with the firm's ability to sell this novel. As to that, of course, my opinion would have no value, and all I can do is to repeat my request that they will decide one way or the other and let me have a wire as soon as the decision is taken. . . .

I ask you to excuse any typographical errors in the letter. They wont be fundamental and I want you to get it as soon as you come to your office.

Sincerely,

Upton Sinclair

———————————

Before fully exploring the *relettering* in *Another Pamela*, let us look at the *lettering*. I ask myself, considering my own contentions that the letter form is so often a site of response encouraging self-referential, self-affirming, self-creation: are these highly intertextualized letters a vehicle especially capable of carrying the heroine to a redefined future and redefined self she could not otherwise have reached? My initial answer is that Sinclair's use of the epistolary form emphasizes the idea that all writing matters and that writing is an important form of action. Sinclair devoted his life to writing: fiction, nonfiction, pamphlets, articles, letters, petitions, plays. Although a man of action, his actions were often in written form or were recorded in written form so that writing still left its mark on his every worldly encounter. His letter-writing heroine, no artist or journalist, no writer in any public or academic sense of the word, is still a writer. In the modern Pamela's letters we follow changes she instigates in self and others through writing (and other acts) as she strives to integrate new and old values, to bridge the space between self and world. The letters become a physical trace or certification of those efforts, but are also often the site of those actions. As she consolidates her thinking, she discovers her future self.

Writing is critical to this Pamela. Her physical actions and speech are, by her circumstances, limited. If she could not write, if she could not voice her doubts, fears, achievements, changes, and needs, she could not see herself as someone capable of control in the midst of so much new stimulation, negative and positive. In a way, her letters (like those of the original Pamela) are a form of confession. In confessional narrative, according to Dennis Foster, the subject "cannot . . . find out who [s]he is by questioning [her]self, but must seek [her] confirmation in the reply of another who can say, 'I know you'" (9). At the same time, the confessing speaker has an overwhelming need to "master [her] story" (Foster 4), which seems exactly what the epistolary heroine must do. Sinclair's Pamela is isolated by class, religious, and ethical differences from those around her, and she is physically separated from her family. Writing letters—confessional and reflective—becomes a necessary, logical way to personal evolution.

Sinclair's use of the letter form gives the heroine the private space of letters within which to legitimize her sense of herself. The modern Pamela, a Seventh Day Adventist whisked from her mother's humble four-acre goat farm to a mansion (through the fortuitous accident of a wealthy woman's car breaking down at the farm and that wealthy woman needing a new maid) uses the writing of letters to her mother and sister to confirm for herself and them the values and beliefs of home and church against those of her new environment. In addition, the letters are a safe space within which to try out new "liberal" ideas that she finds intriguing. As she writes long, confessional confidences to her sister, who is studying to be a doctor at a church-related medical school, this Pamela tests new water, re-creating and redefining herself by incorporating facets of her new world and even offering changed perceptions to her loved ones. What Elizabeth L. Berg finds true for the nun Mariane in the *Portuguese Letters*, that prototype of epistolary novels, seems true also for our Pamela: "Through her interaction with the narratee, Mariane finally arrives at a dismantling of the self that frees her from the relationship the letters serve to describe" (214). In the case of Mariane, the narratee (I prefer the term *addressee*) is her lover, whose dominion she has longed for but finally must reject. In Pamela's case her narratees are her mother and sister, who represent a narrower definition of behavior than Pamela is finally willing to accept, a definition that, if adhered to, would prevent her from education, travel, and marriage to a man much different from herself.

Sinclair's heroine struggles with class conflict and personal values, and writing letters allows her to resolve those struggles. The novel can be read in terms of Fredric Jameson's assertion that novels take "a significant role in what can be called a properly bourgeois cultural revolution—that immense process of transformation whereby populations whose life habits were formed by other, now archaic modes of production are effectively reprogrammed for life and work in the new world of market capitalism" (152). As Sinclair's heroine writes her letters, gaining control over the new environment into which her job throws her, she sorts out the benefits and detriments of rampant materialism, radical politics, and social liberalism, juxtaposing those with her agrarian, stoic upbringing, and finding a way to enter the world of her employers without betraying her own value system. The letter form of this novel propels the heroine toward a self and perspective she could reach only by writing, given her background and circumstances.

The letter form of *Another Pamela* serves the protagonist well, but it also serves Sinclair in a special way. Although the novel is most obviously Pamela's account in letters of her isolation, self-doubt, puzzlement, and gradual assimilation/reformation of new people and forces, it can also be understood as a ciphered correspondence between the author and a public he had consistently tried to reach in assorted media. If we experience this novel as Sinclair writing to us, the letters' contents become allegory for his own missionary goals, and different characters stand for various groups Sinclair encountered in his struggles for social justice.

Mrs. Harries, the wealthy, well-meaning employer of Pamela, represents the rich "bleeding heart" liberals of America, pulled hither and yon by one cause after another, with good intentions and strong convictions, but often shielded from reality by their wealth. Charles, Mrs. Harries' spoiled, alcoholic nephew (whom she has raised), then stands for the dissipated, cynical youths of America. Pamela's mother and grandfather, back home on the four-acre marginal farm, stand for the agrarian and religious values of the past. Pamela represents idealistic youth, with her enduring faith in human goodness and spiritual power. She is the traditional female guardian of morality, but she also represents ideals held by Sinclair —he who pictured his heart inscribed with the words "Social Justice" (*Autobiography* 329).

Throughout his life, like his heroine, Sinclair attempted mediation between what he perceived as a corrupt, greedy, capitalist society and the ideals held in his heart. The modern Pamela's letters to her mother and sister become, in a sense, Sinclair's letters to *us;* will we take from the rich and give their art and technology to the poor? Will we learn from the hardworking, religious poor, helping ourselves and others to their extolled values and discipline? Yes, the characters and concepts are reified, but the letters in this novel, in their own corny way, are letters to us too.

Sinclair's application of the letter form in *Another Pamela* provides the protagonist a safe space within which to explore her responses to a changing world and self. At the same time, the form serves Sinclair's own didactic need to critique his society. Now it is time to return to the question of how *relettering* works in this novel. How does the consistent use of a prior text open up new spaces of response?

All that I have said so far about the power of epistolary address has implied that the letter writer uses writing to act on some preexisting experience of the "real" world, thereby controlling that experience. Of course, concepts and ideologies "always already" shape our mental representations even as "raw" data enters our nervous systems. A seemingly new sensation is instantly processed, so that we are always, to use David Bleich's language, "symbolizing" and "resymbolizing" (39). A piece of paper, for example, may exist for a split second before our eyes and under our fingers as unmediated sense data. Then, almost instantaneously, we will categorize the kind of paper and its condition, usefulness, relationship to other paper and other materials, and so on. It is thus initially placed in the mental "file" labeled "paper," but subsequently it is shifted to a more exact or resymbolized file. A prior text drawn into a current text permits, at an obviously more complex level of cognition and emotion, the same unfolding of resymbolizations. Intertextuality of any kind encourages in the reader a heightened awareness of the ways written texts of any kind resonate against each other; intertextuality then reminds us that "all writing exists in a larger world of *writing*" (Foster 1; emphasis added). *Another Pamela,* with its major incorporation of another text, reinforces a reader's awareness that a great deal of writing is rewriting. (Much of reading is also rereading, but more of that in chapter 9.)

Sinclair's novel was published in 1950, although it is set at the end of the 1920s. The story in this novel comes to the external reader layered with its interlarded prior text, but flavored also by the context of the time of its composition and publication. The heroine of *Another Pamela* lives in rural California in the 1920s, a period in America of both runaway growth and economic decay. In the post–World War Two period in which Sinclair wrote the novel, U.S. actions in Hiroshima and Nagasaki had proved the massive power of atomic weapons to blow up humanity. The hydrogen bomb had just been approved for development by President Truman. At the same time, the McCarthy hearings and Cold War paranoia were beginning to expose our power to blow ourselves up ideologically.

As with any novel set in the past, soundings of meaning occur as the reader compares and contrasts social and historical issues of the moment (the moment of reading the novel), of the time when the novel was written, and of the time when the fiction takes place. In *Another Pamela,* however, Sinclair adds a fourth time layer. Interweaving his own heroine's time and place with that of her predecessor, Richardson's Pamela, Sinclair has further opportunities to look at truths that last and truths that die, conflicts continuing and conflicts, to some extent, resolved. A primary capacity of the letter, its "function as a connector between two distant points" in space and /or time (Altman, *Epistolarity* 13), is reinforced by the reader's connections of different moments in what we could call historic time.

I see Sinclair's use of relettering within the context of Jameson's discussion of narrative as the "central function . . . of the human mind" (13). Narrative is interpretation, whether we name it as such or not. Novelists, we say, represent individuals, language, social systems, and historic events—they invent those individuals, language patterns, social systems and events. Nevertheless, these inventions are not new, not independent. Shaped as they necessarily are by previous writings, previous events, these representations are themselves conceptualizations that become "cultural artifacts," providing the material for the reader's further interpretation. We are that reader, but so is Pamela Two.

Sinclair's heroine, when she reads and then summarizes or copies out parts of the original *Pamela,* comes to see that her dilemma is not hers alone. As she makes connections between her situation and that of Pamela One, she gains understanding of the power that class structure, materialism, and property distribution have had and continue to have over women's lives. Richardson's text held out to its eighteenth-century readers the hope that "if a servant girl could claim possession of herself as her own first property, then virtually any individual must similarly have a self to withhold or give in a modern form of exchange with the state" (Armstrong 118). The privacy of her missives is essential to Pamela Two's sense of herself as her own "property" too and also necessary if she is to speak out fully against the spiritual, economic, and personal wrongs she observes and experiences.

Richardson adopted a female voice and a domestic theater of operation, opening up possibilities for cultural critique (Armstrong 28).[2] Through Pamela's letters he sought social change. Altman discusses the way that the original Pamela's missives function against moral standards of her correspondents: "The letter thus becomes a symbol of virtue for Pamela, and her reader-consciousness is none other than consciousness of a moral monitor, be it future self or parents, who shape her writing to the extent that they influence the actions that she writes about" (*Epistolarity* 104). What I am finding is that Pamela Two's letters have a similar placement against the consciousness of her mother and sister and that, at a secondary level, the letters are placed by Sinclair against the external readers' consciousness. They are didactic and bathetic, but also provide a carnivalesque play with bourgeois, aristocratic, technological, and spiritual values, asking us, with a little poke in the ribs, to consider the notion of virtue, of conduct.

Sinclair's "reincarnation" of Pamela Andrews (vii) draws insights from Richardson's novel and uses that text (in combination with the character's own experience) to criticize not only her "master" but also the upper-class society in which, as a newly hired parlor maid, she finds herself. Although she has some freedom to speak aloud concerning her objections to the ways of her new society, Sinclair's protagonist is one of the hired help and therefore is limited with regard to outspokenness. If she offends her employers she loses her job. Her paycheck not only supports herself, but also is important to her family. If she loses her job her mother must go back to being overworked and her sister must return to wage work that would interfere with her medical studies.

Sinclair's Pamela, however, is no mere copy of her predecessor. Ingrid Kerkhoff finds that "Sinclair turns Richardson's social structure topsy-turvy. Pamela Two is not only virtuous; her station in life is a good and happy one" (191). She comes from a family that, although poor, does manage its own little four-acre goat farm. In addition, although she may be a servant, the second Pamela has freedoms unknown to the 1740 protagonist. Pamela Two can be assertive about what she wants and does not want. The original Pamela suffers much greater constraints. Her only way to obtain good fortune is to maintain her purity; her virginity and integrity are her dowry, her only property. She *is* her sexuality; she is woman as object, as commodity. Nevertheless, as Nancy Armstrong makes so clear, the 1740 Pamela transforms acts of sexual assault into words, and her letters become as desirable to Mr. B. as her physical body: "The pleasure she now offers is the pleasure of the text rather than those forms of pleasure that derive from mastering her body" (Armstrong 6).[3]

The epistolary heroine of Sinclair's novel learns of her fictional namesake from Mr. MacKenzie, a friend of her employer's (Mrs. Harries) family. Intrigued by Pamela's name, he posits Richardson's heroine as her "great-great-great-grandmother" (123). When he learns that the living Pamela's situation is so much like that of Richardson's creation, he offers to lend her a copy of *Pamela*. Her objections to reading a novel, because her Seventh Day Adventist church forbids such dissipation, are overcome when she learns this book is composed of letters—a form she is allowed to read and write. Mr. MacKenzie assures her that "it is the most virtuous book that could be imagined and will strengthen [your] resistance" (125). From this point in the novel, Pamela's letters to her sister Rachel are intermixed with summaries of or quotations from the novel (some of which cover many pages).

Richardson did indeed promote his letter text on the basis that it was *not* a novel (his title page assured readers the book was not a "romance" designed to "amuse") and thereby marketed it as acceptable, instructive reading for women. Through this strategy he "used fiction for redefining the desirable woman" (Armstrong 97). Sinclair likewise mobilizes fiction to teach his public what his heroine knows and learns. Through this female voice he uses a domestic arena to critique a larger field, as did Richardson. This novel's intertextual nature places it within the tradition of domestic fiction that is, in actuality, reformist. What Armstrong says of earlier domestic fiction, such as Richardson's *Pamela*, I find applicable to Sinclair's novel also: "Narratives which seemed to be concerned solely with matters of courtship and marriage in fact seized the authority to say what was female . . . in order to contest the reigning notion of kinship relations that attached most power and privileges to certain family lines" (5).

A central function of Sinclair's relettering of the 1740 novel is to let us see the differences between the two Pamelas with regard to attitudes toward marriage, morality, and social mobility. Richardson's heroine had little freedom to *speak* her criticisms of those with power over her; she had no money of her own to provide mobility; she had little freedom of movement. The modern Pamela has choices, and she is not shy. Therefore she cannot believe that after all the indignities Pamela One suffered, Richardson's heroine could accept Mr. B. in marriage. Mr. MacKenzie (the gentleman who first gave Pamela Two the novel to read) explains that the British class system prevented the kind of social mobility Pamela Two herself has experienced (she has risen "from parlor maid to secretary in a year" [225]), that marriage in eighteenth-century Britain was usually based on property, and that the unfortunate preponderance of brutality among men of that time would create in eighteenth-century women readers a sense that Mr. B. "was not much worse than the one whom they had wedded for the same property reasons" (226). Mr. MacKenzie's instructions, Pamela Two's subsequent commentaries on the first Pamela's situation (mostly to her sister), and the juxtaposition of the 1740s and 1920s events give Sinclair's text a useful perspective on history.

One area where the changing perspective is obvious involves sexuality. The modern Pamela's sexual "purity," although as bathetic as that of the original Pamela, is something she can choose and therefore is part of her resistance to beliefs not her own. The twentieth-century Pamela is virginal, but not under the constant threat of violation experienced by the first Pamela. The chaste state of heroines in eighteenth-century epistolary works stands "for a more profound inviolability, for being able to hold onto one's convictions and not buckle under pressure" (Perry 21). Pamela One *must* maintain her chastity or lose *all* her virtues. In the world of Pamela Two—at least as far as the society around her is concerned— this situation is no longer true. For Sinclair, the temptations his Pamela must resist are as much about materialism, alcoholism, and mental lassitude as about sex; she comments that her ancestress's "persecution was so much more terrible than mine. Hers is more of the body, while mine is of the mind and soul" (225). Sinclair's heroine has information on birth control (and approves of it) and is circumspectly given permission, even encouragement, by Mrs. Harries to sleep with Charles. Pamela sees that many around her enjoy sexual freedom, wealth, alcohol, and idleness—all of which have been anathema to her family. Her protestations against all these temptations are harshly ridiculed by Charles and gently mocked by others in her new world. Regardless of differing mores, chastity is central for both Pamelas, and for both it represents integrity and selfhood.

The perfect symbol of the difference between the two Pamelas is the bedroom. Richardson's heroine had no privacy, no "room of her own." Her shared sleeping quarters were invaded by conniving women and the rapacious Mr. B. (Even her clothes, the only space in which she could hide her letters, could be ripped away by Mr. B.) Her letters, a material representation of her own body, could be (and were) stolen or taken. The 1920s Pamela has her own bedroom, unshared with other servants, and she also has the power to use a screwdriver and drill to install a "good stout bolt" on its door when Charles becomes obstreperous (144). Within her secured room she freely reads, writes, prays, and sleeps without disturbance. In addition, this Pamela's letters are not intercepted; she is the one who mails them.

The 1920s Pamela can recount her own experiences of and ideas about marriage and personal freedom by contrasting them with the earlier Pamela's recountings, affirming through this exercise that as a woman she does have a good measure of self-determination. Sinclair's Pamela is upwardly mobile; presumably she could have advanced monetarily and socially even had she not married Charles. Richardson's Pamela would have had no such opportunity; only marriage to one above her could provide social advancement. In truth, an eighteenth-century woman had "little chance for economic self-sufficiency," so "marriage was one of the very few legal occupations open to her" (Perry 29).[4]

Relettering serves Sinclair well concerning the changing roles of women, but it also fosters on-going critiques of a class system that distributes wealth and opportunities unfairly. Few employers of parlor maids have the progressive ideals of a Mrs. Harries, who is interested, for instance, in the Russian revolution and sympathetic to the Wobblies. At Mrs. Harries' gatherings Pamela Two is exposed to the ideas and ideals of communists, anti-Communists, socialists, Greenwich Village poets, proponents of various religions, the Industrial Workers of the World, and Eugene V. Debs himself. As she writes her sister: "You will see that your little Sister is becoming what the Socialists who come here call class-conscious" (138).

Materialist and social justice issues are explored by Sinclair's letter-writing protagonist not only via the intertext of Richardson's *Pamela* and the speeches and discussions that take place at her employer's salons, but also within the context of her religious beliefs. Of course, Richardson's Pamela was a woman of religious virtue too. However, Pamela Two not only is more religious than her progenitor, she also is more schooled in her religion: a more literate believer. Richardson's heroine certainly believes in Divine Goodness and the power of prayer, but her particular beliefs and practices are unspecified and uninvestigated. She is an adept reader but surprisingly seldom is shown finding moral instruction within the Bible itself.[5] Pamela Two is a Seventh Day Adventist, studies the Bible and the writings of the actual Adventist William Miller, and is missionary-like in her religious zeal. Pamela Two upholds and proselytizes moral values—she is cast in that moral guardian role women have held for centuries.[6]

Pamela's letters report the arguments she has with Charles concerning theological and moral/ethical points. They also explore her own acceptance or rejection of elements of religious belief with which she was raised—so much so that parts of the letters she writes to her sister have qualities of religious tracts. What I think we are seeing in this novel's use of religious belief is a somewhat weary Sinclair turning to the hope that because social reform was agonizingly slow and uncertain, spiritual advancement could be a supplementary "salvation" (Leon Harris 332). *Another Pamela* was written after the Lanny Budd novels. In that commercially successful series of eleven works (one of which was a Pulitzer Prize winner), Sinclair had combined history and fiction to synthesize his picture of America throughout the first half of the twentieth century. Evidently, as Sinclair says of his 1952 nonfiction *A Personal Jesus,* "having been brought up on the bible, in later years I was tempted to go back to those old stories and old formulas and see them through a modern pair of spectacles" (*Autobiography* 298). Bloodsworth writes that Sinclair wanted to believe that "spirit" can "bridge the gaps created by wealth" (151).

By making religion a focal issue in *Another Pamela,* not just an unexamined undercurrent as in Richardson's novel, Sinclair presents the possibility that religion can be as radical as any political credo, and he has Pamela see this too. Throughout this novel, Sinclair frequently connects social justice and religion as when, after hearing a presentation by two Wobblies working to organize the fruit pickers, the heroine reads James 5 about the "hire of the laborers who have reaped down your fields" (96). Pamela finds another passage, " 'Go to now, ye rich men, weep and howl for your miseries that shall come upon you' " which is startlingly similar to the radical ideas espoused by some of Mrs. Harries' Sunday speakers (72). Pamela's religion gives her a sense of justice, mission, and even self-worth. It shores her up against pressures from the upper crust because she believes that "those of us who have the true faith are better" than the rich (9).

Although Richardson's Pamela avows a simple, generalized belief in God's power and protection, she lacks the voice and community support to analyze her religion and to see that it contributes to her subjugation. The religion that Pamela Two preaches to Charles, although initially unquestioned also, becomes more complicated in its argument as time passes. She comes to accept some alternative ways of interpreting what God or a religious spirit may be. Without losing her convictions, she does broaden her conceptual base and her ability to articulate the complexities she realizes are inherent within her religion. Although early on she finds herself confused by Charles's arguments, so that she calls herself "ignorant" and unable to "dispute" with educated people (44), she gains a voice through the practice of arguing in person and on paper. Eventually she can report to her sister that she has been able to engage in give-and-take discussions about ways of understanding different concepts of God, heaven, and hell (212).

It would seem that religious conviction and reflection give Pamela Two a sense of herself as a willing human being, entitled to her own desires (within the parameters of her religious beliefs) and able to refuse others whose desires contradict her own. Her own sexual appetite, however, confuses Pamela; she admits to her sister, after her first outing with Charles, that she is "shocked to discover" she likes him holding her hand and cannot deny, when he draws her to him, the "awful fact that I like to have him do it" (42). His kisses are all too exciting to her, and her own feelings scare her as much as Charles's potential to force her into actions she does not want (88). The ambivalence she expresses is not unlike that encoded in the original Pamela's letters.

Nobody has ever accused Sinclair of being a psychological novelist; his focus was usually on action, on the "exterior world" (Bloodsworth, preface np). Yet, in *Another Pamela* we see him turn to the letter form—a form that allows exposure of the private feelings and thoughts of an individual. Here, as in his other epistolary novel (the 1961 *Affectionately, Eve*), and like Richardson before him, he attempts to portray a woman's point of view. Sinclair's Pamela writes to her sister and mother, revealing her experiences, elations, and fears to the sister while maintaining a decorous, unsurprising persona for her mother. He used the same pattern in *Eve*, with that protagonist opening her heart to her best friend Janey in some letters, writing other, less-open letters to Janey that can be shared by relatives, and carefully selecting the news she sends to her mother. Although he never delves deeply into the darker side of his epistolary heroines' psyches (in either *Another Pamela* or in *Affectionately, Eve*), Sinclair uses two confidantes and two levels of revelation in each novel, efforts that demonstrate his interest in at least acknowledging the complex and constructed nature of the female self.

Sinclair called himself a "feminist"; in a 1944 letter he wrote: "I have been a feminist all my life, and I don't think I make any distinctions between my attitude toward women and that toward men. . . . I dislike women who argue persistently and in loud voices. I have known several such women, but then I have known men who do the same, and I find it equally unpleasant in men. I dislike women who are prejudiced and unreasonable, and I dislike men of the same sort equally as much" (qtd. in Leon Harris 97). How does this "feminism" emerge in the relettered *Another Pamela*?

Kerkhoff traces Sinclair's attitude toward women through a few novels and his own life events. She finds that after his affair with William Noyes's wife, Anna, and his adoption of socialist principles, he decried the institution of marriage (181). He explored birth control and venereal disease in his two "Sylvia" novels (1913–14) as well as in the second volume of his self-help *Book of Life*. The latter work declared that women's passions were as deep and long lasting as men's and that economic and sexual liberation of women was necessary for social health (Leon Harris 184–85). In *Co-op*, a 1936 novel, "self-assertive" women characters take leadership positions on the basis of their political and economic knowledge, not on the basis of their ability to be emotional supports or ego-boosters for men (Kerkhoff 190). Also, in his own long life of social protest, Sinclair met and knew well many strong, active women, from the tireless socialist Ella Reeve Bloor, whom he first met while working on *The Jungle*, to Mother Jones (*Autobiography* 120–21). His second wife,

Mary Craig, was committed to outspoken statements of her political and social preferences, whether her positions agreed with Sinclair's or not. In addition, Kate Crane Gartz, a wealthy leftist whose money and actions supported many socialist and communist causes, was a forceful woman friend—she is the model for *Another Pamela*'s Mrs. Harries.

Kerkhoff notes that Pamela is one of a number of Sinclair's later female characters who are not "clinging vine types" but are "self-assertive" (190). Certainly Sinclair's relettered Pamela is a far cry from her sexually resistant but otherwise so often submissive predecessor. A few examples will make the contrast clear. Pamela One consistently refers to Mr. B. as master, even after they are pledged to marry, and tells Mrs. Jewkes that she will continue the practice: "This is a language I shall never forget: he shall always be my master; and I shall think myself more and more his servant" (319–20). When Pamela Two detours his love attempts, Charles says: "You always know exactly what you want, don't you?" Pamela answers: "You have taught me that I am no longer to call you Master" (117). It is a teaching she hardly needs because, although obedient in her role as servant, Pamela Two is not personally servile to Charles.

At another point, Charles asks, "What would you say if I asked you to marry me?" (241); Pamela Two has already given this thought and so can assertively set forth her conditions: he would have to give up alcohol, he would have to accept that she would go on working for his aunt and earning her own money, and although he would not have to accept her faith, he would have to make some effort, for love of her, to study and understand it (242). In contrast, the earlier Pamela, even when asked simple questions about such things as ordering new clothes, can barely assert any desires; rather, she tends to leave things to her bridegroom's "good pleasure" (290). She does aver that the marriage would be best performed in a chapel, has some say in designating the date, and requests permission to send her parents news of the upcoming event (291). Nevertheless, her desires are never overt assertions.

Although I am not as confident as Kerkhoff that Sinclair is a "feminist," I do find that his espoused views support various feminist positions. In the novel under discussion his sympathies for women's historic oppression prompt him to create a character whose religious and moral beliefs give her certain strengths. That character's readings of an earlier text, Richardson's *Pamela,* empower her by increasing her knowledge of her own role in society. Still, one senses that much of the time Sinclair is "using" his character, having fun at her expense as the text he creates questions the "astonishing" virtues Richardson wished on his heroine (Sinclair, foreword viii).

Fairly early in *Another Pamela*, the heroine tells her sister about discussing Richardson's novel with the newspaper editor who gave it to her. She reports that he finds her identificatory way of reading just what Richardson's own audience experienced, but he tells her she can learn to read with "critical sense," remembering that the characters "are the creation of a man's mind." She can learn to appreciate the "art" Richardson uses to affect her, decipher the author's own beliefs, and gain knowledge of another time and culture (256). The editor points out that within the 1740 *Pamela* one finds emotional inconsistencies, quick transformations, and impossibilities of plot and psychology. When Pamela Two admits that she has "swallowed every word of it and never had a doubt but that it was all happening while [she] read," he says that is the experience of most readers. The editor character is surprised to see that Richardson's "old story can still exert its spell" (256); yet, clearly, one of his goals in giving Pamela Two the book is to use that enchantment to help her become a better reader of much more than fiction. Pamela One became an improved reader of people and events as she gained experience and as she attempted, through writing, to seize some control of her life. Her letters, read by Mr. B., did allow her to rewrite or redefine herself in his eyes so that she could become more than just a sexual morsel. Pamela Two not only has her own experience to build on but also has that of her ancestress as presented in the novel she reads. As she moves between written and "real" world texts, she has increasing opportunities both to read more expertly and to have each kind of reading inform the other. Her letters, especially those to her sister, with their interwoven segments of the earlier novel, offer a rewriting of self that allows her to change and adapt to her new world.

As I reflect on Pamela Two's reading and Editor MacKenzie's critique of it, I find myself plunged back into a consideration of my own reading. What *is* the relationship between the canonical *Pamela* and the noncanonical *Another Pamela*? For all the craft I have discovered in *Another Pamela*, by no standard is Sinclair's novel enduring art-with-a-capital-A. Why must I write a sentence like that? After all, here I am, reading and rereading the book. Why this worry about standards; why these judgments? What hierarchies or controls am I protecting?

Patrick O'Donnell and Robert Con Davis, introducing their essay collection *Intertextuality and Contemporary American Fiction,* ask us to consider that "intertextuality challenges those systems of signification which allow us to mark off the formal terrains of 'literary period,' 'genre,' 'author,' 'subject,' 'nation,' 'text' " (xiv). Alignments among the world of Pamela One, Pamela Two, and the moment/space of our own reading create slippage of period and nation. Sinclair's relettering of Richardson's *Pamela* and his many Biblical references challenge our compartmentalization of literary artifacts. The two novels' didacticism and stiffness, their equally overly virtuous heroines, and those heroines' equally unbelievable habit of "writing to the moment," make me begin to question the ease with which I had judged Sinclair's book. In what category do I put Richardson's "classic" if it shares so many qualities with Sinclair's reputation-less novel? More than ever, I find myself questioning how we derive our categories of "literary" and "popular" fiction, and how we create hierarchies for texts.[7]

Another Pamela's doubled epistolarity and long quotations playfully question distinctness of texts and the separation between author and subject, along with notions of authority and originality. Sinclair's relettering, like other forms of intertextuality, makes us see that all our texts "involv[e] the continual play of referentiality between and within texts" (O'Donnell and Davis ix–x). Pamela Two is not the isolated, self-contained being she might have initially thought herself to be, and her letter-texts, although "private," do not exist without context either. In *Another Pamela* the simple tools of reading and writing enable the heroine's growth. Sinclair, however, enlarges Pamela's space of response through the device of relettering; the ancestral *Pamela* becomes a vital part of this Pamela's education and self-transformation.

9

Remapping the Territory: Ana Castillo's *The Mixquiahuala Letters*

Epistolary novels place primacy on the acts of writing and reading. I have contended that as they write to others of various events, feelings, and thoughts and as they read others' responses to their letters, characters in these novels rewrite or redefine themselves. In addition, they offer to themselves and others the possibilities of rereadings. That is, the epistolary heroine may use the letter as a place to solve mysteries, undo misconceptions, and perceive patterns previously hidden from her view, discovering new interpretations of past happenings that she can present to herself and others. We might call this use of the epistolary response site *remapping,* for it takes ground that has been gone over and changes the way characters and readers see it. This term seems apropos for *The Mixquiahuala Letters* because its letters recount adventures and trips in many locations. The term *remapping* also appeals to me because it responds to the historic link between conquest of land and conquest of the female body that has characterized patriarchal societies.

Ana Castillo's epistolary novel[1] features only one letter writer: the poet, Teresa. Undated letters address her close friend, Alicia, but we know nothing of that artist friend's reading and little of her writing, for Teresa seldom refers to communication from her. Teresa's letters, as succinctly explained by one reviewer, "reflect on [the two women's] experiences in order to confront the ghosts that often haunt women" (Lawhn 1392). Those ghosts, however, are as much internalized attitudes and approaches as external elements of the patriarchal society in which Teresa dwells, as Castillo's epigraph hints: "I stopped loving my father a long time ago. What remained was the slavery to a pattern." This epigraph, a quote from Anaïs Nin (*Under a Glass Bell*), who was famous for her ground-breaking personal diaries, forecasts that Castillo's novel will also use a personal writing style to explore troubled relationships with male figures and that it will investigate conformity and nonconformity and the concept of pattern—in art and consciousness itself. The poet/writer heroine and her sketching/painting correspondent must use their arts, both public and private, to repattern or remap the land of former assumptions. Letters function well in such a revisionary effort, but clearly Castillo sees them as but one method.

The responses documented in this particular epistolary novel then are not redefinitions or restorations or regenerations of the protagonist's self. Rather, at the level of story, the letters encompass a search for new ways Teresa and Alicia can perceive, understand, and live with their continuing, conflicted, and known selves. In addition, as Teresa explains to Alicia, this personal effort may serve others: it may become "pertinent, not just to benefit our lives, but womanhood" (47). For this study of pattern, Castillo chooses a highly patterned form—the letter novel—and enacts her call for change by playing with that form.

Castillo reinforces the importance of pattern with introductory material that provides three tables of contents for reading the novel's letters, telling us to decide which plan to follow. Labeled "For the Conformist," "For the Cynic," and "For the Quixotic," these lists leave out certain letters, rearrange their sequence, or both. Of course they also ask that the external reader label herself, thus setting up the expectation that part of Castillo's project is to question the reader's role. What label applies to the reader who, because of the cover-to-cover reading habit, reads letters one through forty in that order, a pattern Castillo does not recommend? Is such a reader to see herself as the ultimate conformist or, in this particular case, relative to the author's instructions, a nonconformist? After providing the three labeled reading strategies, the author also advises us that each letter is a short story in and of itself, and she opens the door to our own participation by wishing us well no matter what pattern of reading we select: "Good luck whichever journey you

choose!" Regardless of which path one follows, an initial letter focuses on journeying. In letter 1, Teresa plots the complications of a
trip the two women hope to take to Mixquiahuala, Mexico; in letter
2, she refers to a trip to Mexico ten years earlier; in letter 3, she
details the two women's first meeting during a summer culture and
language course in Mexico City. Thus the notion of pattern becomes
intertwined with trips south of the border.

This is very much a quest novel, subsequent letters leading us
on various journeys and visits to Mexico, New York, California, and
Chicago, but with form and explanation taking us into the women's
emotional and artistic searches. The quest here is not for a grail of
selfhood, but for a way to live out that selfhood. Eliana Ortega and
Nancy Saporta Sternbach assert that Latina writers, when depicting
a "search," usually do so in terms of "a search for the *expression* or *articulation* of that identity, but not for . . . identity itself" (3). Indeed,
Castillo's heroine never expresses doubts about her sexuality, desires, pleasures, her mestizo background, or her career choice. Her
letters demonstrate, however, that she does struggle with discovering the writing self's best modes of expression, questing for more
suitable patterns (in writing and living) than the ones the past has
cut.

Castillo's prefatory ploy emphasizes the difference between story
and novel because, as Barbara Dale May explains, each approach
yields "a very different resolution and interpretation of each life"
(314). Castillo's strategy also calls into question the whole notion of
letters' verisimilitude and forces the external reader to question his
or her own reasons for and ways of reading the novel. Reading as
quest (and for what?), reading as linear journey (and to where?)
enter the situation, and again Castillo comments on reading processes through introductory material, for her book is dedicated "In
memory of the master of the game, Julio Cortázar." If reading and,
by implication, writing are games, then they amuse, they have rules,
but they also can leave behind losers and winners. For these games,
the winning strategies, I believe Cortázar and Castillo would agree,
are those that open up self-awareness and choice.[2]

In this highly self-reflexive novel, strangely enough, the relationship between experience and language goes largely unquestioned.
The narrative's Chicana protagonist seems to accept experience
as the precursor to language and language as an adequate trans-
mitter of that experience. Castillo, however, undercuts this convic-

tion somewhat through the work's epistolary form and through her postmodern tactic of alternative orderings for the letters. No matter what a letter novel is about ostensibly, its letter quality makes it about giving and withholding information, about language's ability to transmit thoughts and feelings or to mask them, and about how we construct or misconstruct meaning from language and how we are constructed or misconstructed by language. In the conventional epistolary novel, pen-wielders write "to the moment," providing their addressees with incomplete, new, fragmentary sections of experience. In this novel however, Alicia knows most of what Teresa writes. The communication focuses not on passing information but on reworking that information, making new sense out of it. Also, if one does not perceive that Teresa seeks new responses to old patterns—that this goal is at the heart of *The Mixquiahuala Letters*—then its epistolary format will seem very strange. One puzzled anonymous reviewer wrote: "What is not clear is why anyone would write such elaborate letters simply to retell, without analysis, what the recipient already knows" (*Rocky Mountain Review* 128). Analysis does exist, however. The reviewer neglects the highly reflective quality of the content, along with the possibility that writing here functions to reexamine the experiences, cultural norms, and selves with which the two women have lived. Castillo's heroine participates in the integrative process Ortega and Sternbach claim for Latina writers, in their particular bicultural situation: "She [the Latina writer] accomplishes this integrity by the act of writing itself. This process constitutes an affirmation, and then definition, of that inter-cultural self and serves as her way of returning to the community those stories they have collectively and historically shared with her, recreating them now into new imaginary worlds" (17). In a way, Teresa writes for a small community—that of herself and her best friend—but she also blazes a trail for others.[3]

The affirmative work of *The Mixquiahuala Letters* documents the woman writer's ability to overcome patriarchally imposed conformity and quiescence of women, particularly minority women. Writing itself becomes a way to reach understanding of both the near past, involving unresolved jealousies and needs these two women experienced during their twenties, and the farther past, involving their separate youths and family backgrounds. Letter writing also affirms a bond between these two women in a society where, typically, women's friendship is seen as a pallid substitute for marriage or heterosexual relationship. Teresa writes that society decrees a woman should be satisfied by male sustenance: "Her needs had to be sustained by him. If not, she was to keep her emptiness to herself" (29). Nevertheless, for the two women in this novel, unsatisfied by their relationships with men (yet very much involved in heterosexual pursuits), writing can fill some of the emptiness. Teresa creates letters and poems; Alicia prefers visual arts. Words and artwork alike trace new patterns, new understandings, and new supportive lifelines between them.

The self-reflexivity typical of all letter novels is especially strong in *The Mixquiahuala Letters*. Because, as James Watson reminds us, a letter is always about writing as much as anything else (8), and because Teresa herself is also a professional writer, her letters not only interrogate the stories of her own and her confidante's pasts but also question the telling of those stories. The letter form's particular claim to authenticity—as a document of the writer's heart, as fiction that is nonfiction, as private confession—all of this is questioned in the complex of recollections, imaginings, stories, poems, and diatribe produced by Teresa. For some letter-writing characters, writing is a way to uncover or reveal the truth about an idea or event; for others it is a way to imagine it. As Barbara Hardy observes in her study of narration, any kind of narrative can be compounded of "lies, truths, boasts, gossips, confessions, confidences, secrets, jokes" (7). Castillo and her heroine run the gamut.

In *The Mixquiahuala Letters,* Teresa goes over experience (her own, her friend's, their shared times) to try to discover what did happen. The character occasionally questions the probability that this process will yield truth. For example, recounting a time when she rescued Alicia from aggressive males, assuming that her friend would be grateful, Teresa admits that her perception of Alicia's reaction may have been off the mark. Perhaps Alicia did not really want to be rescued: "perhaps, you hated me too" (79). However, such expression of doubt is rare in the protagonist. It is primarily Castillo who questions the difficulty of ascertaining the truth, signaling her doubts through the novel's game plan. Norma Alarcón finds that "Castillo mocks [Teresa] . . . by framing her with the 'reading charts' offered to the reader" (100).

Although Castillo's format takes potshots at the notion of some knowable, fixable truth, this author is clearly dedicated to the idea that writing clears paths to experiences otherwise unavailable, for her protagonist can write herself into new understandings and into others' experiences.[4] For instance, letter 4 recounts for Alicia material about Teresa's relationship to the Catholic Church, giving the addressee a specific event to experience as her own; letter 5 recounts Alicia's background, clearly unnecessary information for Alicia but presumably an exercise in which the writer is wondering whether her comprehension of her friend's past is accurate. Letter 33 includes a poem Teresa writes from the point of view of an old lover, Alexis, expressing his reactions to seeing Teresa after five years, and in letter 40 Teresa imagines what Alicia must have seen and felt at her lover's suicide. In this exploratory, imaginative use of writing, the character and her author seem fully agreed, confident that the writing act is a powerful transformative enactment of desire and subjectivity, a way to create and maintain human bonds.

Epistolary characters will transmit the belief either that writing is a direct way to express emotion or that it is a way to master emotion. In discussing Jane Austen's novel-in-letters, *Lady Susan*, Patricia Meyer Spacks sorts out the two ways epistolary characters write emotion. The traditional emotive and sentimental character, whose emotions are represented as overwhelming, supposedly transfers emotional content directly to the letter's recipient. The nontraditional, aggressive character, whose emotions are elements to be mastered or disguised, uses writing as an artifice by which to manipulate the recipient (64–67). In Castillo's novel, the protagonist, although never manipulative of her addressee, takes both the traditional and nontraditional roles in relationship to the letters' emotionalism.

One way Teresa exorcises remembered events and their pain is by writing. She can explain and reflect on Alicia's and her own conflicts over a particular man or over their ways of dealing with strangers. Expression of feelings is sometimes unbearable, however; exploring a shared experience in Yucatan, Teresa explains to Alicia that "to be rid of it, i must create distance" (64). Recounting events is a way to control the emotions that would otherwise overwhelm her. Yet, at times she reaches an impasse and has to admit loss of control: "i don't want to go on with this story. You know the rest" (68). Sometimes story, in the classic sense of beginning, middle, and end, is more than Teresa can, or perhaps wants to, impose on experience and emotion.[5] In such instances Castillo allows her poet-protagonist to shift (within the letters) into other forms: dreams, poems, third-person fiction, and reporting of uninterrupted dialogue. Here we find Castillo extending the epistolary format, crossing genres to re-pattern the discourse form itself and the content it represents. She exploits the form's power to communicate emotion, modifying the protagonist's letter content and writing style, so that either can communicate changing motives, states of mind, and so on. As has been noted in earlier chapters, the formal aspects of writing can represent complex emotional relationships even when the relationships themselves are not the precise content of the letters: "to write a letter is to map one's coordinates—temporal, spatial, emotional, intellectual—in order to tell someone else where one is located at a particular time and how far one has traveled since the last writing" (Altman *Epistolarity* 119).

Emotional conflicts can also be implied in terms of the materials and circumstances of writing itself. This inscription has a long history. In *Clarissa,* for instance, Lovelace's ability to control the heroine's access to pen and paper, his easy interception and reading of her correspondence to others, and his forging of letters all represent his control of her body and his power to control the relationship (Castle 22–23). Teresa's dedication to the writing act and the lack of letters from her addressee imply a conflict over much of how the two women understand the past, a conflict Teresa wants to resolve because she continually asks Alicia to "recall" and "remember" the past. These letters form a bond, one Teresa insists she can create in spite of the men who come and go in both their lives, in spite of the miles between them.

Teresa's letters to Alicia, undated, but covering we are told at least a ten-year period, clearly demonstrate the writer's desire to affirm and continue a relationship. A variety of closings indicate a wide range of feelings. "Amen" closes a letter that recounts a night in a haunted house during which Teresa's background of mixed Catholic and folk faiths assisted the two women (84). A letter that delves into the difficult topic of how women attract men and confesses her own docility before men is signed with an unassuming "T" (113), whereas a letter hopeful about the future of both women inscribes futurity with "Always, / Tere" (119).

The letters' salutations similarly encode a variety of emotional ties, moving within three letters, for example, from nothing at all to "Querida Alicia" to "A—" (104–11). Not only is the emotional tone of the letters subject to fluctuation; presumably silences or nonverbal responses (such as the drawings or small gifts Alicia reportedly sends) are tenable parts of the relationship as well. Although the emotional content of Teresa's letters may vary, their steadfast commitment to retelling the past and clarifying it for both women is indicated by the fact that none of the letters is a note: each entails a substantial allocation of space and time. Teresa's persistent effort to rewrite the past for herself and for Alicia could be termed, to borrow a phrase from Nancy K. Miller, an effort to "unwrite the text which keeps her prisoner" (*The Heroine's Text* 95). Miller finds that the early "feminocentric novel in letters . . . is the locus of an exchange of desires unauthorized by the fathers" (150). Certainly this generalization about earlier texts applies to Castillo's novel, for it is the world of their fathers which both characters struggle against and which Teresa attempts to rewrite.

Of Teresa's biological father we hear nothing, other than that he was "a migrant worker or a laborer in the North" (21)—her uncertainty is a comment in and of itself. Another father, the priest to whom she confesses, interrogates her, probing suggestively, and providing no guidance or comfort (24). Alicia's father plays no part in the story. The art instructor under whom Teresa and Alicia study in Mexico City is "an adequate instructor, could be charming," but teaches them little and flirts with the blonde students (20). Rather than actual fathers or father figures, what Castillo's heroine rails against are authoritarian, male-dominated social systems that constantly threaten women's autonomy and freedom. Thus she writes that in Mexico "society has knit its pattern so tight that a confrontation with it is inevitable" (59), and the confrontations there with men young and old, college educated or street smart, seldom yield anything but pain. America is no better: a place where women's lives and hopes are constantly at risk. Husbands and lovers are ineffective at best, brutish or self-destructive at worst. Thus, although both women crave "a family, to share life with a steady man, children to sit around the table together, hold fast to each other during winters, and to go out to play in better days, always as one unit" (106), each must find another life pattern, one that does not revolve around male figures, to satisfy their needs for community and communion.

Castillo's novel gives us a body of letters addressed to one individual, in a pattern typical of much epistolary fiction. By frequently positioning personal correspondence within a broader social context this novel also accepts epistolary tradition. The social (and political, economic, and historic) commentary in letter novels, as

Spacks and others have pointed out, can subvert given social norms or contribute to their inculcation, or it can critique some aspects of society while accepting others.[6] It can also explore an individual's ideas and feelings about social freedoms.

For the protagonist of Castillo's novel, social and personal freedoms must be wrested from the patriarchal power system, a system she evidently presumes will endure. Teresa is a young Chicana who has experienced the so-called liberation of the sixties and seventies and yet not found herself freed of psychological or social burdens, and because her sole correspondent is another woman of similar experience (though of Spanish, not Mexican, descent), this novel's letters are very much a critique of the patriarchy. Repeated incidents detail the psychological and physical freedoms men take with women, liberties patterned into both the American and the Mexican social systems. Yet the letters always return to the personal, focusing on the protagonist's relationship to her correspondent Alicia, who can be seen as both an alter ego and an Other with whom the writer experiences conflict.

Depending on how one reads this novel, the letters resolve the writer's relationship to herself and to her friend in different ways. If one ends with letter 1 (the "quixotic" route) one sees the letters as working toward a new resolve and maturity, but facing an unknown outcome. The two women seem to be planning a new trip to Mexico, a place of past adventures. However, Teresa seems to accept her own situation: "At thirty, i feel like i'm beginning a new phase in life: adulthood" (15). At the same time, she wonders if the reason that the women seem not to have reached their idealistic goals is that they "were not furious enough" (16).

If one ends with letter 34 (the path recommended for "the conformist") one is left with the picture of both women entering new phases of their lives with determination and assurance. Alicia has just had her first one-woman art show, a show Teresa praises for the works' power to perform "the exorcism of the artist's rite" (118). The artist-friend has survived the past and become capable of expressing her anger at and rejection of the existing social power structure. Teresa, meanwhile, has chosen a different path. She announces to her friend that she is "going home" to Mexico, where she and her son will be enveloped in the love and acceptance of the boy's grandparents and where Teresa's husband (from whom she has had long separations) will play a vaguely benevolent nonthreatening role (119). Teresa will teach, but mentions nothing about her poetry. This version of the story is for the conformist because it plots a divided womanhood: either one is the artist or one is the domestic, as so often in the past. The alter ego splits off. Alicia goes to Europe, to art; Teresa turns to motherhood, teaching. This is the plot that women have known for years.

If one follows the "cynic" track of this novel, then letter 8 closes the story. In this angry letter Teresa asks Alicia, "How long did you think i would tolerate your growing pains?" (125). Teresa is jealous of Alicia's flirtation with Vicente, once her own companion. Here is another trapping plot: the one that says a man will always come between women.

In letter 40, placed at the end of the physical novel, Teresa recounts the christening of her son and Alicia's participation in that ritual. This letter, written after the suicide of Alicia's lover, includes a second narrative of participation, for in it Teresa creates an account of the events surrounding the suicide, events she, Teresa, never witnessed. In this writing, Teresa makes herself into Alicia and demonstrates to Alicia her empathic understanding of the friend's terrifying experience. The telling of the story is the making or proving of the relationship. Writing becomes a way the correspondent creates herself and her friend and their importance to each other.

The internal reader in *The Mixquiahuala Letters* is the nonwriting painter friend Alicia. Yet one realizes that the other internal reader of Teresa's letters is Teresa herself. These recountings of the past are as much self-directed as other-directed. For this protagonist (as for many other epistolary protagonists), writing a letter is an opportunity to read herself, an "interpretive rereading" (Irigaray 75). Thus both of the posited readers in this text assume that reading a text can change the way one sees the events reported in that text and, consequently, can change one's beliefs or actions. Castillo, in spite of her metafictional and postmodern stance, seems to have considerable faith that language can reconstruct reality.

The third letter in the novel states that the two women's earliest letters were "passion bound by uterine comprehension" (18), associating friendship with a maternal bond. Sexuality and physical action are inscribed in the letter too, for Teresa refers to their then correspondence as a way they could know each other and themselves:

"We needled, stabbed, manipulated, cut and through it all we loved, driven to see the other improved in her own reflection" (23). Reading is here intimately tied to writing, and both acts are metaphors for physical violence and love. Verbal acts are also related by Teresa to the exchange of other items: jewelry, poems, and sketches (23). The metonymy of the letter as a piece of the self is as strong for the reader/receiver as for the writer/sender. Teresa and Alicia serve various roles for each other: friend, quasi-lover (one might say a sexless lesbianism), colearner, sister, confidante, guide, guardian (in the case of Teresa, who sees herself as rescuer of the more delicate Alicia), rival, alter ego. Castillo here follows a model common to Latina artists. As Ortega and Sternbach explain: "In Latina writing, the entire extended family of women—mothers, daughters, sisters, aunts, cousins, godmothers, lovers, neighbors, fortune-tellers, *cuanderas* (healers), midwives, teachers, and friends, especially girlhood friends—makes up a cast of characters" (12). Teresa's mother, other female friends, her grandmother, and Alicia in a multitude of roles fill out that circle of female characters. Latina "writers have often displaced a central patriarchal figure, replacing it with a woman-headed and woman-populated household" (Ortega and Sternbach 12). Yet Castillo is clear on the heterosexuality of the two women, their desires for and interest in men, even as she establishes the two women's distrust of particular men and anger at a male-dominated society.

In spite of her discursive strength, Teresa worries that a woman's words can never make enough difference to another woman. When she frets that her attempts to help Alicia see herself as beautiful have failed because they are not a man's words (45), is she not casting doubts on the whole project of convincing Alicia of anything? Here she questions the power of her woman's voice to use society's language to dismantle that society, a questioning she shares with many feminists. Although Teresa seems content that she can reread the world around her, she fears that Alicia will not be able to do so. These doubts do not deter her, however; she continues to write, "fighting" (127).

It seems logical for Teresa to place her most intimate trust in another woman. Although Alicia may not read Teresa's texts with complete accuracy, and although Alicia is capable of keeping secrets and deceiving her, still this old friend is more likely to understand

Teresa's experience (and her own) than any man. Castillo gives her protagonist the implicit belief that, as Judith Fetterley puts it, "Women can read women's texts because they live women's lives; men can not read women's texts because they don't lead women's lives" ("Reading about Reading" 149). Throughout *The Mixquiahu-ala Letters* men are depicted as imposing egotistical or sexual needs on women, and they do not perceive the women as separate or distinctive from themselves. Teresa reports a simple instance of this in a scene between herself and her uncle Chino early in the novel: "i said i was going in to get a beer as an excuse to get away. He said, no thanks, he already had one. i said, it wasn't for him, but for me. The look i got could've stopped a charging bull" (13). Chino, like most of the other men both Alicia and Teresa have known, is incapable of perceiving that women have their own needs—their own stories. The men here are like the men in Susan Glaspell's "A Jury of Her Peers." As Fetterley explains, "It is not simply that the men can not read the text that is placed before them. Rather, they literally can not recognize it as a text because they can not imagine that women have stories" ("Reading about Reading" 147–48). For Castillo, women have many stories, and, presumably, other women will best understand them.

In *The Mixquiahuala Letters* both the pleasure of the quest and the pleasure of the text are deliberately frustrated by the author's refusal to create a plot of conquest or a set timeline. In addition, tension arises because of confusion the external reader will probably experience concerning the possibility of a lesbian relationship between the two women. Various letters suggest such a bond, but at one point Teresa pointedly denies it, affirming to Alicia that "you and I had never been lovers" (121). What to conclude? The external reader may discover that he or she becomes complicit with a culture that refuses the possibilities of intimacy or sensuality without genital sexuality.

With its content-level focus on the ways women interpret the actions of men and women, *The Mixquiahuala Letters* forces reflection on how women readers respond to texts by women versus texts by men (and, consequently, how men respond to male- and female-authored texts). Castillo's novel encourages us to think about whether we read for mastery and knowledge or for intimacy and the sharing of experience. Castillo incorporates her own theory of reading that highlights indeterminacy, multiple interpretations, and the need for re-readings. Then too, as Patrocinio Schweickart explains about feminist reading in general, this text heightens one's awareness of how the woman's text exists in its social context. What Schweickart says of feminist reading is true of this feminist text: it stresses "the difference between men and women, . . . the way the experience and perspective of women have been systematically and fallaciously assimilated into the generic masculine, and . . . the need to correct this error" (39).

Nonetheless, although *The Mixquiahuala Letters* presents a woman-centered reading of society, it does so while also situating that reading within the specifics of place and history. To read this novel is necessarily to delve into how one reads individual women affected by their class, race, ethnicity, education, and roles as artists, teachers, mothers, and so on. Because Teresa's letters are preponderantly retellings of past events and fastidiously rooted in the particulars of places and times, Castillo does not seem to dictate to each reader what she should think about women in general. Rather, she asks each of us to read as we wish. We can take each letter as a short story, follow one of the three patterns the author recommends, or read from cover to cover. The hope of recovering the personal past to repattern the future will still exist. Reading Teresa's letters could encourage one's own act of redefinition, but would ask that we consistently confront stereotypes with particular experiences, just as Teresa does.

The letters in this novel permit us to see that Teresa can read herself and Alicia in different ways, just as society can interpret either woman's actions in different ways. To see with one's own eyes becomes not only the goal of the artist but also the goal of the socially and personally responsible individual who wants to move past sexism and prejudice of all kinds. Yet, reading this epistolary novel, as Alarcón notes, "brings into question our own reading practices, for the apparently unconventional suggested readings actually lead to resolutions that are more conventional than the handful of letters attributed to Tere" (105). Alarcón believes that each of the suggested reading maps provided by the author actually provides "an ideological nexus . . . that forces us to reconstruct the meaning of Teresa's letters as always and already leading in that direction," thus countering the notion of play and choice that her introduction apparently introduced. That is, each of us carries textual reading patterns in our heads that we need to question, just as Teresa carries patterns for "reading" relationships which she very much wishes to question.

The Mixquiahuala Letters uses various techniques to repattern our assumptions about the epistolary novel. The most obvious, certainly, is the "hopscotch" possibility of alternative reading routes. Just as important is Castillo's demonstration that letters need not contain "news." Kauffman notes that "it may seem quixotic to study 'epistolarity' . . . when letter writing has practically become a lost art, supplanted by telephones, fax machines, computers, camcorders and tape cassettes" *Special Delivery* xiv).[7] Yet we see here that the letter form retains specific helpful properties not provided by newer technologies. The writer of a personal letter requires no special equipment or special training. Letters can be adapted to the needs of the individual (formal, informal, including poems, sketches, and so forth); they pass from writer to reader, carrying the touch of one individual to the other, and they can be kept and reread. No other means of communication combines these particular qualities and is so readily available to the poor and rich, the itinerant and the stay-at-home, the radical and the conservative. For Castillo's protagonist what other means would do?

Whether we see Teresa's struggle for a new life pattern as successful or not, we will necessarily focus on the sources of accepted or considered patterns. Alarcón refers to the protagonist being "framed by certain 'semantic charters,'" using terminology borrowed from Pierre Maranda (100).[8] Such charters exist within each of us, but, if we follow Castillo, the hope exists that they can be restructured. Through the writing act, which entails also acts of rereading the self, others, and experiences, we may discover new maps of understanding, new patterns of greater freedom. To adapt DuPlessis's well-known book title, we could engage in *reading* as well as "writing beyond the ending."

When I began working on Castillo's novel, I wrote to her with various questions, inviting her to respond with a letter that would then form part of this chapter. Among the topics I suggested she might explore were the way that Teresa uses writing to retell her own and her friend's experiences and how the character of Alicia functions—did Castillo see her mostly as Teresa's construction or as

her alter ego or as her friend? I also asked what influenced Castillo
to choose the epistolary form. The letter I received, echoing *The
Mixquiahuala Letters'* use of narrative as a reflective tool, tells a story
of its own.

Yes, dear critic, there really is an Alicia:

The last time I saw her—head bobbing just above the crowd,
predictably slender, Alicia was taking brisk New Yorker strides to-
wards me. I was standing katty-corner from Washington Square
Park in front of my hotel. We spotted each other and smiled what
could be said to have been sad smiles, then we each looked away.
She was hardly recognizable, not only to me, she remarked later, but
to everyone who knew her. Her hair, which as long as I had known
her, she had always kept waist length, was now in a crew-cut.

The color of that hair, which matches her shiney coal black eyes,
comes from her father's side, the Andalusian gitana grandmother,
the one who retired in a trailer park in Pensacola and who called
herself "exotic," who knew a rosary of men after the brief marriage
to Alicia's grandfather in New York, after she disappeared one day,
leaving husband, children behind and emerging decades later in
that peninsula of exiles, Florida. Eyes and hair and tannable skin,
all made my friend the non-fit of her mother's family that came from
Eastern European stock. Alicia, the foreign-looking child whose blood
must surely be darker. She remembered a family member remarking
once, as dark as a monkey's, the relative joked at a family gathering.
Alicia's mother did not laugh—her mother and her Czech grandmother who never learned English very well and therefore had not
understood the "joke."

On her own Alicia would never have cut that straight sheet
of dark hair, never. That was the Latina side of her, the one tell-
tale betrayal to her feminism, keeping her hair so long because men
loved it so much. Maybe it was the Eastern European side of her, too,
inherited from her mother's mother, the one who hid her flaxen
braids under babushkas when she cleaned houses in Queens in the
early decades of this century, wrapped tight and covered like Alicia
does when she is at the potter's wheel and the way she looked the
very first time I saw her in Mexico, studying art in a gringo summer
program, nearly two decades ago.

We were having orientation and all the students were sitting outside on metal fold-out chairs beneath the sheathed Mexico City sun.

A little restless, maybe bored, for sure already disappointed in the summer program I had worked so hard and traveled so far for and had dreamed of attending for so long, I turned all the way around, to take a glance at my soon-to-be classmates, who had turned out to be mostly all gringas, and my gaze fell on her who later was to become known to me—and to you, as Alicia. Her chiseled cheekbones, the bandanna tied around her slender head, black eyes and lashes, in a Georgia O'Keefe kind of way, she was utterly stunning. That Stieglitzian image has been locked permanently in my memory bank. That is, that young woman who was at that moment a stranger to me had, not the kind of beauty that turns heads on the street, but a photographable remarkableness, chiaroscuro, black and white, hung in galleries later where you might find yourself staring, wondering, *what was she like?* I asked myself that question that afternoon, twenty years ago. And not long after that, perhaps starting that same afternoon, because of the fusion fomented by an instant friendship, I was no longer wondering. She was funny. She was difficult—an incorrigible Yo-Se-Todo. She was too frugal for my comfort. (She'd rather wait at night for a bus in the pouring rain than spring for a cab for us.) And she was formidably talented. At not quite twenty-one years of age she was—compared to my urban provincialism—well travelled—from art school in Rome to pottery classes on a Navajo reservation. She could find her way around New York like I, a young renegade Mexican-American wife, knew my way around my apartment kitchen in Chicago. She was sharp as a tack. And after that summer, I loved her for years.

Ronnie, a good friend, having known me for many years said he had observed that I invent myself as I do the characters in my novels, or rather transform my image: stylish vintage in Chicago, fluorescent beachwear in Southern California and yes, Tony Lamas in New Mexico. And once, this same poet friend told a third party when I had taken up residence in San Francisco and having seen me go through these various stylistic reincarnations living in different cities, "Ana is like a chameleon, she blends right into any environment she inhabits."

But Alicia, to my knowledge, is not a chameleon. You, above all the readers of *The Mixquiahuala Letters* I think, would agree to that. She was born in New York and has never lived elsewhere. Her life is a constant, the daughter of New York liberals, she was raised a vegetarian, as a child with her mother walked the UFW picket lines, growing up as an only child, studied karate and guitar and for a long time, as a young adult, lived alone. She is the product of an American city that belongs to the world. A Manhattanite through and through, she is anything but American and everything American. She has been an artist her whole life and although she has never been terribly ambitious, over the years she made a name for herself around town—a town where no doubt to make your mark as an artist is nothing to sneeze at. She still loves to dance as she did in dancehalls and nightclubs from Puerto Rico to Puebla, Mexico, merengueing from Santo Domingo to San Francisco, although as she settled into her thirties, she did less and less of it. Her art, the man who stayed who does not dance and is also an artist: her life, mostly a quiet one. For complicated reasons, no children, because of allergies no pets and as a matter of preference perhaps rather than economics, her life became a stable affair, unfettered by the kind of spontaneity that is usually attributed to the artist's nature.

Alicia and I embraced and then walked to find a café open for lunch. She immediately took note of my post-modern sunglasses, asked to take a look at them and said she didn't like them. I inquired about her health. Alicia, as I've already mentioned, has always eaten organic; she has never smoked ciagrettes not even tolerated cigarette smoking in her living quarters. She never cared for the taste of alcohol, not even a glass of champagne on New Year's Eve. A glass of sparkling apple cider at the stroke of midnight and then off to bed. She has never been into caffeine, no café au laits, no Cokes, nothing but herbal teas for our Alicia. But she still breathed New York City pollution all her life. And she still drank New York City tap water, at least on occasion, I would guess. In short, she was a product of this neo-civilization of ours and like one out of every four U.S. residents today, she got cancer. The crew-cut was one of the results of recent chemotherapy treatments. "You lose *all* your hair," she said to me sardonically, over lunch, "everywhere."

Four years after the publication of *The Mixquiahuala Letters* Alicia was fighting cancer, my friend Ronnie—who I met the day after Reagan was first elected—tested HIV positive, and I was grateful to be biting the heels of "almost 40" with both breasts, uterus and ovaries intact, no surgical scars, no "positive results" on any of my annual tests. So far a virtual model of good health. Considering the odds, a miracle in itself.

There are certain almost perfunctory questions I am always asked concerning my first novel, *The Mixquiahuala Letters*. The most common one usually comes from students, those poor innocents whom I always fear will be turned off to my writing altogether because of having to develop a critical eye for interpretation, being prodded to find hidden meaning in the text in order to satisfy aca-

demia rather than simply enjoying or not enjoying the stories I en-
joyed (as well as in some passages did not enjoy) telling. The most
popular question concerning that text has to do with the use of the
lower case "i" for the personal pronoun. Although the letters are not
dated, one letter does clearly set the time of the novel which is in the
mid-seventies. As you may know, the use of the lower case "i" for
poets was at that time a trademark of protest poetry. Teresa saw herself as a political activist and hoped to become a poet.

Different languages do not give different names for the same
thing, they give different names for very different things. In Teresa's
other language, Spanish, the personal pronoun is not capitalized.
However the abbreviated formal "you," *Ud.,* is. You,—Ud.—are important, i—yo—am no one, simply your humble servant—Spanish,
baroque and elegant, a tango of reflexive verbs and reversed syntax,
perhaps falsely humble but provocative and charming nevertheless,
a veritable concert of courtesies. The Spanish yo of the poor, the
agricultural pickers and factory workers was a we—at least then, at
least in spirit, at least in our stories.

The second most common question refers to the authenticity
of the events told in the novel. In other words, is *The Mixquiahuala
Letters* autobiographical? My standard answer is that approximately
forty per cent of the novel is based on actual occurences; however,
it is up to the reader to decide for her/himself what in the novel
comprises autobiography and what is only and always possibility.

As to the ingenuous opinion of one of your colleagues, who
wrote in a review that it is "unclear as to why anyone would write
such elaborate letters simply to retell, without analysis, what the recipient already knows," I would have to suggest for that scholar to
do as he most surely demands of his students and that is to kindly
take the time for a more careful reading of the text.

To my knowledge, Alicia herself has never read *The Mixquiahuala Letters*. I never asked why or if I did she did not answer. She told
me that afternoon over lunch that she kept the copy I sent her in a
closet, hidden from view.

After lunch Alicia gave me a small gift of a pair of pastel flow-
ered socks. I picked up the tab. We hugged, arms wound tight
around each other, breasts to breasts, and then let go. As we parted
in front of the restaurant I remembered to give her *saludos* from
Teresa, who still lives in Chicago. "Oh yeah," Alicia replied, smiling
a bit and seeming suddenly to be caught up in private reflection, "By
the way, is she still gaining weight?" she asked.

"Oh no!" I said, as usual a little put off by Alicia's bluntness
and this unshakable feeling that she can be, for all her political cor-

rectness, catty. "The last time I saw her, Teresa looked fantastic—beautiful, in fact—as always!" I added. Alicia shrugged her shoulders, or maybe it was a reflex, and waved good-bye and turning around, was immediately sucked into the mesh of the Manhattan lunchtime crowd.

Another question I have frequently been asked regarding the book is what I think about what critics think about it. Well, for a long time, I didn't. But increasingly there is a tendency for that entity known as the critic to split and multiply; and with time, appear in all manner of shapes, tones and sizes everywhere I go. There are critics who believe that without them my work has no meaning. I am sure, dear critic, that you are not one of them.

Franz Capra in his book *The Tao of Physics,* states " . . . In atomic physics, we can never speak about nature without, at the same time, speaking about ourselves." Likewise, no matter how sure of himself or herself a critic may feel behind the illusion of an empirical argument, I think the critic cannot speak on a text without revealing him/herself. Susan Sontag, critic and novelist, in her essay, "Against Interpretation," states that ultimately all thought is interpretation. Therefore, I feel that even my own comments here on my novel several years after its publication are very likely interpretations of others' interpretations of *The Mixquiahuala Letters,* rather than untainted reflections of my own. I can only add that the writing process was an experience that I would like to remember as being one of unselfconsciousness, having been a self-taught and relatively unknown poet at the time that I completed the second version of the manuscript and with not so much as a presumption about my first novel's potential publication. I close with a simple thanks for your interest in my work.

Te deseo mucha suerte con tu proyecto— Siempre,

Ana Castillo

July 18, 1992 / 'Burque, Nuevo Méjico
y June 6, 1995, Gainesville, Florida

An "Epistolary Fix":
Dear Reader, Once Again

Dear Reader:

For nine chapters now, this book's discourse has marched along, discursive at times, supplemented in places by letters from others, but in general following the conventions of scholarly prose. Although early on proposing that this book could function as a letter, inviting your responses (in the form of your readings and writings), I've managed to resist the urge to address you directly. Like Germaine Pitt in Barth's *LETTERS*, however, I need an "epistolary fix." If you don't, skip ahead to Chapter 10. You've probably already skipped a chapter or two, anyway! (Isn't it funny that, as we carefully structure books we write, we "forget" how seldom we follow the structure of others' texts—how often we "use" rather than "read" a book—ignoring chapters, skimming introductions, sometimes jumping over whole sections of a book that concern authors or periods or texts in which we hold no immediate interest?) Maybe I need the epistolary fix because within it, YOU is an acceptable mode of address—a connecting pronoun, the one we're forbidden to use in academic discourse. With the increasing acceptance of personal criticism, especially in the humanities, "I" has become legitimate, but the person at the receiving end of the text is still "the reader" or "one." *You* do not exist.

The letter form makes explicit a need to connect. As a feminist, I need/want that sense of connecting to take precedence over the sense of proclaiming *a* point of view, arguing for an interpretation, displaying how well I've uncovered new materials. I need a space for trial balloons, for questions (the kind you ask someone else, not the kind you pose and then proceed to answer yourself), for incomplete discussion. . . . Switching to the letter form helps me remember and recover what I believe should be motivating the critical impulse—my desire to connect with the various "you's" who may read what I write. The informality of the letter also allows a delicious fluidity; here the discursive tendencies of my writing style are no sin.

In Chapter 3, Dorothy Hill wrote with regret about the way involvement with academic life has all but eradicated the time and energy for letters. Many of my colleagues say the same thing. Their "letter" activity these days, if it exists at all, is likely to take place via electronic mail—which is a fantastic system, I admit, with qualities all its own. In spite of what some of my colleagues call my "romantic" attachment to the old-fashioned letter, like many of you I use e-mail all the time. For a while, when first turned on to the joys of this new correspondence method, it was my primary mode of correspondence. Especially when interchanging messages with friends and family in Europe, e-mail's speed allowed a sense of connection that letters' pokiness often blocked. Also, I liked the almost sloppy way we all wrote using e-mail. Probably because editing was awkward in the early systems, we allowed ourselves misspellings, grammar slippage, and shortcuts that seldom blemished prose dispatched via word-processing, typing, or even hand writing.

I remember once sending off a rather long e-mail letter to my daughter in Finland just before teaching a class. I'd rushed to finish it, punched Control E to leave the composing mode, pressed Enter at the query Send now?, gathered books, pen, grade book, and keys, flicked the light switch, closed the office door, and dashed down to the classroom, plunging instantly into a discussion with about 25 students—"Bartleby, the Scrivener" was our reading for that day, I think. The hour flew by and then, once again, I was in my office. Because the computer was still on and within the Mail function, I nonchalantly clicked the keys that would call up any new mail—and there was a letter from my daughter. The hair on my neck rose, for it seemed almost as if she had magically entered the room. While I'd been on the second floor of the building, teaching an American Lit. survey class, she—well, her words—had electronically flown into my third floor office (sort of), responding to me, to us, to our history as mother and daughter.

For a while the wonder of e-mail's immediacy stayed with me. It remains a nifty way to exchange ideas with colleagues, but it has its limits. (Right, all modes of communication do—of course.) Now my daughter in Finland and I still use e-mail, and we talk on the phone as our budgets allow; however, we also write long letters, and when the "snail mail" arrives it's precious—it's saved and reread, it's a true gift. Maybe I want us to slow down, to value our private worlds, to make ourselves stop for a few more minutes and luxuriate in creating a letter that will travel enclosed in its envelope—private, anticipated, carrying the scent and the fingerprints of the writer to the reader.

Even though criticism in letters can only imitate the nuances of authentic correspondence (*this* letter has been edited and printed on a press, for heaven's sake, it goes out not to one YOU but many), there are times when using the epistolary form brings a new (old?) immediacy and presence to the critical undertaking. It's certainly not the only way to "connect," but for some of us, it's a powerful way. Okay, I feel better now.

Anne

10

Epistolary Responses
to the Critical Act

Although we have long had letters to editors and letter columns within our scholarly journals, criticism in letter form has been relatively scarce.[1] Nevertheless, some critics, especially since around 1980, have capitalized on letters' particular virtues to assert the dialogic side of scholarship and promote revised notions of the scholar's self and audience. Such uses of the letter form seem part of a broader discontent with traditional academic writing, a discourse some "have come to see as pseudo-objective, impersonal, and adversarial," as Diane P. Freedman, Olivia Frey, and Frances Murphy Zauhar write in the introduction to *The Intimate Critique: Autobiographical Literary Criticism*.

This chapter studies the particular benefits that the epistolary form offers contemporary critics. I want, like Nancy Newton in a 1989 article on the professional practices of teachers and critics, "to call into question some of the games we play and urge collaborative efforts to alter the rules of these games as we reconstitute them, even while they—inevitably—reconstitute us" (23). In addition, like G. Douglas Atkins, author of *Estranging the Familiar*, I want "a courageous criticism that records personal encounter, evincing an author's or a text's power and the reader's powerful, whole response" (97). "Personal" criticism in letter form provides those of us who find the standard argumentative article alienating or combative or uninteresting with an alternative and stimulating means of responding to the critical act.

Most of us take personal criticism to mean that which brings into the discussion some aspect of the critic's life or experience. We assume that personal scholarship will contain the autobiographical, demonstrating the writer's own reactions to a place, event, or experience relative to the material under discussion. Alicia Ostriker's *Writing Like a Woman* includes many passages that function this way; Jane Tompkins' "Me and My Shadow" and Diane Freedman's *An Alchemy of Genres* centrally intertwine the scholar's lived experience with her literary work. Personal criticism can also show one's own process of working with texts, as does Susan Howe's *My Emily Dickinson*. It can speak directly to the author whose texts are under investigation, as in Barbara Christian's "Layered Rhythms: Virginia Woolf and Toni Morrison," which begins, "I see your face, Toni Morrison" and consistently addresses Morrison as "you." Personal criticism might acknowledge the importance of certain ideas within a text to one's own moral, emotional, or intellectual development or even the centrality of a certain edition of a text to one's own reading of that work. In this context, one thinks of Norman Holland's "Recovering 'The Purloined Letter' " in which he asserts that "I can give you my feelings and associations and let you pass them through the story for yourself to see if they enrich your experience" (372). Holland resists the "celibate state of mind" that denigrates or eliminates the emotional (373), finding that a "transactive" approach that deals with all aspects of the reading act restores "stories [and one assumes, other texts] to their rightful owners—you and me and all of you and me, our emotional as well as our intellectual selves" (373).

Important and stimulating as such connective *content* may be, another intriguing aspect of personal criticism is its exploration of *forms* that diverge from the standard critical essay so that the body of the text is clearly marked by a different, personalized presentation. One has but to look at "Stabat Mater," with its shifting margins, to know that Julia Kristeva ventures into new territory. Spaces on the page, incomplete sentences, shifting type faces, and interjected personal responses with signatures let us know that, in "For the Etruscans," Rachel Blau DuPlessis and members of Workshop 9 are using formal differences to signal a multivoiced, collaborative literary criticism. When personal criticism appears as one or more letters, that formal choice clearly marks its author's entry (or attempted entry) into a world of give and take, of the fragmentary, of a desired one-to-one-ness ("dear" and "sincerely"), of *recognized* distance and absence that will never be overcome completely. In addition, although the letter form does not necessarily allow us access to revolutionary content, it usually signals an attempted shift in attitude toward our material, ourselves, and our readers.

"The spectacle of a significant number of critics getting personal in their writing, while not, to be sure, on the order of a paradigm shift, is at least the sign of a turning point in the history of critical practices," writes Nancy K. Miller in *Getting Personal* (x). She then mentions numerous variations scholarly writers have introduced into critical discourse—from autobiography to narratives of exploration to personal anecdotes—finding that such elements create linkage between the article writer's own life and her or his subject (2). Surprisingly, among the many formal experiments she notes, letters as such are absent (2–3).[2] Here I refer not to "Letters to the Editor" or "Forum" sections of journals, nor to republished letter exchanges between authors and/or critics, all of which I do of course value, but to books or articles or essays cast in epistolary form.[3]

In trying to understand why personal criticism has marked the 1980s, Miller brings up four factors: reactions against the antisubjectivity of some contemporary critical modes, the need for critical styles that permit entry to a greater range of voices, a questioning of the basis for critical authority, and feminism itself, which in many instances privileges the personal (20–21). I would add a fifth factor: an exploratory pressure for the new, which leads to the rupturing of genre boundaries.[4] These factors overlap, of course, as will become evident in the following discussion, where I apply Miller's categories to an exploration of recent epistolary criticism.

As I suggested above, Miller finds that one impetus toward personal criticism comes from "the gradual, and perhaps inevitable waning of enthusiasm for a mode of Theory, whose authority—however variously—depended finally on the theoretical evacuation of the very social subjects producing it" (20). I take this to mean that poststructuralism's questioning of such concepts as unitary character, textual coherence, voice, and agency, although provocatively opening up interpretive strategies, has also created, for many, a depoliticized, decontextualized, and antihuman milieu. Letter criticism posits (though it may do so playfully) a "signed" writer producing a text out of his or her individuality, reaching out for some sense of community—a response to an other or others and a desire for further response from that other. This approach to critical work confronts emptiness by taking dialogic action rather than the action of individual mastery or combat. Letter criticism also works against "theoretical evacuation" by permitting conventions of coherence that are less divorced from the rhythms of daily life than the standard essay.

Dialogism, intimacy, and personal commitment are key elements in Fay Weldon's *Letters to Alice on first reading Jane Austen,* in which Aunt Fay writes letters to her niece Alice about school, family, writing, and literature, including concentrated discussions of Jane Austen's works. The second sentence of the first letter invokes the give-and-take of epistolarity: "You ask me for advice" (7). Who does not like to be *asked* for her opinion? Normally no one asks a critic for advice, but we are quick to hand it out, neatly disguised, of course, in almost everything we write. Once it is given, most respondents, that is, other critics, insist on refuting, denying, and decrying it. Michael Rifaterre once praised this combative aspect of critical work by stating that "debate is a contact sport," but many of us wonder whether that is a desirable model.[5] Rather, why not use a model of conversation, construction, or correspondence?

Weldon's use of the letter form reminds us that her text is one person's response penned for another person. Her book's letters function rather like Susan Koppelman's "authentic" letters—ones she sends to friends and colleagues rather than publishing her ideas in articles (although at times Koppelman does publish). In a letter to a group of friends, Koppelman asks, "Why do you write long essays that are speeches or position papers instead of writing letters to each other?" and asks further whether it is "the patriarchy that teaches that discussion of literature has to take that kind of impersonal form, that nondialogic form, that emotional-after-the-fact form" (76–77). Weldon's format takes the more personal approach, presenting literary criticism (in fictionalized form) with an appealing level of humility, ostensibly shaped for just one young reader, with obvious subjectivity behind its generalizations. As external reader I find that what Miller calls "social subjects" come into existence vividly through Weldon's strategy. Three individuals—Jane Austen, the letter-writing Aunt Fay (the advising critic), and the letter-receiving Alice (Fay's niece)—emerge as powerful personalities who are contextualized, each in her own separate community, yet here brought credibly into relationship with the others.

In *Letters to Alice* the contexts are achieved in various ways. Austen's context comes from Aunt Fay's attempts to place this famous author within her sociopolitical-historical setting; Fay provides Alice with considerable informative data on Austen's works and life. Alice's resistance to Austen and to literary study is also contextualized, for Fay includes references to the niece's letters and their detailing of the young woman's preferred activities. Aunt Fay's own physical location, occupation, preoccupations, and prejudices are informally included in her letters, so we easily see how they shape her reactions both to Jane Austen and to her niece. The tension between Aunt Fay's private life and her "literary advice" erupts into the letters, and when Fay disparages too much intrusion of the personal into her discourse, it is but proof of the connection between personal life and cultural production.

The critic's authority within this text lies in her ability to make connections among herself, her niece, and Jane Austen. Using the letter form highlights the distance among these individuals, but also underscores the possibility of making them more present to each other. The letter's nature also underscores the physical work of reaching out to the other, which Weldon emphasizes by bringing into Aunt Fay's discourse speculations on the ways we write, including such things as choices of pen versus typewriter or computer. The letter further allows a productive tentativeness as when Fay, doubting that one argument will persuade her reader, suggests: "Let's try another way. Let me put to you another notion. Try this" (10–11). In an amusing way, too, the letter form permits the writing authority to set herself up and then show herself mistaken. For example, in one letter she firmly proclaims, in anonymously authoritative language, that Jane Austen's contemporaries typically began menstruating quite late: "In 1750 we know it [the age for onset of menarche] to have been between eighteen and twenty" (28). Two letters later she discovers her mistake, offhandedly reminding her niece that facts are slippery things: "Well, you can't trust anyone. In an encyclopedia published in 1813 I find . . . that the age of menstruation in the human female is sixteen" (49). She warns her protegé that "I mention my error out of conscience and as a general warning that we all (especially me) tend to remember what it is convenient to remember, and forget what we want to forget, and manage to deduce from given facts what we want to propose" (49). The epistolarity of the form within which Weldon writes accentuates this question of authority, for the "mistaken" data stood uncontested for a number of pages (representing a certain block of time) and was only then undone by personal admission.

In " 'Bold, But Not Too Bold': Fay Weldon and the Limits of Post-structuralist Criticism," Alan Wilde proclaims that both in her critical work and in her fiction Weldon "hearkens back, in some ways at least, to earlier models." He explains that her fictions "do not, *formally* (as metafictional novels do) contest the notion of a 'shared reality' " (408). I find myself agreeing and disagreeing. On the one hand, *Letters to Alice,* which is after all presented as a fiction, participates in the conventions of stable characters and assumes unquestioned faith in language's power to refer safely to a known and shared world out there. The text manifests a standard chronological timeline, uses an old-fashioned form (letters), and, although not exactly a "page-turner" of a novel, does have a chartable plot. Nevertheless, should we call it a novel when it is as much a reading of Jane Austen as anything else, when it is so often devoted neither to character nor to plot but to straightforward exposition concerning the writer's craft? Is not Weldon undertaking some quite metafictional, metacritical moves here?

I conclude that this author chooses to present a basically critical and pedagogical work in fiction's costume to emphasize personal, subjective connectedness, to underscore literature's palpable role in and relevance to the life of a woman and her female descendant.[6] In this text, the three characters (Aunt Fay, Alice, and Jane Austen) remain separate, the epistolary form accentuating the isolations of time and space and circumstances that prevent any easy sharing of reality. Yet the form also works to hold out the possibility of contact and interchange among the three, even though that contact is tenuous and conditional. Of course, Weldon's text is not limited to a three-fold contact. Through Aunt Fay, Weldon writes to us too. I presume she wants her external readers (you and me) to occupy the writerly position of Aunt Fay, the readerly situation of Alice, or, most advantageously, shift back and forth. In this configuration, we are given multiple opportunities to think about our own subjective relationships to fiction and to criticism.

Jacques Derrida's "Envois," a book-length section of *The Post Card,* is another epistolary critical work that presents itself as a fiction. Derrida explains, in a letter on *The Post Card*'s rear cover, that he has produced "a satire of epistolary fiction," which he describes as "farci, stuffed with addresses, postal codes, crypted missives, anonymous letters, all of it confided to so many modes, genres, and tones." Much of the content of the letters is about writing, reading, and sending letters. Letter novels traditionally have included meta-commentary, in the sense that the letter writers dwell on their reading and writing acts, but in Derrida's text the metacommentary satirically outweighs the story aspect of the letters.

In the introduction to "Envois," Derrida remarks about these letters, "I do not know if their reading is bearable" (3). Depending on one's taste, to read this work as a novel may be unbearable, and yet one cannot ignore its fictional elements, simply call it criticism, and then feel comfortable bringing to the reading act one's literary-critical-analytical skills. Derrida's text insistently projects the general form of a letter novel: the letters, many of them love letters of sorts, mostly dated and arranged in chronological order, cover approximately two years of a relationship of some sort. A tenuous but nonlinear plot hints at possibilities of known or fixable characters (possibilities that remain unsatisfied), but the letters, although frequently dated, carry no signatures. The fictionality of the fiction constantly interposes itself as the text's deconstructive, critical commentary surges forward, but the possibility of a fiction/novel shape never disappears.

Mocking the convention in epistolary novels that the letters were written by other "real" people, Derrida wonders about the authorial identity of any kind of writer: "Who is writing? To whom? . . . I owe it to whatever remains of my honesty to say finally that I do not know" (5). Thus, in this work that is both criticism and fiction, Derrida attempts to deconstruct the concept of scholarly or critical identity, an act typically directed at authors of fiction, drama, and poetry. Is he declaring the "death of the critic," contending that all writerly identity is equally undecidable, equally a construct? Also tenuous is the identity of the addressee, for the "you" written to may be a fictitious character, the external reader, or perhaps, by implication, a real friend or lover (one or more people!) (5–6). Finally, Derrida asserts that the uncertainties and correspondences within "Envois" are linked to "the movement of the posts and to the psychoanalytic movement, to everything that they authorize as concerns falsehoods, fictions, pseudonyms, homonyms, or anonyms" (5)—a considerable claim, but one that, once more, puts this text within the field of critical discourse as much as within the field of fiction. And all of this within that most personal of forms, the letter.

Shari Benstock introduces her detailed analysis of Derrida's text by explaining that " 'Envois' reflects and refuses to be constrained by literary form: it is relentlessly self-conscious, unable to take for granted the structure and conventions letter writing employs" (88). She then proceeds to show that the choice of letter form allows Derrida to take apart all assumptions concerning genre and gender (and even assumptions about such a "literary" element as the postal service). "The existence of a historical line that separates letters from literature or distinguishes authority through generation is the first casualty of *The Post Card*" (120). Derrida himself has claimed, in "The Violence of the Letter" chapter in *Of Grammatology*, that "in its syntax and its lexicon, in its spacing, by its punctuation, its lacunae, its margins, the historical appurtenance of a text is never a straight line" (101). This is certainly true for epistolary texts. It makes perfect sense that Derrida, after exploring in essay form the ways that "the letter" (meaning writing in general) violates and is violated by its readers/writers, would move on to practice on himself, on the text, and on his readers the violence of the letter (meaning the epistolary genre). The fact that the letter is the postal letter (and actually, often a post card) in the "Envois" section of *The Post Card* is not only the elaboration of Derrida's sense of humor, but also his insight that genres are fairly arbitrary divisions. Linda Kauffman not only finds that this text deconstructs story, plot, character, and identity, but also sees that through its form it demonstrates that "one need not choose—indeed, it is not even a question of choosing—between language and experience, deconstruction and psychoanalysis, poststructuralism and materialism" (*Special Delivery* 130). Derrida's breaking of genre and gender conventions attempts to deauthorize these dichotomies.

An issue central to Derrida's text is connection. How interesting that this scholar, known for dense, abstract, philosophic prose, chooses the most traditional "novel" shape to play with ideas of breaking down the unbreakable separateness of person from person, now from then, the act of engendering from the being (or thing) engendered, signifier from signified. This overarching desire for connection is exemplified in "Derrida's" letter of September 9, 1977, which includes a statement about the writer's superabundance of mailings: "These are memories that I am sending to you, the essential remaining that I send to you, that I touch you by sending you whatever, even if it is nothing, even if it is without the slightest interest" (79). Not only is the writing act seen as a desperate attempt at connection; reading too shares that motivation. "I am spending my time rereading you" (50), writes the protagonist. In fiction the received letter is the other person, and so to reread the letter is to reread the person. This is true theoretically, too: to reread someone's text can equal rereading the person. So, as much as Derrida in other texts and even in this one may theorize away the concepts of person, body, and presence, here he inscribes the need and desire for the subject—the person.

The protagonist of "Envois" also relates letters to that essential situation of connection and communication, the *"fort:da"* of childhood: "for finally the *fort:da* is the post, absolute telematics" (44). The letter-writing character speaks to his addressee on the phone and refers often to seeing or planning to see the addressee in the flesh, yet he writes continuously, often twice or more a day. There seems no way to bridge absence; the addressee's absence is but a representation for an alienated state: "She is not here but there, she is speaking to me, she brings me near to myself who am so far from everything" (56). Presence is always slipping away: "Do I write to you in order to bring you near or in order to distance you, to find the best distance—but then with whom? The question is posed when you are in the next room, or even when in the same room, barely turning my back to you, I write to you again, when I leave a note under your pillow or in the letter box upon leaving, the essential not being that you are absent or present at the moment when I write to you but that I am not there myself, when you are reading, that is, still there, myself" (78–79). Although absence is so pervasive, the existence of a sensed other (and here we can substitute text for person to move the discourse back to critical theoretical practice, should we so desire) establishes one's subjectivity, one's existence. "You mark for me both reality and death; absent or present moreover (you are always there, over there . . .), all this amounts to the same, you mark *me,* you signify reality as death for me, you name them or show them with your finger" (181). Derrida's "Envois" speaks to an urgent desire for dialogism within theoretical work, doubts about our motives and processes, and undeniable connections between the intellectual and the physical.[7]

The epistolary form serves Derrida elegantly because, as Kauffman writes in *Special Delivery, The Post Card* (in which "Envois" appears) tries "to go beyond totalizing theories—including even poststructuralism" (81). The form maximizes exploration of many literary issues, which, according to Kauffman, include "defamiliarizing the production of the text" and demonstrating that even emotions such as love are constructed by language (82, 83). This text also stresses, through content and form, the arbitrary and subversive acts of readers; the "undecidable" nature of the text, writer, recipient, and contents of the letters; and the central role of the reader's expectations and desires for plot, consistency, and "authenticity" (84, 85). In addition, as elsewhere in his more overtly theoretical works, Derrida here works against neat genre classifications (89). The external reader shifts back and forth between fiction and criticism, unsure (pleasantly or unpleasantly) which reading strategies to bring to the text, questioning the very existence of separate types of writing: the critical, the creative. Taking into account Derrida's many puns and word games and putting those in conjunction with his deconstruction of character, identity, emotion, and event, Kauffman seeks a new way to place "Envois," concluding finally that this book is not "*on* literature but *to* . . . literature," and thus it "abandon[s] the fiction of authoritative interpretation" (103).

Derrida's text, like Weldon's, uses book length to elaborate various critical positions and issues. In contrast, epistolary articles are being used by some critics to accomplish work on more limited topics. In "Citing the Subject," Gerald MacLean creates five unmailed letters that respond to the content and form of Jane Tompkins's "Me and My Shadow." Tompkins's nonletter, personal essay calls for the integration of public and private voice, the epistemological valuing of emotion and personal experience, and discourse forms that will inscribe connections, cooperation, "appreciation," and others' voices (Tompkins 126–27). She states that the "authority effect" of most academic prose leaves out "the human frailty of the speaker, his body, his emotions, his history; the moment of intercourse with the reader—acknowledgment of the other person's presence, feelings, needs" (129). In her analysis of why the personal attracts her, Tompkins realizes that "what is personal is completely a function of what is perceived as personal," and this depends on what "strikes one as immediately *interesting*"; she then further decides that "for women, the personal is such a category." That is, she believes that for women, the personal is necessarily interesting (134). Not all women find the personal consistently intriguing, however (see, in particular, Linda Kauffman's "The Long Goodbye: Against Personal Testimony, or an Infant Grifter Grows Up" and Daphne Patai's "Sick and Tired of Scholar's Nouveau Solipsism"). Even those who are drawn to the personal may find it inappropriate or uninteresting in certain settings, texts, and moments. Rather than generalizing about women's interests, I would contend that the personal—one's own emotion and experience—forms *one* important category of what interests many women (and men). Because the academy has so often devalued the personal, however, we need to reaffirm this aspect of ourselves and our work as vital to the epistemology and availability of whatever wisdom we offer. By responding to Tompkins's call with letters, MacLean would seem to emphasize criticism as response, each scholar's contribution but a part of the on-going and incomplete whole.

MacLean's first letter states his puzzlement at the form he is using. Because these "letters" have footnotes and were not mailed, he wonders whether they really are letters. As in Derrida's "Envois" the fiction of these letters—just what they are and how to define them—becomes a problem, but one that productively moves us to keep questioning our uses of texts. Yet, he finds writing to "Dear Jane" compelling; it inscribes that keeping "in mind" of the addressee. To his credit, MacLean queries his own use of the informal epistolary form, wondering whether he is not "covering my criticisms of your essay by using an informal style, and insinuating my will by doing what you asked, by seeking to give you pleasure [through the use of the personal]" (140). In addition, he knowingly questions how much presence the personal can have anyway (141).

Despite his doubts, MacLean retains the epistolary form. His struggles with the form are amusing and somewhat discomforting. The second letter (chronologically the first) opens by declaiming, "This is not a journal" (141)—shades of "This is Not a Pipe." Just as Magritte's title and picture war against each other, proclaiming the odd slippage between object and language, MacLean's disclaimer sets up the notion that his discourse *is* a journal and, at the same time, declares the arbitrariness of all naming of genres.

I find myself becoming annoyed with MacLean toward the end of this letter, when he explains what he thinks Tompkins has in mind, using the very language and style to which Tompkins has raised certain objections. To tag her desire for wholeness "the displacement of the authority of the text by the supplement of the writer" (142) may not be to miss her point entirely, but certainly removes from her point the pleasure and body originally there. Moreover, his references to Tompkins in the third person here mitigate against effectively connecting with Tompkins; presumably it was that connection that in part elicited his use of the letter form. As Nancy Miller puts it, out of frustration at MacLean's patronizing tone, vocabulary, and extensive and academic footnotes: " 'Dear Gerald,' I feel like writing back. 'Try a letter *to a person*' " (*Getting Personal* 17).

MacLean's fourth letter (recall that we know from letter one that these missives were never sent) thanks Tompkins for sending him an essay. How is one to read that? Is it a maneuver aping the personal, just another form of "This is Not a Pipe," or a deconstructive challenge of the letter's authority? One feels a tension between the denial of authority embraced through use of the letter form and the assertion of authority maintained by much of the content, which repeatedly asserts MacLean's interpretations of Tompkins. A footnote to this letter doubly demonstrates MacLean's prejudices about the personal, especially within a feminist context. First, the existence of footnotes makes clear that he is a "real" authority who only plays with the letter form; Tompkins is but his titular addressee. Second, this footnote's content, which reminds Tompkins that "this belief in the irreversible 'self'—a symptomatic ideal of bourgeois individualism—fails to meet the post-structuralist denial of the subject position" (155), simply reiterates the problem with which Tompkins herself has been working. The self within a text is expressed as voice, and investigations of the notions of self and voice have particular importance for those groups who have been denied access to the full exploration of either. Feminist explorations of voice grow out of a history of imposed silence; MacLean loses sight of that factor. As Susan Lanser puts it, "Despite compelling interrogations of 'voice' as a humanist fiction, for the collectively and personally silenced the term has become a trope of identity and power" (*Fictions of Authority* 3).

In his final letter, after considerable advice to Tompkins on ways to see her anger, her history, and her desire for the personal in what to him are more acceptable terms (collective, Marxist-oriented critiques of institutions, for example), MacLean finally attempts to redeem himself by facing up to his own actions of authority. "So here

I am, doing what I was trained to do, telling 'women' what to do, how to think and behave. And I am doing it in that body-less 'objective' language" (148). Presumably, to recuperate Tompkins's respect, MacLean accepts Tompkins's implicit challenge and moves into a long section of autobiographical writing to explain his own relationship to authority. While actively exploring the connections between his personal (emotional, psychological, physical) experiences and scholarly endeavors, MacLean also strives to show Tompkins (and us) that he, a man, can write the personal. He proudly asserts that he has written about topics Alice Jardine suggests men need to include if they can "learn how to talk their bodies": "I have spoken of my mother, death, madness, paranoia, and desire" (153). It is rather odd to see him taking out the list and checking it off.

MacLean seems intent on demonstrating through his own experience his conviction that the personal does have value. For him, however, this personal writing, if it is to have validity, must be positioned in its socioeconomic context, for he believes it is formed as much by our institutions and the expectations of society as by our individual psychological histories. MacLean seems to believe that expression of the personal can benefit not only the individual writer, for whom its communication may have therapeutic value, but also society at large if only the writer will use theoretical positioning to perform the collective work of undoing or reforming detrimental social institutions. Accepting the feminist position that the personal is the political, it does not seem necessary that every writer of the personal undertake neo-Marxist or new historicist strategies to connect with the socioeconomic situation surrounding his or her discourse. A major advantage of the letter form as a mode of personal criticism is its logical way of incorporating elements that so often result from the conditions that shape our lives: class, race, gender, ethnicity, sexual orientation, and so on.

Nancy Miller, whose *Getting Personal* does mention the MacLean epistolary response to Tompkins's "Me and My Shadow," concentrates on analyzing Tompkins's kind of personal writing and the problems she raises. Miller wonders whether "you have to turn your back on theory in order to speak with a non-academic voice" (5). In terms of Tompkins's essay, which attempts to combine personal-emotional-body responses with critical work, Miller expresses, though with a different tone, some of the same concerns raised by MacLean, asking whether "putting all that into writing and into the world," working "against a language of abstraction," will not function negatively for women scholars, essentializing them back into second-class citizenship in the academy: "How can women get power from this?" (7). Miller decides that the stirring thing about personal criticism is that it is "engaged" (24). It takes risks—"by turning its authorial voice into spectacle, personal writing theorizes the stakes of its own performance: a personal materialism" (24). Engaging in personal criticism certainly puts MacLean at risk. To discuss his own abusive behavior, which he contextualizes in terms of the psychological analysis offered him in therapy and in terms of systemic, destructive "institutional privileges and pressures" (152), takes courage. In addition, although I have objected to much of his essay's style, his willingness to practice what we might call the contextualized personal and to see it as an important way of knowing extends the possibilities of literary critical discourse. That his letters have no closings or signatures, that their dates seem arbitrary, and that they have footnotes and use a language seemingly alien to the letter situation signals to me that he has not yet found the full advantages of the epistolary. Perhaps he will at some point return to the possibilities of the letter, uncovering ways the form itself offers unique contextualizing opportunities.

In explaining the rise of interest in personal criticism, Miller moves from ideas about postmodernism's sometimes antisubjectivity to "the emergence of global movements of liberation," including concurrent "pressure in this post-colonial moment for more complex modulations of agency" (*Getting Personal* 20). The politics of location informs our choice of language and form, and, here again, how we present our ideas can actually inform (or reform) those ideas effectively. Why reproduce within our rhetoric the colonialist economies of conquest and competition? Why always privilege a rhetoric of mastery, hierarchies, and hegemonies when alternatives abound?

Gloria Anzaldúa's "Speaking in Tongues: A Letter to Third World Women Writers" was at one point in its creation an essay, she explains to her addressees. That form, however, was "wooden, cold" and did not allow for the "intimacy and immediacy" she desired (165). As a woman of color and a "Third World woman" she resists academia's pressure to "bow down to the sacred bull, form. Put frames and metaframes around the writing. Achieve distance in order to win the coveted title 'literary writer' or 'professional writer.' Above all do not be simple, direct, nor immediate" (167).

Anzaldúa fears that too many of her "sister-writers" have been tempted to sell out, through the form and content of their writing, and urges that they "not acquiesce" (167). One way she seeks to give them confidence is through the letter form, a form that more than many others can symbolize the message of her content: "You are not alone" (169).

Her letter, dated 21 Mayo and addressed to "Dear *mujeres de color*, companions in writing—," takes advantage of the letter's informal possibilities to permit a sense of the familiar, with home, food, and body very much part of the discourse. Allowing these personal elements into her discourse emphasizes the notion of writing as a liberatory act—an essential part of daily life and a necessary part of surviving, rather than a separate, elitist, professional activity.

For Anzaldúa, power is a central issue: "Writing is the most daring thing I have ever done. . . . Writing reveals: the fears, the angers, the strengths of a woman under a triple or quadruple oppression. Yet in that very act lies our survival because a woman who writes has power. And a woman with power is feared" (171). Yet only if she writes in her own voice and in a form that fully allows her thoughts free rein will woman's power emerge. To write in what we might call predictable forms will not free up new insights or solutions for the reader or writer. If one is to "shock [her]self into new ways of perceiving the world," one must "throw away abstraction and the academic learning, the rules, the map and compass" (172, 173). Obviously no one form can guarantee the kind of radical creative freedom for which Anzaldúa hopes, but I believe that she is modeling a *choice* of form by using the epistolary.

If we see the letter form functioning within the "post-colonial moment," then the interruptions inscribed into "Speaking in Tongues" take on particular significance. That this piece is interrupted and must be written over the course of five days matters. The dates, the extra lines of white space representing time spent not writing, remind us that most women—especially women without professional standing, money, or the self-confidence built up through generations of social status—do not have support systems that allow extended periods of writing time ("No long stretches at the typewriter unless you're wealthy or have a patron—you may not even own a typewriter" [170]). They may also remind us that writing is part of other activities that also must be attended to ("Write on the bus or the welfare line, on the job or during meals, between sleeping or waking. . . . While you wash the floor or clothes listen to the words chanting in your body" [170]). In addition, of course, they remind us that writing is hard work and cannot always be accomplished at one go ("Why does writing seem so unnatural for me? I'll do anything to postpone it" [166]).

In publishing her letter to third-world women writers, Anzaldúa necessarily communicates with many who are not encompassed in her salutation, but her use of form positions the reader instructively. Through the fiction that she writes to a select group alone, Anzaldúa privileges a group that, historically, has had less access to publication and power. Readers who are third-world women writers can take strength from their community with Anzaldúa, they can feel themselves entering the conversation with her. Readers who are not third-world women writers, no matter how sympathetic to the needs and powers Anzaldúa describes, will necessarily feel themselves privy to but outside of the direct conversation. This formal maneuver quietly and nonconfrontationally positions the reader to recognize his or her own location in society and helps highlight each individual's relationship to reading and writing as part of a social structure. Although she permits the external reader—male or female, third world or not, of color or not—a fairly intimate sense of what motivates her own work and that of other third-world women writers, her form of address should keep that external reader particularly self-aware. Each reader—third-world woman writer or other—will presumably begin to question his or her motives for writing and to think about what conditions our choices concerning content, form, and style. Heightening the individual's likelihood for response to her letter, Anzaldúa intersperses her own text with quotes from other writers, but casts most assertions and explanations in her own voice, eschewing generalizations or the citation of authority figures. Her use of an informal first-person voice, combined with the letter form, leaves space for other, alternative explanations.

Within "Speaking in Tongues," many of the motivations Anzaldúa finds prompting her writing seem to echo the empowering and liberating qualities I have asserted letters in fiction most fully support: "I write to record what others erase when I speak, to rewrite the stories others have miswritten about me, about you. To become more intimate with myself and you. To discover myself, to preserve

myself, to make myself, to achieve autonomy. To dispel the myths
that I am a mad prophet or a poor suffering soul. To convince myself
that I am worthy and that what I have to say is not a pile of shit"
(222). For Anzaldúa, epistolary criticism provides the same space of
freedom that epistolary fiction provides many novelists.

Miller's third explanation for renewed interest in personal criticism is what she calls "a crisis over . . . representativity: an anxiety
over speaking *as* and speaking *for*" along with "a massive reconsid-
eration of the conditions grounding authorization itself" (20). In
spite of the "death of the author" and the concept of "intentional
fallacy," some of us still often question an author's intention in the
sense of wondering how this individual is authorized to make certain statements or paint certain portraits. Our own intentions and
authorizations come under scrutiny too, with psychoanalytic and
reader response theories often used to help us understand our reading strategies, or we seek the support of established critics, hoping
they can textually authorize our arguments or interpretations. As
Susan Lanser reveals about her own scholarly work, the critic's "act
of writing a scholarly book and seeking to publish it—is implicitly a
quest for discursive authority: a quest to be heard, respected, and
believed, a hope of influence" (*Fictions of Authority* 7). As we learn
to admit the complexities beneath every category of discourse, it
does get difficult to generalize for whom or as whom or to whom we
speak. Will our own experience legitimate our perceptions? Can the
personal at least ground or substantiate our experiences and help us
explain to a community of others why we read a text a particular
way? Can the personal help us understand our own enactments of
authority and ownership?

Robert Stepto has devised a form of epistolary criticism that explores the issue of what Miller terms "speaking *as* and speaking *for*,"
although, to date, he has not published work in this mode. As part of
a course co-taught with Roberto González-Echevarría at the School
of Criticism and Theory during the summer of 1988, "Fictions of
Representation in the Americas," Stepto presented a lecture titled
"Let Me Tell Your Story: Fraternal Authorship in Narratives of Slavery, Revolt, and Incarceration—Douglass, Montejo, and Wideman."
In this presentation he crafted the *form* of his criticism to enter dia-
logically into the experience of Frederick Douglass's "The Heroic
Slave," Miguel Barnet's edited version of Esteban Montejo's *Autobiography of a Runaway Slave,* and John Edgar Wideman's *Brothers and*

Keepers.[8] Stepto's epistolary form of criticism participates in rather than solely comments on these three texts, all of which involve "writing about heroes who are more precisely brothers in the struggle" (1). In the preliminary part of his lecture, he explained how reading *Brothers and Keepers* led him to new questions about the "biographing" undertaken by Douglass and Barnet. Stepto found that Wideman's earnest textual efforts to create a space for his imprisoned brother's autonomous voice fail because "he can no more give over the narrative to Robby than he can free him from prison" (2), whereas in the earlier texts Douglass and Barnet seem to create "seamless" narratives in which they are untroubled at transmitting another's story (3). Stepto's presentation then looks at the three texts as "distinct examples of fraternal authoring" (3).

Two-thirds of Stepto's presentation is given over to epistolary responses that in content and form creatively confront and complement the work of the three authors whose work he is investigating. As he puts it, his aim "is to offer brief narratives in a fraternal manner; narratives which both explicate and implicate what I am terming fraternal authorship" (7). Each of Stepto's letters uses a different voice. To Douglass, Stepto writes a letter in the voice of the Reverend Henry Highland Garnet and dates it late 1853. To Miguel Barnet he writes in the voice of a Cuban doctor, creating the fiction that Barnet and this doctor shared a flight from New York to Miami around 1959. To Wideman he writes in his own voice in the present time. (A similar strategy of "fraternal authorship" is used by Gerry Brenner in his intriguing "More than a Reader's Response: A Letter to 'De Ole True Huck,' " written "by" John, the sixteen-year-old son of ex-slave Jim to Huck Finn, critiquing "his" novel.)

To write a letter in another's voice would seem an evacuation of the personal: after all, Stepto is not present as himself in two of the three letters he creates; Brenner is not present in John's letter to Huck. To create or re-create their letter writers, however, Stepto and Brenner must immerse themselves in the lives and situations and language of their "characters." They must get personal with the texts they explore in a new way, a way that is traditionally associated with fiction writing rather than criticism. I think of Alice Walker's statement about writing *The Color Purple:* "I was sure the characters of my new novel were trying to . . . contact me, to speak *through* me" ("Writing *The Color Purple*" 356). And although the letter texts of Stepto (and Brenner) do not in themselves question the critic's adoption of another's voice, any author's use of voice is very much a central issue in all these letters; as Stepto says, the letters "explicate and implicate . . . fraternal authorship" (7).

In Garnet's letter to Douglass, Stepto concentrates on the issue of authorial control or voice-appropriation, as I think of it. After welcoming Douglass back from England, "(Rev.) Henry Highland Garnet" takes up a critique of Douglass's story about Madison Washington, "The Heroic Slave." Some small historical inaccuracies in Douglass's account come up for passing commentary. "Garnet" then launches into his strong objections to Douglass's erasure from the story of the two black men who assisted Madison in his escape from slavery—Robert Purvis and Garnet himself—and a similar erasure of Madison's wife. He also objects to the invention of a white sympathizer whom Douglass portrayed as cutting Madison's chains and thereby enabling him to lead the revolt aboard the slave ship *Creole*. Stepto's Garnet, although he praises Douglass in many ways (including celebrating his new sympathies with those advocating meeting violence with violence), decries the textual violence within "The Heroic Slave." Garnet also hints that Douglass is plagiarizing earlier versions of Madison's revolt told by Garnet himself.

Two things fascinate me about this fictitious letter. First, to write it, Stepto must immerse himself in the time about which he writes and even study, absorb, and then mimic, to the best of his ability, the prose of a period not his own. Second, he must move out of his own critical mindset and into Garnet's. He must communicate what he imagines would be Garnet's primary objections to Douglass's manipulations of history, objections based on a pragmatic political base within a particular historical moment. Garnet's critique seems motivated not out of any intrinsic interest in discourse analysis, but from his goal of freedom for all slaves—how will Douglass's text help or hinder abolition? Rather than *explaining* how the Reverend Garnet might have reacted to Douglass's text, Stepto *enacts* a form of fraternal authoring for this exercise. The piece is convincing—one slips into thinking this is an authentic letter from Garnet that Stepto somehow discovered hidden in an attic or folded into an old book. This epistolary response creates an effective space of exploration—one experiences "fraternal authorship" within the Garnet letter and is then free to analyze the layered discourse relative to such issues as authority and voice, fiction and "truth."

The second letter, from a mythical Puerto Rican doctor, Edmundo

Figueras, to Miguel Barnet, congratulates the author for "collecting" the story of Esteban Montejo, published as *The Autobiography of a Runaway Slave*. Although expressing displeasure with some of the story's "magic and superstition" and its content about "the bandits and the wenching" (13), "Figueras" admires how effectively Barnet's account of Montejo's experience comments on the events of the 1959 Cuban Revolution, showing how Castro's war is "but the newest chapter in a long struggle against colonialism" (13). Yet "the doctor" quietly suggests that Barnet's text contains its own subtle colonizing: "You say this is Montejo's story, and I believe you. But . . . " (14). That "but" leads to a question about an element of Montejo's story that the doctor conjectures may actually be Barnet's and not the runaway slave's.

By using the epistolary form, Stepto accomplishes various complex critical tasks, each most satisfyingly linked to Barnet's text. To start with, he creates a commentator who is not a literary critic but a black doctor from Puerto Rico, someone who supposedly sat next to Barnet on an airplane trip and only learned of his book through conversation. This means that the book is being critiqued not from the academy but presumably from a member of the audience Barnet would most want to reach—people from the American/Caribbean region whose knowledge of their own history would most benefit from Montejo's story. The doctor's criticism grows from his own experiences of prejudice, of being shunned or silenced, and warns Barnet not to fall into a prejudiced or stereotyping pattern of not fully acknowledging another.

In the explanatory part of his presentation, Stepto had wondered "to what extent is portraiture [in Douglass's "The Heroic Slave" and Barnet's *The Runaway Slave*] self-portraiture or self-projection?" He also wondered how much of such literary projects could honestly be understood as "acts of male bonding, race bonding, and constructions of national identity" (2). The fictional letter to Barnet raises these issues in subtle ways. "Doctor Figueras" comments early on that "all that you told me on the plane about the culture sugar made in Cuba seems to be in Montejo's story. It is important that you could somehow document that simply by having an ordinary man from the country tell his tale" (13). The repetition of "you" quietly emphasizes Barnet's appropriation of Montejo's material and his ability to participate in a political act through the publication of Montejo's story. "It is clever of you to collect his story now since it suggests that the Revolution of '59 is but the newest chapter in a long struggle against colonialism, and that black men like Montejo have helped to write every episode" (13–14), Stepto has his doctor continue, again highlighting Barnet's well-intentioned use of the Cuban's story.

Toward the end of this letter Stepto's fictitious doctor becomes more directly critical of his addressee's textual manipulations, questioning whether a particular description and related insight belong to Montejo or Barnet: "Were you quoting Montejo or yourself? Was that observation made in 1905—or in 1959?" (14). Although Barnet's published version of *The Runaway Slave* appears to be "true to" its original, in fact, at least in one place, it may be inventive. This implies the possibility of other inventions or reshapings. Also under interrogation is the editorial role: what is left in and what left out, what is footnoted and what stands alone. All such editorial acts evince the power relationship between editor and original author. As Stepto explained, Barnet "attempted to minimize his authorship by declaring himself merely the editor" (4). Although seeing this as a truly "brotherly act," Stepto also finds that the assumption of "deference" Barnet shows to Esteban Montejo is a way of keeping him in his place. "Deference to Montejo is another form of authoring him, especially in the context of written discourse, and that raises the question of how brotherly the narrative is after all" (5). Such positioning "works to keep people in place: Montejo is the 'real author' only because the Real Author has made him so" (5).

An important benefit of the letter form here is that it emphasizes the idea of correspondence—of two people exchanging ideas and reactions: of individuals reacting to each other not for the sake of some recognition by others (the field of scholarship, publication, academic status) but on a one-to-one basis. The "doctor" has nothing to gain from writing the author except greater understanding of issues important to them both; if we imagine Barnet responding to the doctor, we must see that he would garner from such involvement no publicity, no critical or commercial recognition, only further exploration of issues raised by his text and his authoring of that text. Through the polite voice of Doctor Figueras, Stepto's epistolary criticism effectively explores the editorial aspect of "speaking *as* and speaking *for*."

In his third letter, Stepto assumes his own voice to address John Edgar Wideman. An element of fiction remains, however, because the external audience will not know whether the posited friendship with Wideman is fictitious or real. This letter, the longest of the three, most openly dwells on the correspondences between writer and writer, between Stepto and Wideman, opening with reminders of conferences both men have attended, mention of their similar collegiate experiences, and references to texts they both have read (from *Huckleberry Finn* to *Invisible Man*). These affiliations presumably set up a sense of community and trust that can open possibilities for textual intimacy.

The focal point of the letter is its emphasis on listening, an active listening that Stepto explains he regrets not having done when the two men were face to face: "I think I write to you now because I finally want to listen to you in all the ways I didn't years ago" (22). True listening is difficult, and many of us discover that, as Stepto puts it, "it's easier to learn to read than to learn to hear someone out" (16). Stepto wants to elevate the reading act by making it as close to the listening act as possible. Just as Wideman's own text begins because he "needed a listener" (18), just as Ellison's invisible man assumes a listener (18–19), Stepto wants a listener too, but he also wants to prove himself a listener. By choosing the epistolary form, he emphasizes personal give and take; many places in his long letter even serve as substitute active listening gestures. Remembering Wideman's outfit at a conference, remembering an incident when Wideman began to "talk-story" (15), focusing on details of *Brothers and Keepers*, recalling ideas and phrases that Wideman used in that text (18–19), serve as nods of approval or acknowledgments of what Wideman has accomplished. Enclosed in a letter, these remembered acts take their power from their ability to impress *one* person only—the letter's addressee. Stepto and Wideman are imagined here as the beneficiaries of the letter process, each growing personally and professionally from the correspondence.

Of course my statement instantly becomes problematic because Stepto's letter to Wideman was read to an audience of hundreds. Perhaps it is partly because of such a conceptual knot that so far Stepto has resisted "publishing" this letter (or the other two) in a journal or book. In the presentation that preceded his letters, Stepto explained that Wideman's "narrative strives to fashion the voices of both brothers" (2), which I would take to mean that Wideman wants to see himself as a good listener, someone who gives the dialogic partner equal access to the space and time they share. Wideman's efforts, ones that Stepto's epistolary acts also explore, search for ways we can speak for others without erasing them, ways we can speak with authority yet give authority to other voices within our own texts.

Choosing the epistolary form to some degree allows Stepto to address these issues because of the "private" nature of letters. The letter acknowledges by its very form that a separation exists between Wideman and Stepto and that Stepto's assertions are vulnerable to Wideman's response. This form seems to be Stepto's own effort to perform critically what he believes Wideman also attempted in his nonfiction exploration of his own brother's experiences and their relationship. It makes sense that Stepto admires James Clifford's ethnographic aim of opening "the textualized fabric of the other, and thus also of the interpreting self" (qtd. in Stepto 6); the separation of writer and reader implied in letters heightens acknowledgment of the other's subjectivity.

Stepto investigates questions of voice and authorization within a "fraternal" context. Douglas Robinson's "Dear Harold" focuses on issues of the paternal. In doing so, his epistolary criticism, published in the autumn 1988 issue of *New Literary History*, highlights in a different way the problem of scholarly or critical authorization. This letter opens with the writer positioning himself in relationship to the letter's intended reader, Harold Bloom. Robinson lists areas of scholarship the two share, but admits that academic commonality does not yield intimacy: "I don't feel entirely comfortable addressing you as Harold" (239). Robinson states that he has chosen epistolary address in particular because of its informality, hoping to create some "dialogic equality" (239). Instead of the "abstraction or depersonalization or transcendentalization of voice, context, human reality" usually identified with "a 'straight' critical style" he wants to use the personal letter form to question the Oedipal power relationship between established critic and newcomer, "sidestepping" the conflict rather than "resolving" it—which is to say, reseeing the nature of the conflict itself (240).

Much of the letter concerns Bloom's buying into the Freudian concept of the Oedipal triangle, which leaves out so much and, in particular, in this context of critical influence, leaves out women and what Robinson calls "nonaggressive relationships." After all, we need not "reduce all relationships to one or another form of conflict and aggression" (242). As if to support the possibility of a different relationship between himself and Bloom, the bulk of the letter provides alternative readings of power relationships in texts that Bloom has explicated within the Oedipal dynamic. Finally, Robinson asks why critics put themselves in the "submissive [role] before the great fathers and mothers of literary history," reminding himself and Bloom that "mere temporal priority doesn't make writers parents; *we* do. If we want to" (249).

Robinson's letter is a formal positioning, with its "Dear Harold" marking off, if uncomfortably, his desire *not* to see Bloom as a parent, not to see prior critics or literary artists in the Oedipal position, not to see literary investigation in terms of mastery and conflict and aggression and proving of the self, but to move it into a conversation between siblings—regardless of reputation or age of those involved. Interestingly, Robinson claims that the "awe" he felt for Bloom when he began his letter was "dissipated" through the dialogic form of the letter, even though in fact it was a "one-sided" process. He closes the letter by asking Bloom, "care to join the dialogue?" (250). Whether or not Bloom ever replied, the possibility of dialogue is enforced not only through the content Robinson relays but also through the form he used, a form that always looks for a response.

The last explanation Nancy Miller offers for the rise in personal criticism is that within more recent feminism[s] "the personal is part of theory's material" (21). Although other experts too "read" the personal in some ways—folklorists, anthropologists, and sociologists interpret artifacts and activities from bargaining rituals to corsets to supermarket behavior, and art historians read significance in hats and household articles as well as paintings—feminist approaches in various disciplines have extended our readings of material culture, the body, relationships, and subjectivity. Feminist studies, for instance, have taught us new ways to read quilts, objects always appreciated for their function and attractiveness but only as a result of many feminist studies now perceived as having textual readability.[9]

A distinctly feminist, personal, epistolary text, "We Write Letters," consists of one rather long letter from Kady Daughter of Ann Daughter of Kate Daughter of Anna, framed by shorter letters from Celeste West, editor of *Words in Our Pockets: The Feminist Writers Guild Handbook on How to Gain Power, Get Published & Get Paid*. The entire book is informal in style, as befits a book intentionally created as "a woman writer's survival chest, a collection of spiritual and economic tools," an "unabashedly woman-to-woman wordsmithing" (2). The book's components include standard informational articles, interviews, resource lists, recipes, fiction, and anecdotes; many of the pieces critique current writing and publishing practices in down-to-earth, often first-person, prose. Part III, called "A Spectrum of Genres," includes two articles in the form of letters: Gloria Anzaldúa's stand-alone "A Letter to Third World Women Writers," which I have already discussed, and Kady's and West's correspondence, "We Write Letters."

Celeste West opens "We Write Letters" by explicitly valuing letters as a form of woman's writing: "the art, passion, and real power of women writing letters to each other," an art form that allows one "to break the silence, without any 'submission.' " West also states her belief "that women can well consider letters a form of publishing, which means 'to make public' " (211). In these statements West links herself with those many literary historians (feminist and other) who have seen the letter as a special province of women (by choice or necessity).

Kady's answering letter pushes against West's notions of women's letters. She thinks of letters not as a form necessarily endowed with "art, passion, and real power of women," but as a form chosen out of dire necessity. She writes letters and journals not because those are the best forms available but because "that's what you write when nobody offers you money for words" (213). In addition, although she agrees that letters do avoid the problem of submission—of suiting your words to a particular audience, that is, "an advantage of writing letters is / you can write it the way you want it," letters also have major limitations. "A big disadvantage is that only one woman sees it / and I often dump myself onto a page for one woman / who does not have a working mind" (214). Kady's blunt language integrates into her statements about letter writing the conditions of her life, contextualizing for us her perception of letter writing as part of her feminist writing practice and part of the life of a radical feminist. She is a poor, older, "radical lesbian feminist," who will not wear the "slave uniform" and accept jobs such as chicken sectioning or live-in domestic service and who knows herself to be among the huge number of women who somehow survive without property, space, or leisure (213).

West writes about letters as if they were a valuable art form in and of themselves, but Kady thinks of them differently. For her they are not necessarily discrete packages, fragmentary forms that carefully frame select information, reflection, description, and questions. Kady reveals to her correspondent that letters for her are also part of a writing process, for she periodically takes "hunks" of her letters and journals and retypes them in standard prose format ("I string them together / and I put in punctuation / and I run the words all the way across the page the way they want you to" [213]) and finds that certain small feminist presses publish this work. Although this publishing yields no income, it does allow her to "break out of silence," with her feelings and ideas communicated to more than one woman at a time (215).

Kady uses her letter not to perform literary criticism as such, but most centrally to perform cultural critique. Her anger is a communicative tool that harnessed, that is to say, published, has the power to plant ideas, inspire action. "Our pens are dangerous weapons. / We speak. We listen. / We tell each other what we know / any way we can" (216). Thus, in this letter to Celeste West that, being published in *Words in Our Pockets* becomes a letter to other women too, she offers pragmatic instruction from her own experience (for instance, dollars and cents information about self-publishing), and she offers her energy and anger as inspiration.

Kady's interweaving of the daily and the artistic, the personal and the political, grows out of her experience as a feminist. Her letter exemplifies the move within various areas of feminist criticism to explore the many ways in which the lives we live are an integral part of our literary production. She does not extol the letter as the best or only form in which to present her discourse, but finds it imminently suited to the kind of public/private dialogue she needs to undertake with West and suited also to reflect, through its fragmentary nature, the disjointed way of life that social and economic pressures still inflict on all too many women.

A thank-you letter from West ends this "article," acknowledging the special nature of letter performance: "Your letter flew into my heart. And into the book" (217). The letter is private, but public as well.

To Miller's four-part rationale for recent interest in personal criticism, I earlier suggested that we add a fifth impetus: a continuing interest in the experimental—the new. Postmodernism has included a consistent broadening of topics for discussion (in "creative" and critical work) and a studied questioning of rhetorical conventions, including that of neatly divided genres. In its impulse to challenge

boundaries, postmodernism is no different from earlier literary and
critical movements. Particular interests, such as genre and gender,
questions of language referentiality, and unitary notions of subjectivity, however, distinguish postmodernism's interest in "the new"
from the interests of other literary/critical movements (various contemporary approaches, including feminism, share some of the same
concerns). The breaking down of boundaries between fiction and
nonfiction, poetry and prose, verbal and graphic, and private and
public discourse forms logically extends to a loosening of the boundaries between letters and other texts. To make the personal letter into
a form of critical analysis may appeal to some of us just because we
have not tried it before. For some scholars the form's freedoms and
constraints may then permit new levels of expression. For, as Audre
Lorde says of poetry, "within structures defined by profit, by linear
power, by institutional dehumanization, our feelings were not meant
to survive" (127). The structure of the letter can stimulate access to
new concepts and insights.

In no way am I suggesting that the personal or the letter is some
panacea for rhetorical rigidity or the anomie and destructive com-
petitiveness often encountered in the academy. As Miller reminds
us, the personal can make its readers feel left out through a "chum-
miness" of "institutionally authorized personalism," of "privileged
selves who get to call each other (and themselves) by their first names
in print" (*Getting Personal* 25). Still, when it works, what Miller values
is that "the personal in these texts is at odds with the hierarchies of
the positional—working more like a relay *between* positions to create
critical fluency" (25). For me, it is that "betweenness" that letters
underscore.

Mary Ann Caws hopes that personal criticism can yield mutual
markings. In a class at the School of Criticism and Theory in July of
1988, she explained that the critic should influence the text, but
that the text should also leave its mark on the critic. She looks for a
"buckling" together, a criticism that is "at the pitch of the work [pri-
mary text] itself"; she wants "thick criticism." Similarly, what Robert
Stepto seeks through a more personal writing method, he explained
during a question-and-answer period following a lecture at the same
institution, is "the creation of comparable texts that honor rather
than compete with existing texts" and that permit the critic more
artistic leeway.

Letters in critical writing provide sites of response where "buckling" is possible—in the sense of connecting to texts, to concepts, to people. Buckling, however, also includes the possibility of bending, warping, or crumbling; for every "presence" a letter creates, an "absence" hovers nearby. Every letter delivered, "understood," and responded to initially included the possibility of nondelivery, misunderstanding, and lack of response. Thus, letters, as a form of personal writing, although offering the writerly self opportunities for intimacy and engagement, can promise neither. Still, use of the form, at some level, manifests awareness of distance and lack of different kinds of connections and implies the desire to bridge that distance, to make a connection, to have one's mind changed, to mix up private and public forums, break boundaries. Criticism in letter form seeks some form of response, some intimacy with or acknowledgment from an addressee. In part, the letter writer may also be addressing him or herself, attempting thereby to redefine the critical/scholarly self. In addition, the letter writer's address to a particular human positions us, as external readers, in a world of particulars rather than an abstract world of generalizations. At one or more levels—emotional, psychological, political, intellectual—"lettered" criticism holds the potential to change the writer, the reader, the critical act, and the relationships among them.

Notes

1. Introduction

1. Georges Poulet describes the alluring power of texts to engage us and move us beyond our known experience: "Because of the strange invasion of my person by the thoughts of another, I am a self who is granted the experience of thinking thoughts foreign to him. I am the subject of thoughts other than my own. My consciousness behaves as though it were the consciousness of another" (44).

2. I do not mean to overstate some separation between "content" and "form"; Susan Lanser, in *The Narrative Act,* brings narrative components together well when she reminds us that "ideology is not simply a content 'poured into' the text but is the very fabric of textual organization" (101) and when she shows the interrelationships between point of view, content, and form (98–101).

2. Epistolary Fiction: Space to Respond

1. The form actually originates in the seventeenth century; Aphra Behn's 1689 *Love-Letters Between a Nobleman and his Sister* and the 1669 *Lettres Portugaises* (translated into English in 1678) are the best known early examples. For solid historical background various sources are helpful; see, for example, Natascha Wurzbach's *The Novel in Letters: Epistolary Fiction in the Early English Novel 1678–1740* or Robert Adam Day's *Told in Letters: Epistolary Fiction Before Richardson.*

2. Which is not to say that every twentieth-century epistolary novel stars a female protagonist with a feminist agenda: see chapter 6, note 1.

3. Interpolated drawings may also symbolize what words cannot state or may supplement those words; in addition, drawings may reveal qualities of the letter writer, such as whimsy, special perceptions, or a desire to charm. In Webster's *Daddy-Long-Legs,* Judy frequently includes simple drawings in the letters to her trustee. The sketches remind letter recipient and external reader alike that the letter writer, although eighteen, is in some ways a child who needs more than some official at the other end of her correspondence.

4. Borges's "Pierre Menard, Author of the *Quixote*" encourages one to question whether reproduction of an earlier text is an act of interpretation or not or, as Edward Said puts it, to think about "the question of how an uninterpreted text differs from an interpreted text" (194). Said offers the notion that an interpreted text, worked and "partially purged . . . of its problematics" becomes more itself, more canonized, than the uninterpreted but repeated text. The uninterpreted, merely reproduced text retains full potential to take on new meanings (194).

5. The same question could be asked of the movie version of Walker's *The Color Purple*.

6. For instance, before I began studying epistolary fiction, I never noticed the letter quality of *The Adventures of Huckleberry Finn*. How many times had I read over the novel's last words without considering their implications: "The End. Yours Truly, Huck Finn"?

3. *Fair and Tender Ladies*: Letters as a Response to Absence, Presence, and Property

1. Terry Castle's thorough deconstructive work with *Clarissa* (in *Clarissa's Ciphers*) focuses on the novel's figurations of reading and writing, but favors the former. Clarissa's extreme isolation (her own alienation from even her own body) means that she is much more dependent on others' readings of her than is Ivy. Castle's concentration on reading tropes therefore makes good sense.

2. François Jost (along with others) distinguishes between active and static (or passive) letters, active referring to those letters that enact the narrative, passive referring to those that merely relate events that have occurred before the time of writing (see "Le Roman épistolaire et la technique narrative au xviiie siècle"). This distinction may be somewhat hard to see at times because the two modes can overlap.

3. In all quotations from *Fair and Tender Ladies* I have reproduced Smith's orthography. The author gives her heroine a limited vocabulary

and erroneous spelling and grammar that seem logical given Ivy's upbringing. With education, reading, and her own maturation, Ivy's later writing becomes more "correct," and Smith allows her to gain analytic powers as well.

4. Desire is always more than can be encompassed in speech or writing; this condition is central also to Derrida's "Envois," a novel/critical work (published as part of *The Post Card*), which I discuss in chapter 10.

5. For excellent examples of metonymic and metaphoric representations, see Altman's *Epistolarity,* page 19.

6. Not all of the letters attempt connection. As Altman points out, letters can reinforce absence as well as presence; they can emphasize the "distance" or difference between correspondents (*Epistolarity* 13). Sometimes Ivy attempts to separate herself from family or acquaintances whose conceptions of her or her family are painful or, by her lights, mistaken. These letters allow Ivy to be more present to herself as she rejects others' ideas or actions.

7. Lennard Davis seeks the origins of the English novel in ballads and chronicles (see especially pages 57–72 of his *Factual Fictions: The Origins of the English Novel*). It is interesting to note that Ivy functions both as balladeer, telling the important stories of her family and region, and as chronicler, telling the "news" of her community.

8. How history is told and by whom is a central concern for feminists. "Feminists have argued persuasively that we can't get adequate accounts of women's lives through theories constructed by men that are geared to direct us to the lives of men and away from the lives of women. But by the same token we should be skeptical about any claim that theories constructed by and for one group of women will automatically enlighten (rather than deeply mislead) us about all women's lives. Have we thought enough about what kind of knowledge and skill are necessary in order for one woman to speak about another? In order to speak in behalf of another?" (Spelman 9). Placement of "history" in Ivy's letters makes that history highly contextual and personal and thus prevents it preempting another woman's or group of women's historical vision.

9. We can see Ivy's yearning for Silvaney as a longing to merge back into a preverbal state, that connected state of early mother-child fusion that Nancy Chodorow has detailed so effectively throughout *The Reproduction of Mothering*. Her mother never having been fully present for Ivy has exacerbated the protagonist's hunger for maternal acceptance. Communication with Silvaney is a way of re-creating and appropriating the missing body of the mother.

10. Ivy's and Silvaney's names signify here; ivy certainly occurs in both wild and domestic states, but the sylvan is only present in the woods—in what we might call the "wild zone."

11. *Not* telling that story is a frequent component of late twentieth-

century epistolary fiction; in Updike's *S.*, Bob Randall's *The Fan,* Natalia Ginzburg's *The City and the House,* and Amos Oz's *Black Box,* for instance, nothing in the letters themselves or any preface relates or implies some method for the letters' collection. Other contemporary letter fictions do reenact the traditional incorporation of the collection/publication story: Barth's *LETTERS* posits a John Barth character who solicits the letters that then compose, in a metafictional maneuver, his newest novel; the nondelivery of letters and their collection by the wrong party is a central issue in Walker's *The Color Purple.* Castillo's *The Mixquiahuala Letters* sets up a situation, with all letters going to one correspondent, that logically implies their collection at the designation point; the publication of these documents, however, is given no explanation within the fiction, effectively mocking the old story of pretended reality for letter novels.

12. An excellent example of this kind of gynocritical, historically based work is Susan Coultrap-McQuin's *Doing Literary Business,* which details the material difficulties of nineteenth-century American women writers.

13. A. S. Byatt's novel *Possession* engagingly depicts the property value of letters. An academic, Roland Michell, discovers two letters by the poet Randolph Henry Ash hidden in a book in the London Library and steals them before he thinks through his action. These letters are the hinge of the whole novel, for they symbolize the ways in which letters can, as property, yield wealth, status, and power.

4. "Help! Love me! I grow old!": The Central Role of Germaine Pitt in John Barth's *LETTERS*

1. Ruth Perry believes that "in epistolary novels, it is not the maturing of character which is presented, but rather the testing and defining of character" (95). I find it rather difficult to make such a clear-cut distinction between self-definition and change, as if to define self were not at times to change. In the case of Germaine Pitt, one sees that she is not a radically different person or personality at novel's end, but much about her and her goals has undergone major transformation.

2. Oddly, Aldridge also ignores the historical apparatus the John Barth character introduces that so clearly historicizes the novel and so effectively connects the novel as construct to the world of events around it.

3. In its major commitment to history, *LETTERS* also shows a preoccupation with regeneration.

4. Various critics concentrate on Barth's novel in terms of its commentary on how history is narrated; in particular I think of Kim McMul-

len's "The Fiction of Correspondence: Letters and History," Linda Hutcheon's "Historiographic Metafiction: Parody and the Intertextuality of History," and Thomas Carmichael's "John Barth's *LETTERS:* History, Representation and Postmodernism."

5. Germaine often uses Ambrose's language to refer to his daughter; she is "his backward daughter," "dear, damaged daughter," "the d.d'd daughter," and "damaged Angela" (227, 337, 238, 244). When Germaine finally meets Angela she wants to change her language: "I can't use the ironic epithet any longer" (245).

6. Part of the style Barth gives Germaine is an epistolary flirtatiousness, even lasciviousness; her sexual language contrasts with that of earlier epistolary heroines. One might assume that her erotic nature and blunt narratives of sexual activity are set up to fulfill male fantasies, but that would stereotype notions of male and female eroticism.

7. The novel, of course, does not reproduce the individualized handwriting; we have only standardized print and our imaginations.

8. Carolyn Heilbrun opens *Writing a Woman's Life* by defining the four ways a woman writes her life: in autobiographical writing, in fiction writing, in actions (available for others' "reading" just as much as any text), or as subject of another's biography (11); Germaine seems to participate in all of these. Her letters contain considerable autobiographical material, yet she knows the author-character plans to use them within a fiction and that her biography is important to him. She also reports on her own (and others') actions and how they are read by others.

9. Lydon writes: "It is important for us not to know our place, not to rush to occupy it when we are being ushered into it. . . . Let us borrow from Foucault the word *esquive,* and the strategy it implies, from *esquiver,* 'to dodge or to feint,' as in fencing, the reflexive form of which, *s'esquiver,* means 'to slip away' " (139).

10. At one point, affirming the need for her addressee (confidant? stimulant? authorization? father confessor?), Germaine refers to a previous letter she had sent via certified mail and states that "Barth's" signature on the receipt was her "Go now and sin some more" (197). I take this as a comment that even for the most confident of individuals, change cannot take place in a vacuum. We all need something to bolster our determination occasionally.

11. This language cannot help but remind one of Roland Barthes's eroticized relationship to the text in *The Pleasure of the Text,* although Germaine's analysis at this particular point is slight. The "abrasions" that Barthes takes particular pleasure in placing on the text's surface and the disruptions caused by the nature of language itself (11–12) are not central to the female character's metaphor here, although elsewhere she plays with the elusive nature of language.

5. Restoration and In-gathering—*The Color Purple*

1. Including reviews, dissertation chapters, articles, book chapters, essays within edited collections, and interviews with Walker about *The Color Purple,* I estimate that well over 250 responses to the novel have been published. Additional materials, of course, address the movie version, and many of those also discuss the novel.

2. Walker writes at length about her relationship to the spirits of her ancestors and to the spirits of her novel's characters in "Writing *The Color Purple*" and "Coming in from the Cold."

3. Wendy Wall consistently terms Celie's letters to God "diary letters," presumably because they would never be posted. Although that term works well enough, it does have a tendency to erase the symbolic value of the letter—of the reaching out and desire for a return. Wall notes that Celie wants "a reciprocal sign that will order her life and thus constitute her as whole" (84). I will argue that the sign is the letters themselves that remain to her as testament of her own will and action.

4. Gates explains the black tradition of "double-voiced" discourse in the introduction to *The Signifying Monkey* and shows throughout that book the fascinating ways that black literature is constantly addressing its own tradition as well as a particular current issue and audience.

5. Nick Bantock's attractive *Griffin & Sabine, Sabine's Notebook,* and *The Golden Mean* all play on the reader's desire to intercept others' mail; these beautifully printed books detail two artists' correspondence (literal and figurative—they write each other, and Sabine can "see" what Griffin paints). Both postcards and letters are exchanged. In the case of the postcards, the external reader always sees the stamped pictorial side of the postcard first and must turn the page to see its verbal aspect. In the case of the letters, the external reader first sees the stamped, addressed, and decorated face of the envelope (printed on the book page) and then, on turning the page, is presented with an actual envelope pasted onto the book's page and must withdraw from it either a letter from Sabine ("handwritten") or one from Griffin ("typed"; typos neatly corrected). The books' subtitles, respectively, "An Extraordinary Correspondence," "In Which The Extraordinary Correspondence of Griffin & Sabine Continues," and "In Which the Extraordinary Correspondence of Griffin & Sabine Concludes," have multileveled applications, not the least being that these epistolary novels' physical presentation is out of the ordinary. In spite of rather slim content matter, both books have met with surprising commercial success, attributable, I suspect, to their physical appeal to our senses and to our voyeuristic desire to read others' mail.

6. Various critics discuss *The Color Purple* in relation to *Clarissa.* One recent such article is Linda Abbandonato's " 'A View from "Elsewhere" ':

Subversive Sexuality and the Rewriting of the Heroine's Story in *The Color Purple*," in which she discusses the many ways Walker's text "attacks" the "bourgeois morality" that for her is upheld by Richardson's text.

7. For other discussions of the parallels between *The Color Purple* and slave narratives see Michael Awkward's "A Circle of Sisters," Valerie Babb's "*The Color Purple:* Writing to Undo What Writing Has Done," and hooks's "Writing the Subject: Reading *The Color Purple*." Especially interesting is hooks's explanation of why she believes that Walker's text is a parody of slave narratives.

8. Keeping in mind that Walker's text also works to create parallels between African American and African customs and traditions, Awkward finds another implication in Celie's changing addressees. He sees a call and response pattern in Celie's letters. The first one asks for a response from God (209), yet writing to God provides "no sense of exchange or engagement with her specific Audience" (209) after the first letter. "In order to become an effective Black storyteller, it is necessary for Celie to develop, as does her fictive forebear Janie [in Zora Neale Hurston's *Their Eyes Were Watching God*], a more acute sense of audience. . . . In a real sense, then, Celie's quest involves the development of an understanding of an audience's essential role in Afro-American textual communication" (211–12).

9. In *Discourses of Desire* (chapter 3) Kauffman discusses at length the shifting gender identifications critics have placed on the book's author; in *Special Delivery* she reprises the "three-century debate" about this text's author (104–5). Nancy Miller argues strongly for a male author because she reads the letters as part of "a patrilineal line" in which "the textualization—hence glamorization—of female suffering around the male" is central ("The Text's Heroine" 49).

10. For Wall, the almost overwhelming unity pictured at the novel's end is "qualified" by the fact that the only reason the whole family can come together is because on the fourth of July whites do not demand the services of African Americans; this seeming unity derives, in part, from having in the whites "a common enemy" (92).

11. I am filling a gap here, imagining that Nettie has with her, on returning to the States, whatever letters she recently received from Celie; potentially these could be given to Celie.

6. John Updike's *S.*: Gender Play

1. "Writing as a woman" is not necessarily a feminist practice. Elizabeth Forsythe Hailey's *A Woman of Independent Means* is but one example of a female-authored epistolary novel without feminist underpinnings.

The letter-writing protagonist in this novel assertively conquers domestic and corporate difficulties, making herself a rich, mainstream purveyor of American patriarchal centrist values, but never questioning those values in any significant way. *A Woman of Independent Means* uses market-tested clichés of language and plot, rather than truly exploring or expressing a female's efforts at self-development or transformation.

2. Discussions of the stylistic differences between "masculine" and "feminine" communication abound. Essay collections such as Eisenstein and Jardine's *The Future of Difference,* Miller's *The Poetics of Gender,* and Showalter's *The New Feminist Criticism* provide various approaches to the topic.

3. For an article that tackles the latter crossover, see Elaine Showalter's "Critical Cross-Dressing," which analyzes the works of various male feminists, questioning motives and results of such practice. A recent collection of essays, *Men Writing the Feminine: Literature, Theory, and the Question of Gender,* edited by Thaïs Morgan, offers various perspectives on feminist theorizing as practiced by male scholars.

4. Discussions concerning plot as a manifestation of social ideology occur in many feminist books and articles. Susan Lanser's "Toward a Feminist Narratology," Susan Stanford Friedman's "Lyric Subversion of Narrative in Women's Writing: Virginia Woolf and the Tyranny of Plot," and Rachel Blau DuPlessis's *Writing Beyond the Ending: Narrative Strategies of Twentieth-Century Women Writers* are wonderful examples of this critical investigation.

5. Updike's "Scarlet Letter Trilogy" includes *A Month of Sundays, Roger's Version,* and *S.*

6. Also, perhaps aware of feminist writing about characteristics of *l'écriture féminine,* Updike has Sarah's writing acknowledge the importance of the gaps and disruptions between words. From the beginning of her voluminous writings, her prose is enlarged by the space and time it cannot but tries to incorporate: "The distance between us grows, even as my pen hesitates," she begins her first letter. When she continues, "the engines drone in the spaces between words" (3), one knows that words on a page cannot capture or conquer full experience. We see that she wants to explain herself, retain contact, fill empty space, in a kind of verbal hysteria that proliferates for a dozen pages. Updike gives similar body to at least one male writing protagonist. In *Roger's Version* the main character discovers much about his own repressed feelings through his typographical errors. Here the body (the typing hands) forces the writer to own thoughts and sensations he might otherwise suppress. We can see the use of such writing as a "feminine" characteristic—an opening of the self to understanding derived from the body as well as the mind.

7. The novel comes equipped with a twelve-page glossary of Sanskrit terms.

8. Perhaps what Updike is attempting to show here is the same "lesson" that Margaret Atwood finds emerging from *The Witches of Eastwick*—which she compares to *The Wizard of Oz*. The three female protagonists of *Witches* "go back, in the end, to the equivalent of Kansas—marriage, flat and gray maybe, but at least known" (40). That Sarah cannot imagine herself without romantic attachment to Myron or some male figure may simply show the dominant culture's ability to prevail.

7. Delettering: Responses to Agency in Jean Webster's *Daddy-Long-Legs*

1. Most of Webster's extant letters are held by the Vassar College Library.

2. It is a mark of popular fiction that little of its *popularity* depends on its form, says Morris Dickstein (47).

3. In an actual survey of all letter fiction ever written, one might find almost as many male epistolary characters as female, but many more of the memorable characters are female. This sounds horribly subjective, yet think about it: most of us can recall the Portuguese Nun, Pamela, Clarissa, Evelina, and, in more modern times, Celie (from *The Color Purple*) and Lee Smith's Ivy Rowe (from *Fair and Tender Ladies*). Males write letters in *Humphry Clinker,* and in *Les Liaisons dangereuses* both males and females correspond. But other men in letter fictions? Werther perhaps. More recently, Nick Bantock's Griffin? John Barth's *LETTERS* contains six male and one female epistolarian, but the only character created new for that novel is the woman—the males are recycled from earlier novels and hardly have the vibrancy of Germaine Pitt, a.k.a. Lady Amherst.

4. In *Discourses of Desire*, Kauffman points out that although earlier writers had experimented with the letter form and with writing from the female heroine's point of view, Ovid's *Heroides* was the first work to create distinctive personalities writing sequences of interrelated letters that told the woman's story from the woman's point of view (20). Kauffman credits Ovid with inventing the "genre of amorous epistolary discourse" (21).

5. A daddy longlegs is not a spider, I am relieved to tell you. Although the daddy longlegs is an arachnid, it belongs to the order *Phalangida* (spiders are in the order *Araneida*). According to *A Field Guide to Insects,* "Most [daddy longlegs] feed on dead insects or on plants." They do not produce either the silk or the venom that true spiders are known for (Borror and White 54). Whether Webster realized this distinction I cannot say, but she was an enthusiastic nature lover, so it is possible.

6. Webster herself worked for reform of orphanages and prisons and was a "drawing-room" socialist, according to the Simpsons (132). She sketched out her ideas for orphanage improvements in *Dear Enemy,* a second epistolary novel, published in 1915.

7. The play was extremely well attended, but reviewers had mixed reactions: the *Washington Post* celebrated the "deeper sighs of happiness and satisfaction" expressed by the audience at each of the play's four acts, but the play was termed a "slushy, smushy, rather nauseatingly sentimental, amateurish effort" when it toured in Saint Paul, Minnesota (Flandrau).

8. *Daddy Long Legs* was the first property Pickford produced with her own company. The film, as attested to by reviews in *Variety* and the *New York Times,* drew large crowds. Pickford's previous films, such as *Tess of the Storm Country* (1914), *The Poor Little Rich Girl* (1917), and *Rebecca of Sunnybrook Farm* (1917), established her as an appealing beleaguered child-woman.

9. Surely it was no accident that the Roxy Theatre's accompanying live stage show was "Modern Cinderella" (Hall 15). Why does each transformation of Webster's novel bring it closer to the modern versions of Cinderella, deauthorizing the heroine? Reading Louise Bernikow's work on various versions of the Cinderella story makes me think that Webster's novel lodges the "good mother" figure within the orphaned Jerusha herself; she helps herself to her future. (The figures of Fairy Godmother and Prince Charming also merge in the anonymous trustee—Jervis Pendleton.) The dramatic version and subsequent film adaptations remove this force, giving power more and more to luck and the "prince." That the Judy figure is less and less a writer symbolizes this shift. (The 1931 version was a Fox production, directed by Alfred Santell. One of the few extant prints is held by New York's Museum of Modern Art.)

10. With words, glances, and physical contact, the younger sister "woos" Edward Morgan. Molly Haskell reminds us that this was often Temple's role: "Generally, her flirtatiousness with her daddy figures was outdone, in precociousness, only by the patronizing way in which she treated contemporaries." She was "an ideal post-Production Code sex kitten, her attraction politely shrouded in the natural interplay of family feeling" (123).

8. Relettering: Upton Sinclair's *Another Pamela* Responds to Samuel Richardson's *Pamela*

1. In the last chapter of *Discourses of Desire,* Linda Kauffman presents an excellent discussion of *The Three Marias.* She summarizes its method by saying that the authors "revisit and revise the original nun's letters, cast-

ing them in a new light that illuminates their subsequent literary history" but also using the earlier text to prompt political, personal, and moral arguments germane to their own time and place (281–82).

2. Armstrong explains that "the explicitly female narrators of *Pamela, Evelina,* or *The Mysteries of Udolpho* are more effective in launching a political critique because their gender identifies them as having no claim to political power" (28–29).

3. Richardson presents Pamela's capitalizing on her charms as unconscious. An early response to Richardson's novel, Henry Fielding's 1741 *Shamela,* mocks the original's naiveté, for Shamela knows full well (or takes advice from other women on) what ploys and tactics will best capitalize on her attractiveness and net her marriage with the wealthy employer.

4. Perry makes clear that the growing concept of marriage for love provided more opportunity for crossing class boundaries through matrimony (58–59), but matrimony still was almost the only way for a woman to move up. Personal improvements could actually be a hazard to social advancement. Richardson's Pamela, in her opening letter, expresses the fear that "as my lady's goodness had put me to write and cast accounts, and made me a little expert at my needle, and otherwise qualified above my degree, it was not every family that could have found a place that your poor Pamela was fit for" (3).

5. Richardson's Pamela has permission to read books in the household to "improve" herself (5), is skilled at reading aloud to others (9), and is termed "well read" by her master (26), but she is not shown studying or recalling Biblical passages.

6. I had to chuckle when, looking up reviews of *Another Pamela,* I found a fine demonstration of woman's continuing role upholding morality, reforming recalcitrant or degenerate figures, and tempering (male) power with (female) sensibility. On the front page of the June 3, 1950, *Christian Science Monitor* in which appeared a review of *Another Pamela,* I read the following headline: "Eight Republican Senators Repudiate 'McCarthyism' "; the article explained that Margaret Chase Smith (the only female then in Congress) took the moral lead by presenting a "declaration of conscience" signed by herself and six other Republicans, objecting to Senator McCarthy's anticommunist tactics.

7. In *Highbrow/Lowbrow,* Lawrence W. Levine beautifully analyzes the ways in which notions of high and low culture have been constructed in the service of power maintenance for certain segments of the society. Toward the end of his study, he concludes that "we have in recent decades begun to move gradually but decisively away from the rigid, class-bound definitions of culture forged at the close of the nineteenth century" (255). Still, if we are to read well (books, other cultural productions, ourselves) we need to keep these lines of investigation open.

9. Remapping the Territory: Ana Castillo's *The Mixquiahuala Letters*

1. The novel was published in 1986 and won the 1987 American Book Award. Published originally by Bilingual Press, the book is now more widely available in a paperback edition from Doubleday.

2. One of the strongest statements I have ever read about reading strategies comes from Patrocinio P. Schweickart, discussing feminist approaches. "The point is not merely to interpret literature in various ways; the point is to *change the world*. We cannot afford to ignore the activity of reading, for it is here that literature is realized as *praxis*. Literature acts on the world by acting on its readers." Reading and writing are critical aspects of "interpreting the world in order to change it" (39).

3. Although Teresa's primary community for her writing is herself and her best friend, the letters' content mentions other outlets. Because both Teresa and Alicia actively produce art (Teresa teaches and writes, although she does not mention publishing; Alicia meets with success as a visual artist), their artistic products can influence others. Teresa also self-consciously and humorously notes the possibility of others reading the letters (88).

4. Given Alicia's art, Castillo presumes that nonverbal and verbal processes can yield new insight. Alicia's one-woman exhibit (described by Teresa in letter 34, the final letter for "the conformist" reader, but absent for "the cynic" and "the quixotic") contains a project titled *La casita*—mixed media pieces that analyze stereotypes of domestic women (118).

5. Norma Alarcón analyzes the way this distancing is linked to the emotions surrounding "romantic love" that "cannot be spoken of, intimately or directly" (103).

6. Spacks contends that most epistolary novels have "reinforced the status quo by assuming it. Declaring in their reliance on epistolary form their concern only with 'private' matters, women novelists apparently accepted the necessity of the system under which they suffered" (75). Janet G. Altman also finds that little epistolary fiction of the past "overtly challenged the privilege accorded to male conqueror figures" ("Graffigny's Epistemology" 173). Like Jane Austen, whose epistolary Lady Susan is a "female character capable of play and mastery through play" (Spacks 75), Castillo invents a heroine who uses word play and verbal mastery to explore a range of public and private issues.

7. Note, however, that fax machines, e-mail, and computers still often use the basic letter form. One difference is the speed of the letter's transmission. Video and audio recording devices certainly depart radically from the letter format, especially the first, which (especially when edited) can become nonlinear and contains different ways of reflecting on or analyzing its material.

8. Maranda proposes that "semantic charters condition our thoughts and emotions. They are culture specific networks that we internalize as we undergo the process of socialization" and "have an inertia and a momentum of their own" (qtd. in Alarcón, 106).

10. Epistolary Responses to the Critical Act

1. Virginia Woolf's *Three Guineas,* published in 1938, presents an early application of letters to critical work. At first this text may not appear epistolary—no dates or headings or formal address begin any of its three parts; no signatures close them; the text even includes footnotes. Nevertheless, the text makes clear that Woolf is responding to a letter inquiry concerning ways to avoid wars, and consistent references to her own work as letters and to others' letters reinforce the understanding that, indeed, this is an epistolary work. Woolf's three letters move between the small scale and the large, between the privacy traditionally associated with women's letters and the publicity associated with (male) political polemic.

2. Miller does cite *This Bridge Called My Back,* in which Anzaldúa's "Letter" first appeared, but she does not bring up the letter itself at this point. In recollecting a recent course she taught, she mentions that this piece was on the syllabus (*Getting Personal* 7). Another feminist critic interested in personal criticism, Diane Freedman, specifically mentions letters and diaries as forms available to critics. In *An Alchemy of Genres: Cross-Genre Writing by American Feminist Poet-Critics,* she extols the crossing of genres and disciplines in critical writing, particularly praising the work of feminist poet-critics who intertwine "poetry, autobiography, testimony, literary interpretation, and politics with women's so-called private genres (diary, letter), all bearing on and bearing out issues of gender, race, class, and sexuality" (97).

3. In the May 1990 issue of *PMLA* devoted to the special topic of "The Politics of Critical Language," I was pleased to see "An Exchange of Letters between Emil Staiger and Martin Heidegger" included as part of an article titled "A 1951 Dialogue on Interpretation: Emil Staiger, Martin Heidegger, Leo Spitzer." However, these letters are not the bulk of the article (they are safely sandwiched between other essayistic prose), and the journal's table of contents gives no hint of their existence.

4. Perhaps now that almost no holds bar any subject matter, pushing on the limits of the possible may have more to do with form than content. The valuing of innovation is evident in a *College Composition and Communication* special issue devoted to "Personal and Innovative Writing," published in February 1992. Although none of the essays included is epistolary, all of them experiment with other forms of the essay.

5. Riffaterre's comment was overheard at the School of Criticism and Theory, following a particularly heated floor discussion of a colloquium paper presented by Nancy Miller in July of 1988.

6. Whether Fay Weldon really has a niece named Alice does not matter here; the fiction of an actual blood relative I take as stand-in for the connection to the next generation imagined by any teacher or critical writer.

7. In further elaboration both of writing's uncertainty and of its concomitant, contradictory materiality, Derrida also points out (in "Envois") that all writing is subject to intervention, misdirection, and, by implication, misinterpretation. For Derrida, the possibility that the letter can be lost or intercepted means that "in advance it is intercepted." He finds, however, that everyone denies that misdirection is always the fate of texts, especially "the guardians of the letter" who range from mail carriers to "the literature people" (51). Then, a few pages later he plays against this: "I repeat, my love: *for you*. I write for you and speak only to you. . . . I am writing it to you, you are touching it, you are touching the card, my signature, the body of my name, me" (73).

8. Wideman's *Brothers & Keepers* was published in 1984, Barnet published his edition of Esteban Montejo's *Autobiography of a Runaway Slave (Biografía de un Cimarrón)* in 1966 (trans. Jocasta Innes, 1968), and Douglass first published "The Heroic Slave" serially in his own newspaper in 1853 and then in *Autographs for Freedom,* a collection of poetry and prose.

9. Elaine Hedges's "The Needle or the Pen: The Literary Rediscovery of Women's Textile Work," her "Hearts and Hands: The Influence of Women & Quilts on American Society," and Elaine Showalter's "Piecing and Writing" provide excellent analyses and histories of quilts-as-texts. Showalter's recent *Sister's Choice: Tradition and Change in American Women's Writing* includes an essay, "Common Threads," that uses quilting as a metaphor for American literature as a body of work. Also see Cheryl Torsney and Judy Elsley's *Quilt Culture: Tracing the Pattern.*

Works Cited

"A 1951 Dialogue on Interpretation: Emil Staiger, Martin Heidegger, Leo Spitzer." Trans. Sibylle Staiger and Wolfgang Spitzer. *PMLA* 105 (1990): 409–36.

Abbandonato, Linda. " 'A View from "Elsewhere" ': Subversive Sexuality and the Rewriting of the Heroine's Story in *The Color Purple*." *PMLA* 106 (1991): 1106–15.

Alarcón, Norma. "The Sardonic Powers of the Erotic in the Work of Ana Castillo." *Breaking Boundaries: Latina Writing and Critical Readings*. Eds. Asunción Horno-Delgado, Eliana Ortega, Nina M. Scott, and Nancy Saporta Steinbach. Amherst: U of Massachusetts P, 1989.

Aldridge, John W. *The American Novel and the Way We Live Now*. New York: Oxford UP, 1983.

Altman, Janet Gurkin. *Epistolarity: Approaches to a Form*. Columbus: Ohio State UP, 1982.

———. "Graffigny's Epistemology and the Emergence of Third-World Ideology." *Writing the Female Voice: Essays on Epistolary Literature*. Ed. Elizabeth C. Goldsmith. Boston: Northeastern UP, 1989. 172–202.

Rev. of *Another Pamela*, by Upton Sinclair. *New Yorker* 20 May 1950: 119.

Anzaldúa, Gloria. "Speaking in Tongues: A Letter to Third World Women Writers." *This Bridge Called My Back: Writings by Radical Women of Color*. Eds. Cherríe Moraga and Gloria Anzaldúa. New York: Kitchen Table: Women of Color P, 1981. 165–74.

Armstrong, Nancy. *Desire and Domestic Fiction: A Political History of the Novel*. New York: Oxford UP, 1987.

Atkins, G. Douglas. *Estranging the Familiar: Toward a Revitalized Critical Writing*. Athens: U of Georgia P, 1992.

Atwood, Margaret. "Wondering What It's Like to Be a Woman." Rev. of *The Witches of Eastwick*, by John Updike. *The New York Times Book Review* 13 May 1984: 1, 40.

Austin, J. L. *How to Do Things With Words.* New York: Oxford UP, 1962.

Awkward, Michael. "A Circle of Sisters." Diss. University of Pennsylvania, 1986.

Babb, Valerie. "*The Color Purple:* Writing to Undo What Writing Has Done." *Phylon* 47 (1986): 107–16.

Bakhtin, Mikhail. *The Dialogic Imagination: Four Essays.* Ed. Michael Holquist. Trans. Caryl Emerson and Michael Holquist. Austin: U of Texas P, 1981.

Bantock, Nick. *The Golden Mean: In Which the Extraordinary Correspondence of Griffin & Sabine Concludes.* San Francisco: Chronicle Books, 1993.

———. *Griffin & Sabine: An Extraordinary Correspondence.* San Francisco: Chronicle Books, 1991.

———. *Sabine's Notebook: In Which the Extraordinary Correspondence of Griffin & Sabine Continues.* San Francisco: Chronicle Books, 1992.

Barth, John. *The Friday Book.* New York: Putnam's, 1984.

———. *LETTERS: A Novel.* New York: Putnam's, 1979.

———. "The Literature of Exhaustion." *The Atlantic Monthly* Aug. 1967: 29–34.

———. "The Literature of Replenishment." *The Atlantic Monthly* Jan. 1980: 65–71.

Barthes, Roland. *The Pleasure of the Text.* Trans. Richard Miller. New York: Hill and Wang, 1975.

Bateson, Mary Catherine. *Composing A Life.* New York: Plume-Penguin, 1990.

Behn, Aphra. *Love-Letters Between a Nobleman and His Sister.* 1689. Ed. Janet Todd. (*Complete Works of Aphra Behn,* vol. 2.) Columbus: Ohio State UP, 1993.

Benstock, Shari. *Textualizing the Feminine: On the Limits of Genre.* Norman: U of Oklahoma P, 1991.

Berg, Elizabeth. "Iconoclastic Moments: Reading the *Sonnets for Helene,* Writing the *Portuguese Letters.*" *The Poetics of Gender.* Ed. Nancy K. Miller. New York: Columbia UP, 1986. 208–21.

Bernikow, Louise. *Among Women.* New York: Harmony Books, 1980.

Bleich, David. *Subjective Criticism.* Baltimore: Johns Hopkins UP, 1978.

Bloodsworth, William, Jr. *Upton Sinclair.* Boston: Twayne, 1977.

Booth, Wayne. *The Rhetoric of Fiction.* 2nd ed. Chicago: U of Chicago P, 1983.

Bordwell, David. "Classical Narration." *The Classical Hollywood Cinema: Film Style and Mode of Production to 1960.* Eds. David Bordwell, Janet Staiger, and Kristin Thompson. New York: Columbia UP, 1985. 24–41.

Borges, Jorge Luis. "Pierre Menard, Author of the *Quixote.* Trans. James E. Irby. *Labyrinths: Selected Stories & Other Writings* [of Borges].

Eds. Donal A. Yates and James E. Irby. New York: New Directions, 1962. 36–49.

Borror, Donald J., and Richard E. White. *A Field Guide to the Insects of America North of Mexico.* Boston: Houghton Mifflin, 1970.

Bradbury, Richard. "Postmodernism and Barth and the Present State of Fiction." *Critical Quarterly* 32 (1990): 60–72.

Brenner, Gerry. "More than a Reader's Response: A Letter to 'De Old True Huck.' " *Journal of Narrative Technique* 20 (1990): 221–34.

Brown, Homer Obed. "The Errant Letter and the Whispering Gallery." *Genre* 10 (1977): 573–99.

Broyard, Anatole. "Letters from the Ashram." Rev. of *S.,* by John Updike. *The New York Times Book Review* 13 March 1988: 7.

Burke, Jacqueline. " 'Mother I Can Do it Myself!': The Self-Sufficient Heroine in Popular Girl's Fiction." *Women's Studies* 6 (1970): 187–203.

Byatt, A. S. *Possession: A Romance.* New York: Random House, 1990.

Carmichael, Thomas. "John Barth's *LETTERS:* History, Representation and Postmodernism." *Mosaic: A Journal for the Interdisciplinary Study of Literature* 21 (1988): 65–72.

Castillo, Ana. *The Mixquiahuala Letters.* Binghamton, N.Y.: Bilingual P, 1986.

Castle, Terry. *Clarissa's Ciphers: Meaning & Disruption in Richardson's Clarissa.* Ithaca: Cornell UP, 1982.

Caws, Mary Ann. Classroom Discussion 23 June 1988 and 26 July 1988. Problematics of Personal Criticism. School of Criticism and Theory. Dartmouth College.

Cheung, King-Kok. " 'Don't Tell': Imposed Silences in *The Color Purple* and *The Woman Warrior." PMLA* 103 (1988): 162–74.

Chodorow, Nancy. *The Reproduction of Mothering: Psychoanalysis and the Sociology of Gender.* Berkeley: U of California P, 1978.

Christian, Barbara T. "Layered Rhythms: Virginia Woolf and Toni Morrison." *Modern Fiction Studies* 39 (1993): 483–500.

Cixous, Hélène. "The Laugh of the Medusa." Trans. Keith Cohen and Paula Cohen. *Signs* 1 (1976): 875–93.

———. "Sorties: Out and Out: Attacks/Ways Out/Forays." *The Newly Born Woman.* Hélène Cixous and Catherine Clément. Trans. Betsy Wing. Intro. Sandra M. Gilbert. Minneapolis: U of Minnesota P, 1986. 63–132.

Coultrap-McQuin, Susan. *Doing Literary Business: American Women Writers in the Nineteenth Century.* Chapel Hill: U of North Carolina P, 1990.

Curly Top. Dir. Irving Cummings. With Shirley Temple. Fox, 1935.

Daddy Long Legs. Dir. Marshall Neilen. With Mary Pickford. Mary Pickford Co., 1919.

Daddy Long Legs. Dir. Alfred Santell. With Janet Gaynor and Warner Baxter. Fox, 1931.

Daddy Long Legs. Dir. Jean Negulesco. With Fred Astaire and Leslie Caron. Fox, 1955.

Daddy Long Legs. Dir. Bunker Jenkins in association with Nippon Herald. Animated. 3B Production, 1984.

Rev. of *Daddy Long Legs. Variety* 16 May 1919: 54.

Rev. of *Daddy Long Legs. Variety* 9 June 1931: 18.

Rev. of *Daddy Long Legs. Washington Post* 24 Feb. 1914: 5.

Davis, Lennard. *Factual Fictions: The Origins of the English Novel.* New York: Columbia UP, 1983.

Day, Robert Adams. *Told in Letters: Epistolary Fiction Before Richardson.* Ann Arbor: U of Michigan P, 1966.

Derrida, Jacques. "Envois." *The Post Card: From Socrates to Freud and Beyond.* Trans. Alan Bass. Chicago: U of Chicago P, 1987.

———. *Of Grammatology.* Trans. Gayatri Chakravorty Spivak. Baltimore: Johns Hopkins UP, 1974.

Dickstein, Morris. "Popular Fiction and Critical Values: The Novel as a Challenge to Literary History." *Reconstructing American Literary History.* Ed. Sacvan Bercovitch. Cambridge: Harvard UP, 1986. 29–66.

DuPlessis, Rachel Blau. *Writing Beyond the Ending: Narrative Strategies of Twentieth-Century Women Writers.* Bloomington: Indiana UP, 1985.

DuPlessis, Rachel Blau, and Members of Workshop 9. "For the Etruscans: Sexual Difference and Artistic Production—The Debate Over a Female Aesthetic." *The Future of Difference.* Eds. Hester Eisenstein and Alice Jardine. New Brunswick: Rutgers UP, 1985. 128–56.

Edwards, Thomas R. "A Novel of Correspondences." Rev. of *LETTERS,* by John Barth. *The New York Times Book Review* 30 Sept. 1980: 32–33.

Eisenstein, Hester, and Alice Jardine, eds. *The Future of Difference.* New Brunswick: Rutgers UP, 1985.

Elson, Ruth Miller. *Myths and Mores in American Best Sellers 1865–1965.* New York: Garland, 1985.

Federman, Raymond. "Surfiction—Four Propositions in Form of an Introduction." *Surfiction: Fiction Now . . . and Tomorrow.* Ed. Raymond Federman. Chicago: Swallow, 1975. 5–15.

Fetterley, Judith. "Reading about Reading: 'A Jury of Her Peers,' 'The Murders in the Rue Morgue,' and 'The Yellow Wallpaper.' " *Gender and Reading: Essays on Readers, Texts, and Contexts.* Eds. Elizabeth A. Flynn and Patrocinio P. Schweickart. Baltimore: Johns Hopkins UP, 1986. 147–64.

———. *The Resisting Reader: A Feminist Approach to American Fiction.* Bloomington: Indiana UP, 1978.

Fielding, Henry. *Shamela.* In *Joseph Andrews and Shamela.* 1741. Boston: Houghton Mifflin, 1961. 299–370.

Fifer, Elizabeth. "The Dialect & Letters of *The Color Purple.*" *Contemporary American Women Writers: Narrative Strategies.* Eds. Catherine Rainwater and William J. Scheick. Lexington: U of Kentucky P, 1985. 155–65.

Fiske, John. *Reading the Popular.* Boston: Unwin Hyman, 1989.

Flandrau, C. M. Rev. of *Daddy Long Legs* [stage version], by Jean Webster. *St. Paul Pioneer Press* 11 October 1915: n.p.

Foster, Dennis A. *Confession and Complicity in Narrative.* Cambridge: Cambridge UP, 1987.

Freedman, Diane P. *An Alchemy of Genres: Cross-Genre Writing by American Feminist Poet-Critics.* Charlottesville: UP of Virginia, 1992.

Freedman, Diane P., Olivia Frey, and Frances Murphy Zauhar, eds. *The Intimate Critique: Autobiographical Literary Criticism.* Durham: Duke UP, 1993.

Friedman, Susan Stanford. "Creativity and the Childbirth Metaphor: Gender Difference in Literary Discourse." *Feminist Studies* 13 (1987): 49–82.

———. "Lyric Subversion of Narrative in Women's Writing: Virginia Woolf and the Tyranny of Plot." *Reading Narrative: Form, Ethics, Ideology.* Ed. James Phelan. Columbus: Ohio State UP, 1989. 162–85.

Frye, Joanne S. *Living Stories, Telling Lives: Women and the Novel in Contemporary Experience.* Ann Arbor: U of Michigan P, 1986.

Gates, Henry Louis, Jr. "Color Me Zora: Alice Walker's (Re)Writing of the Speakerly Text." *The Signifying Monkey: A Theory of African-American Literary Criticism.* New York: Oxford UP, 1988. 239–58.

———. Introduction. *The Signifying Monkey: A Theory of African-American Literary Criticism.* New York: Oxford UP, 1988. ix–xxviii.

Gilman, Richard. "The Witches of Eastwick." Rev. of *S.,* by John Updike. *The New Republic* 13 June 1988: 39–41.

Ginzburg, Natalia. *The City and the House.* Trans. Dick Davis. Manchester: Carcanet, 1986.

Goldsmith, Elizabeth. Introduction. *Writing the Female Voice: Essays on Epistolary Literature.* Boston: Northeastern UP, 1989. vii–xiii.

Gray, Paul. "Karma in the Sunbelt." Rev. of *S.,* by John Updike. *Time* 29 February 1988: 98.

Greiner, Donald J. "Body and Soul: John Updike and *The Scarlet Letter.*" *Journal of Modern Literature* 15 (1989): 475–95.

Guilleragues, Gabriel-Joseph de Lavergne de. *Lettres Portugaises.* 1669. *Lettres Portugaises, Valentins et autres oeuvres de Guilleragues.* Ed. F. Deloffre et J. Rougeot. Paris: Editions Garniers Frères. 1962.

Gussow, Adam. Rev. of *The Color Purple,* by Alice Walker. *Chicago Review* 34 (1983): 124–26.

Hailey, Elizabeth Forsythe. *A Woman of Independent Means.* New York: Avon, 1978.

Hall, Mordaunt Hall. "The Screen: Charm and Sentiment." Rev. of *Daddy Long Legs. New York Times* 6 June 1931: 15.

Hansen, Miriam. *Babel and Babylon: Spectatorship in American Silent Film.* Cambridge: Harvard UP, 1991.

Hardy, Barbara. *Tellers and Listeners: The Narrative Imagination.* London: Athlone P, 1975.

Harriman, Lee. *The Dublin Letters.* New York: Ives Washburn, 1931.

Harris, Charles B. *Passionate Virtuosity: The Fiction of John Barth.* Urbana: U of Illinois P, 1983.

Harris, Leon. *Upton Sinclair: American Rebel.* New York: Thomas Y. Crowell, 1975.

Harris, Mark. *Lying in Bed.* New York: McGraw Hill, 1984.

———. *Wake Up, Stupid.* New York: Knopf, 1959.

Harris, Trudier. "On *The Color Purple,* Stereotypes, and Silence." *Black American Literature Forum* 18 (1984): 155–61.

Hart, James D. *The Popular Book: A History of America's Literary Taste.* Berkeley: U of California P, 1961.

Haskell, Mollie. *From Reverence to Rape: The Treatment of Women in the Movies.* Middlesex: Penguin, 1974.

Hawkins, Harriet. *Classics and Trash: Traditions and Taboos in High Literature and Popular Modern Genres.* Toronto: U of Toronto P, 1990.

Hedges, Elaine. "Hearts and Hands: The Influence of Women & Quilts on American Society." *Hearts and Hands: The Influence of Women and Quilts on American Society.* Eds. Pat Ferrero, Elaine Hedges, and Julie Silber. San Francisco: The Quilt Digest P, 1987. 11–97.

———. "The Needle or the Pen: The Literary Rediscovery of Women's Textile Work." *Tradition and the Talents of Women.* Ed. Florence Howe. Urbana: U of Illinois P, 1991. 338–64.

Heilbrun, Carolyn G. "Critical Response II: A Response to Writing and Sexual Difference." *Writing and Sexual Difference.* Ed. Elizabeth Abel. Chicago: U of Chicago P, 1982. 291–97.

———. *Writing a Woman's Life.* New York: Ballantine, 1988.

Henderson, Mae Gwendolyn. "*The Color Purple:* Revisions and Redefinitions." *Sage* 2 (1985): 14–18.

———. "Speaking in Tongues: Dialogics, Dialectics, and the Black Woman Writer's Literary Tradition." *Reading Black, Reading Feminist: A Critical Anthology.* Ed. Henry Louis Gates, Jr. New York: Meridian-Penguin, 1990. 116–42.

Hicks, Granville. "Mr. Sinclair's Pamela." Rev. of *Another Pamela,* by Upton Sinclair. *New York Times Book Review* 23 April 1950: 30.

Hill, Dorothy. "An Interview with Lee Smith." *The Southern Quarterly* 28 (1990): 5–19.

———. *Lee Smith.* New York: Twayne, 1992.

Hite, Molly. *The Other Side of the Story: Structures and Strategies of Contemporary Narrative.* Ithaca: Cornell UP, 1989.

———. "Romance, Marginality, Matrilineage: *The Color Purple.*" *The Other Side of the Story: Structures and Strategies of Contemporary Feminist Narrative.* Ithaca: Cornell UP, 1989. 103–26.

Hoffman, Frank W., and William G. Bailey. *Arts and Entertainment Fads.* New York: Haworth P, 1990.

Holland, Norman. "Re-covering 'The Purloined Letter': Reading as a Personal Transaction." 1980. *Contemporary Literary Criticism.* Ed. Robert Con Davis. New York: Longman, 1986. 363–75.

hooks, bell. "Writing the Subject: Reading *The Color Purple.*" *Reading Black, Reading Feminist.* Ed. Henry Louis Gates, Jr. New York: Meridian: 1990. 454–70.

Howe, Susan. *My Emily Dickinson.* Berkeley: North Atlantic Books, 1985.

Hutcheon, Linda. "Historiographic Metafiction: Parody and the Intertextuality of History." *Intertextuality and Contemporary American Fiction.* Eds. Patrick O'Donnell and Robert Con Davis. Baltimore: Johns Hopkins UP, 1989. 3–32.

Irigaray, Luce. *Speculum of the Other Woman.* Trans. Gillian C. Gill. Ithaca, New York: Cornell UP, 1974.

Iser, Wolfgang. *The Act of Reading: A Theory of Aesthetic Response.* Baltimore: Johns Hopkins UP, 1978.

Jacobus, Mary. *Reading Woman: Essays in Feminist Criticism.* New York: Columbia UP, 1986.

Jameson, Fredric. *The Political Unconscious: Narrative as a Socially Symbolic Act.* Ithaca, New York: Cornell UP, 1981.

Jost, François. "Le Roman épistolaire et la technique narrative au xviiie siècle." *Comparative Studies* 3 (1966): 397–427.

Kady Daughter of Ann Daughter of Kate Daughter of Anna and Celeste West. "We Write Letters." *Words in Our Pockets: The Feminist Writers Guild Handbook on How to Gain Power, Get Published & Get Paid.* Paradise, CA: Dustbooks, 1987. 211–17.

Kakutani, Michiko. "Updike's Struggle to Portray Women." Rev. of *S.,* by John Updike. *New York Times* 5 May 1988: C29.

Kauffman, Linda S. *Discourses of Desire: Gender, Genre, and Epistolary Fictions.* Ithaca: Cornell UP, 1986.

———. "The Long Goodbye: Against Personal Testimony, or an Infant Grifter Grows Up." *American Feminist Thought at Century's End: A Reader.* Ed. Linda S. Kauffman. Cambridge: Blackwell, 1993. 258–77.

——. *Special Delivery: Epistolary Modes in Modern Fiction.* Chicago: U of Chicago P, 1992.

Kaveney, Roz. "In the South." Rev. of *Oral History, Fair and Tender Ladies,* and *Family Linen,* by Lee Smith. *Times Literary Supplement* 21 July 1989: 803.

Kerkhoff, Ingrid. "Wives, Blue Blood Ladies, and Rebel Girls: A Closer Look at Upton Sinclair's Females." *Upton Sinclair: Literature and Social Reform.* Ed. Dieter Herms. Frankfurt am Main: Peter Lang, 1990. 176–94.

Kinsella, W. P. "Left Behind on Blue Star Mountain." Rev. of *Fair and Tender Ladies,* by Lee Smith. *The New York Times Book Review* 18 Sept. 1988: 9.

Koppelman, Susan. "Excerpts from Letters to Friends." *The Intimate Critique: Autobiographical Literary Criticism.* Eds. Diane P. Freedman, Olivia Frey, and Frances Murphy Zauhar. Durham, N. C.: Duke UP, 1993. 75–79.

Kristeva, Julia. "Stabat Mater." 1974. *The Kristeva Reader.* Ed. Toril Moi. New York: Columbia UP, 1986. 160–86.

Lampkin, Loretta. "An Interview with John Barth." *Contemporary Literature* 29 (1988): 485–97.

Lanser, Susan Sniader. *Fictions of Authority: Women Writers and Narrative Voice.* Ithaca: Cornell UP, 1992.

——. *The Narrative Act: Point of View in Prose Fiction.* Princeton: Princeton UP, 1981.

——. "Toward a Feminist Narratology." *Style* 20 (1986): 341–63.

Lardner, Ring. *You Know Me Al: A Busher's Letters.* 1916. Cleveland: World Publishing, 1945. New York: Macmillan, 1987.

Lawhn, J. Luna. Rev. of *The Mixquiahuala Letters,* by Ana Castillo. *Choice* 24 (1987): 1392.

Leonard, John. "Bad-Boy Books." *Ms.* January/February 1989: 124, 126.

Levine, Lawrence W. *Highbrow/Lowbrow: The Emergence of Cultural Hierarchy in America.* Cambridge: Harvard UP, 1988.

London, Jack, and Anna Strunsky. *The Kempoton-Wace Letters.* New York: Macmillan, 1903.

Lorde, Audre. "Poetry is Not a Luxury." 1977. *The Future of Difference.* Eds. Hester Eisenstein and Alice Jardine. 1980. New Brunswick, N.J.: Rutgers UP, 1985. 125–27.

Lurie, Alison. "The Woman Who Rode Away." Rev. of *Trust Me: Short Stories* and *S.,* by John Updike. *The New York Review of Books* 12 May 1988: 3–4.

Lydon, Mary. "Foucault and Feminism: A Romance of Many Dimensions." *Feminism & Foucault: Reflections on Resistance.* Eds. Irene Diamond and Lee Quinby. Boston: Northeastern UP, 1988. 135–47.

MacArthur, Elizabeth J. *Extravagant Narratives: Closure and Dynamics in the Epistolary Form.* Princeton: Princeton UP, 1990.

MacLean, Gerald M. "Citing the Subject." *Gender & Theory: Dialogues on Feminist Criticism.* Ed. Linda Kauffman. Oxford: Basil Blackwell, 1989. 140–57.

Maranda, Pierre. "The Dialectic of Metaphor: An Anthropological Essay on Hermeneutics." *The Reader in the Text: Essays on Audience and Interpretation.* Eds. Susan R. Suleiman and Inge Corsman. Princeton: Princeton UP, 1980. 183–204.

May, Barbara Dale. Rev. of *The Mixquiahuala Letters,* by Ana Castillo. *Hispania* 71 (1988): 313–14.

McDowell, Deborah. " 'The Changing Same': Generational Connections and Black Women Novelists." *New Literary History* 18 (1987): 281–302.

McMullen, Kim. "The Fiction of Correspondence: *LETTERS* and History." *Modern Fiction Studies* 36 (1990): 405–20.

Miller, Nancy K. "Arachnologies: The Woman, The Text, and The Critic." *The Poetics of Gender.* Ed. Nancy K. Miller. New York: Columbia UP, 1986. 270–96.

———. "Changing the Subject: Authorship, Writing, and the Reader." *Feminist Studies/Critical Studies.* Ed. Teresa de Lauretis. Bloomington: Indiana UP, 1986. 102–20.

———. *Getting Personal: Feminist Occasions and Other Autobiographical Acts.* New York: Routledge, 1991.

———. *The Heroine's Text: Readings in the French and English Novel, 1722–1782.* New York: Columbia UP, 1980.

———. "The Text's Heroine: A Feminist Critic and Her Fictions." *Diacritics* 12 (1982): 48–53.

Rev. of *The Mixquiahuala Letters,* by Ana Castillo. *Rocky Mountain Review of Language and Literature* 41 (1987): 127–28.

Morgan, Thaïs, ed. *Men Writing the Feminine: Literature, Theory, and the Question of Genders.* Albany: State U of New York P, 1994.

Newton, Nancy A. "Mermaids and Minotaurs in Academe: Notes of a Hispanist on Sexuality, Ideology, and Game Playing." *The Journal of the Midwest Modern Language Association* 22 (1989): 23–35.

O'Donnell, Patrick. *Passionate Doubts: Designs of Interpretation in Contemporary American Fiction.* Iowa City: U of Iowa P, 1986.

O'Donnell, Patrick, and Robert C. Davis. Introduction. *Intertextuality and Contemporary American Fiction.* Baltimore: Johns Hopkins UP, 1989. ix–xxii.

O'Hara, John. *Pal Joey.* 1939. New York: Vintage, 1983.

Ortega, Eliana, and Nancy Saporta Sternbach "At the Threshold of the Unnamed: Latina Literary Discourse in the Eighties." *Breaking Boundaries: Latina Writing and Critical Readings*. Eds. Asunción Horno-Delgado, Eliana Ortega, Nina M. Scott, and Nancy Saporta Steinbach. Amherst: U of Massachusetts P, 1989. 2–23.

Ostriker, Alicia. *Writing Like a Woman*. Ann Arbor: U of Michigan P, 1983.

Oz, Amos. *The Black Box*. 1987. Trans. Nicholas de Lange. San Diego: Harcourt Brace Jovanovich, 1988.

Patai, Daphne. "Sick and Tired of Scholar's Nouveau Solipsism." *Chronicle of Higher Education* 23 February 1994: A52.

Perry, Ruth. *Women, Letters, and the Novel*. New York: AMS Press, 1980.

Poulet, Georges. "Criticism and the Experience of Interiority." *Reader-Response Criticism: From Formalism to Post-Structuralism*. Ed. Jane P. Tompkins. Baltimore: Johns Hopkins UP, 1980. 41–49. Rpt. from *The Structuralist Controversy: The Language of Criticism and the Sciences of Man*. Eds. Richard A. Macksey and Eugenio Donato. Baltimore: Johns Hopkins UP, 1972. 56–72.

Randall, Bob. *The Fan*. New York: Warner Books-Random House, 1977.

Richardson, Samuel. *Pamela, or Virtue Rewarded*. 1740. New York: W. W. Norton, 1958.

Robinson, Douglas. "Dear Harold." *New Literary History* 20 (1988): 239–50.

Roemer, Marjorie Godlin. "The Paradigmatic Mind: John Barth's *LETTERS*." *Twentieth Century Literature* 33 (1987): 38–50.

Romine, Dannye. "This Love Story is Even Better 2nd Time Around." *The Charlotte Observer* 13 Jan. 1991: 5C.

Ross, Daniel W. "Celie in the Looking Glass: The Desire for Selfhood in *The Color Purple*." *Modern Fiction Studies* 34 (1988): 69–84.

Sacks, Karen. "Engels Revisited: Women, the Organization of Production, and Private Property." *Woman, Culture, and Society*. Eds. Michelle Zimbalist Rosaldo and Louise Lamphere. Stanford: Stanford UP, 1974. 207–22.

Said, Edward. *Beginnings: Intention & Method*. 1975. New York: Columbia UP, 1985.

Schmitz, Neil. "Barth on Barth." Rev. of *LETTERS*, by John Barth. *Partisan Review* 48 (1981): 320–22.

Schulz, Max F. *The Muses of John Barth: Tradition and Metafiction from* Lost in the Funhouse *to* The Tidewater Tales. Baltimore: Johns Hopkins P, 1990.

Schweickart, Patrocinio. "Reading Ourselves: Toward a Feminist Theory of Reading. *Gender and Reading: Essays on Readers, Texts, and Contexts.* Eds. Elizabeth A. Flynn and Patrocinio P. Schweickart. Baltimore: Johns Hopkins UP, 1986. 31–62.

Showalter, Elaine. "Critical Cross-Dressing, Male Feminists and the Woman of the Year." *Men in Feminism.* Rpt. from *Raritan* Fall 1983.

———. "Feminist Criticism in the Wilderness." *The New Feminist Criticism: Essays on Women, Literature & Theory.* Ed. Elaine Showalter. New York: Pantheon, 1985. 243–70.

———. "Piecing and Writing." *The Poetics of Gender.* Ed. Nancy K. Miller. New York: Columbia UP, 1986. 222–47.

———. *Sister's Choice: Tradition and Change in American Women's Writing.* Oxford: Oxford UP-Clarendon P, 1991.

Simpson, Alan, and Mary Simpson, with Ralph Connor. *Jean Webster, Storyteller.* N.p.: Tymor Assoc., 1984.

Sinclair, Upton. *Affectionately, Eve.* New York: Twayne, 1961.

———. *Another Pamela, or Virtue Still Rewarded.* New York: Viking, 1950.

———. *The Autobiography of Upton Sinclair.* New York: Harcourt, Brace & World, 1962.

Smith, Dinitra. " 'Celie, You a Tree.' " Rev. of *The Color Purple,* by Alice Walker. *The Nation* 4 Sept. 1982: 181–83.

Smith, Lee. *Fair and Tender Ladies.* 1988. New York: Ballantine, 1989.

———. *Family Linen.* New York: Putnam, 1985.

———. *Oral History.* New York: Putnam, 1983.

Smith, Starr. Rev. of *Fair and Tender Ladies,* by Lee Smith. *Library Journal* 15 (1988): 95.

Sorrentino, Gilbert. *Mulligan Stew.* New York: Grove, 1979.

Spacks, Patricia Meyer. "Female Resources: Epistles, Plot, and Power." *Writing the Female Voice: Essays on Epistolary Literature.* Ed. Elizabeth Goldsmith. Boston: Northeastern UP, 1989. 63–76.

Spiegelman, Willard. "Ornery Ivy, Appalachian Heroine." Rev. of *Fair and Tender Ladies,* by Lee Smith. *Wall Street Journal* 28 Nov. 1988: A11.

Spelman, Elizabeth V. *Inessential Woman: Problems of Exclusion in Feminist Thought.* Boston: Beacon, 1988.

Stepto, Robert. "Let Me Tell Your Story: Fraternal Authorship in Narratives of Slavery, Revolt, and Incarceration—Douglass, Montejo, and Wideman." Public Lecture. School of Criticism and Theory. Dartmouth College. Hanover, N. H., 5 July 1988.

Tavormina, M. Teresa. "Dressing the Spirit: Clothworking and Language in *The Color Purple.*" *Journal of Narrative Technique* 16 (1986): 220–30.

Tompkins, Jane. "Me and My Shadow." *Gender and Theory: Dialogues on Feminist Criticism.* Ed. Linda Kauffman. Oxford: Basil Blackwell, 1989. 121–39.

Torsney, Cheryl, and Judy Elsley, eds. *Quilt Culture: Tracing the Pattern.* Columbia: U of Missouri P, 1994.

Tucker, Lindsey. "Alice Walker's *The Color Purple:* Emergent Woman, Emergent Text." *Black American Literature Forum* 22 (1988): 81–95.

Updike, John. *Roger's Version.* New York: Knopf, 1986.

———. *S.* New York: Knopf, 1988.

———. *The Witches of Eastwick.* New York: Knopf, 1984.

"Virtue Still Excellent Entertainment." Rev. of *Another Pamela,* by Upton Sinclair. *Christian Science Monitor* 3 June 1950: 6 [magazine].

Wagner-Martin, Linda. " 'Just the Doing of It': Southern Women Writers and the Idea of Community." *The Southern Literary Journal* 22 (1990): 19–32

Walker, Alice. *The Color Purple.* New York: Simon & Schuster, 1982.

———. "Coming in from the Cold." *Living By the Word: Selected Writings 1973–1987.* San Diego: Harcourt Brace Jovanovich, 1988. 54–68.

———. "Writing *The Color Purple.*" *In Search of Our Mothers' Gardens.* San Diego: Harvest-Harcourt Brace Jovanovich, 1984. 355–60.

Walkiewicz, E. P. *John Barth.* Boston: Twayne, 1986.

Wall, Wendy. "Lettered Bodies and Corporeal Texts in *The Color Purple.*" *Studies in American Fiction* 16 (1988): 83–97.

Watkins, Mel. Rev. of *The Color Purple,* by Alice Walker. *The New York Times Book Review* 25 July 1982: 7.

Watson, James G. *William Faulkner: Letters & Fictions.* Austin: U of Texas P, 1987.

Watt, Ian. *The Rise of the Novel.* Berkeley: U of California P, 1959.

Webster, Jean. *Daddy-Long-Legs.* New York: Grosset & Dunlap, 1912.

———. *Daddy Long-Legs: A Comedy in Four Acts.* New York: French, 1922.

———. *Dear Enemy.* 1915. New York: Grosset & Dunlap, 1970.

Weldon, Fay. *Letters to Alice on first reading Jane Austen.* 1984. New York: Taplinger, 1985.

Wilde, Alan. " 'Bold But Not Too Bold': Fay Weldon and the Limits of Poststructuralist Criticism." *Contemporary Literature* 29 (1988): 403–19.

Wilder, Thornton. *The Ides of March.* New York: Harper, 1948.

Wilhelmus, Tom. "Knowing." *Hudson Review* 61 (1988).

Williams, Carolyn. " 'Trying to Do Without God': The Revision of Epistolary Address in *The Color Purple.*" *Writing the Female Voice: Essays on Epistolary Literature.* Ed. Elizabeth C. Goldsmith. Boston: Northeastern UP, 1989. 273–85.

Woolf, Virginia. *Three Guineas.* 1936. Intro. Hermione Lee. London: Hogarth P, 1986.

Wurzbach, Natascha. *The Novel in Letters: Epistolary Fiction in the Early English Novel 1678–1740.* Coral Gables: U of Miami P, 1969.

Ziegler, Heide. *John Barth.* London: Methuen, 1987.

Index

Modernism, 11, 12, 47, 50, 51, 56, 57, 115
Molly-Make-Believe, 97
Montejo, Esteban, *Autobiography of a Run-away Slave,* 170, 173, 196 n. 8
Montherlant, Henry de, 11
Month of Sundays, A, 190 n. 5
Morgan, Thaïs, *Men Writing the Feminine,* 190 n. 3
Mrs. Wiggs of the Cabbage Patch, 97
Mulligan Stew, 31
Multiplicity, 86
My Emily Dickinson, 155
Mysteries of Udolpho, 193 n. 2

Nabokov, Vladimir, *Lolita,* 11
Narrative devices, 14
Narrativity, 54
New Feminist Criticism, The, 190 n. 2
New Portuguese Letters, 11
Nin, Anaïs, *Under a Glass Bell,* 133
Novel: avant-garde, 11; metafictional, 159; relettered, 113
Novel form, development of, 70
Novel in Letters, The: Epistolary Fiction in the Early English Novel 1678–1740, 183 n. 2.1

O'Donnell, Patrick, and Robert Con Davis, *Intertextuality and Contemporary American Fiction,* 131
Of Grammatology, 161
O'Hara, John, *Pal Joey,* 13
Oil!, 114
Oral History, 34
Orthography, 14, 23, 86, 184 n. 3.3
Ostriker, Alicia, *Writing Like a Woman,* 155
Other, 54, 162
Ovid, 75; *Heroides,* 100, 191 n. 4
Ownership, 14, 22, 32, 36, 80, 89, 104
Oz, Amos, *Black Box,* 186 n. 11

Pal Joey, 13
Pamela, 10, 19, 30, 57, 70, 114, 115, 121, 123, 126, 129, 131, 193 n. 2
Perry, Ruth, 193 n. 4
Personal Jesus, A, 126
Persona of author, 53
Phone systems, 4, 9, 145, 153
Pitt, Germaine, 17, 42, 53, 55, 58, 187 n. 10
Pleasure of the Text, The, 187 n. 11
Poetics of Gender, The, 190 n. 2
Political Unconscious, The, 7

Politics, feminine, 35
Pollyanna, 97
Possession, 186 n. 13
Post Card, The, 11, 94, 159, 163, 185 n. 4
Postmodernism, 3, 11, 12, 20, 25, 31, 47, 48, 51, 56, 77, 115, 135, 141, 167, 180
Postscript of letter, 49, 52
Poststructuralism, 156, 165
Poulet, Georges, 183, n. 1.1
Power: and delettering, 19; documentary, 56; of epistolary address, 120; female, 85; of language, 16, 52–53; from letter tradition, 9, 111; over life, 99, 101–2; of naming, 69, 101; narrative, 104; over others, 48; from ownership, 32; of protagonist, 30, 93; of signature, 8; of story, 33; of voice, 87; of writing, viii, 4, 5, 6, 8, 12, 64, 67, 68, 71
Prayers as response, 65–66
Presence, 43
Properties of letter, 14
Property, as oral history, 34
Protagonist, delettered female, 112
Psychoanalysis, 68
Puig, Manuel, *Heartbreak Tango,* 11

Quilt Culture: Tracing the Pattern, 196 n. 9

Rabbit Run, 91
Randall, Bob, 11; *The Fan,* 186 n. 11
Reader: as character, 16; as correspondent, 60; external, 17, 20, 22, 30, 50, 51, 54, 59, 60, 62, 79, 80, 89, 94, 104, 110, 120, 122, 133, 143, 157, 159, 163, 169, 181, 184 n. 2.3; imagined, ix; intended, 176; internal, 59, 110, 141; and performative action, 62; unintended, 56; as voyeur, 62
Reader response theory, 3
Reading: act of, 94, 132; feminist, 31, 71, 144; methodology, 66, 94
Realism, 47
Rebecca of Sunnybrook Farm, 97
Receiver, 14
Recipient of letter, 29, 55, 184 n. 2.3
Relettering, 19, 113, 114, 117, 120, 121, 124, 125, 128, 129, 131
Remapping, 132
Reproduction of letters, 30, 31
Resistance to text, 2, 80
Respondent, role of, 59

About the Author

Anne Bower is an associate professor of English at The Ohio State University-Marion. She received her M.A. and her Ph.D. from West Virginia University.